# THE JOY OF

*Grilling*

JOE FAMULARO

BARRON'S

# THANKS

A lot of people have added fuel to this fire— not in alphabetical order, but that's how I'm going to list them. But first, I want to thank as a group the chefs who so willingly shared their recipes and their knowledge of grilling. To so many others who helped in a variety of ways, my sincere thanks: Marylin Bender Altshul, Liz and Simon Bonham, Lou and Howard Erskine, Jerry Famularo, Missy and Chris Fisher, Betty and John Hettinger, Louise, John and Susan Imperiale, Bernie Kinzer, Bob Lei-fert of MECO, Mike McMillen of Preway Industries, Inc., Stephen Leskody, Phyllis Levin, Roberta and George Linkletter, Michael Lowsley-Williams, Victoria Mastalerz of Structo/THERMOS, Joan Muessen, Warrie and Jim Price, Alma Sotel, Alan Steel of Lazzari Fuel, Ed and Karen Towle, Judyth van Amringe, Lady Jane Weir, Margarite and Tom Whitney, and Jerry Ann and Gene Woodfin. Out of alpha order and last but not least, heartfelt thanks to Grace Freedson, who really lit the fire.

All inquiries should be addressed to:
Barron's Educational Series, Inc.
250 Wireless Boulevard
Hauppauge, NY 11788

Library of Congress Catalog Card No. 87–33434
International Standard Book Nos.
    Paperback Edition:  0-8120-4703-6
    Hardcover Edition:  0-8120-5840-2

**Library of Congress Cataloging-in-Publication Data**

Famularo, Joseph J.
    The joy of grilling.
    Includes index.
    1. Barbecue cookery. 2. Fireplace cookery.
3. Broiling I. Title.
TX840.B3F28  1988  641.5'748      87-33434
ISBN 0-8120-5840-2

PRINTED IN THE UNITED STATES OF AMERICA
    8    9770    12 11

# TABLE OF CONTENTS

# INTRODUCTION

America is making gastronomic history. Food trends continue to flourish; some fade away while others make a new mark or reestablish their importance. The state of the art of eating in America is as rich as a Renaissance painting.

Our interest in flavors and seasonings, in regional cuisines (our own and those of other nations), in ingredients and the development of high-quality products with a keen concern for nutritional principles have all become American tradition. The resurgence of "comfort food" is really a renaissance of good home cooking. Let them argue over the derivation of the word barbecue; the important thing is that it is a way of life, and everyone who grills takes great pride in his or her technique.

The goal of this book is to show the state of the art of grilling today. For this reason, some of the recipes are the work of selected outstanding young chefs. Touched by the work of teachers and writers such as Craig Claiborne, Richard Olney and Alice Waters, these young creators across the country are molding American cuisine with a professionalism and love not seen before on the American culinary horizon, and they are grilling food.

Americans have always loved meats, fish and vegetables cooked over fire, and the current love affair with grilling, spit-roasting and smoke cookery reveals our innate love of barbecue. After all, aren't barbecue and America synonymous? Grilled foods may prove to be America's most important culinary contribution of the 1980s and '90s.

People everywhere are grilling, barbecuing, spit-roasting and smoking foods. Cooking over an open fire is a way of life in Scandinavia, as it is in China, Greece, India, Italy, Japan and South America. In the United States, barbecue has become the national cuisine. Once limited to summer, it is now practiced all year long, whenever weather permits. And the grill has been brought indoors. Fireplace cooking is undergoing a revival, and new products such as properly vented indoor gas grills, salamanders, electric grills and gas-fired flattops are advertised and installed daily.

It seems to me that everyone is a grill cook in one way or another. Up-to-the-minute chef Jim Price grills on his modern indoor gas grill. More traditional, Judith McMillen barbecues on a custom-made reproduction of an 18th-century spit. Both are avid grill cooks. As a child, I watched my father and grandfather grill foods at Italian feasts in the parks on Long Island. I can still smell the sausages and lamb they cooked. As a teenager, I thought a day at the beach was incomplete without a portable grill. My first apartment on West 11th Street in Manhattan had a fireplace and in it I cooked many a bird, many a chop.

In a recent letter from the south of France, Richard Olney wrote, "I eat something grilled in the fireplace nearly every day, but grilling has mostly to do with intuition, experience, touch, depth of coals, intensity of heat and so on. It is not easy to transform method into recipe. The wood depends on the time of year— olive in the winter because I heat with it; broom, grapevine, prunings and fruitwood branches during the summer to make a fire that rapidly reduces to a bed of coals."

This short paragraph gave me a better understanding of why so many people love to grill: because we are dealing with an ancient cooking technique, an art and not an exact science, a procedure both rustic and fraught with mystique.

# COOKING TECHNIQUES

Since words and terms mean different things to different people, it needs to be said that five types of cooking are included in this book:

1. GRILLING: Cooking food over heat supplied by charcoal briquettes, lump charcoal, mesquite or logs, on a grid, flattop, or skewer, in a hibachi, brazier, gas or electric grill or any other grill. The heat can be "direct"—that is, right under the food—or "indirect," which means to one or more sides but not squarely beneath the food to be cooked. There is some question whether grilling should be limited to food grilled *over* a flame and not *under* a flame, as in broiling. But I have included some broiling, especially where the recipe adapts easily to one method or the other.

2. COVERED GRILLING: Cooking food under cover, directly or indirectly over a heat source.

3. SMOKE COOKING: Cooking food over very low heat (150°F to 200°F) in a covered container, with water or other liquid vapors or without (dry smoking), and usually with aromatic wood chunks or chips, vine cuttings or herb branches for special smoke flavors.

4. SPIT ROASTING: Cooking food on a rotating skewer with the heat source to one side, almost always with a drip pan under the food. Additional basting can be employed but fundamentally the food bastes itself as it rotates.

5. STOVETOP AND OVEN COOKING: Cooking food on or in an indoor stove, broiler or range, in this case to facilitate the preparation of marinades, sauces or other things required to complete the recipes in this book.

# GRILLING EQUIPMENT AND APPOINTMENTS

There are many shapes, sizes and designs of grilling, barbecuing, and smoking equipment but fundamentally they all have two components: a container to hold the fire (charcoal, wood, electric element or gas burner unit) and a grid or rack to hold the food to be cooked. Here is a brief description of the major types; many are described in more detail on page 2.

FIRST, A FEW BASIC DEFINITIONS:

COAL GRATE: The rack that hold charcoal in a covered charcoal grill. In a gas grill, a lava grate holds lava stones.

FIREBOWL (firebox) A container, generally round, square or rectangular, to hold the fire.

GRID: A metal rack on which the food is cooked.

GRILL: All the above items, arranged in one fashion or another, will make a grill. In other words, a grill is the entire cooking unit.

LID: Also called a hood or cover. It usually has a shutter-type vent and a temperature gauge built in.

VENT: A simple device to ventilate the fire, often in the form of a shutter. When the vent is open, more oxygen gets to the fuel and the fire brightens; when shut, the fire is snuffed out. Some grills and braziers have no vents at all.

WATER PAN: This holds water or another liquid to vaporize as food smokes in a smoker. It may be as simple as a foil pan set in any covered grill.

# USEFUL INFORMATION ABOUT GRILLING

No longer a summertime treat, cooking over fire has become an everyday event whose popularity continues to grow. Today's techniques of grilling indoors and out reflect the ancient art. These days the firebox usually replaces a pit, and rather than a *barbacoa*—a native American greenwood grill—we use a metal grid. Spit-roasting has been simplified with the use of an electric or battery-operated motor, and smoking can now be done in a tiny box instead of a shed. Yes, grilling has been made easy, and this enables us to spend more time on the refinements, especially in two areas: the marinades and the complements to the grilled foods.

This section includes useful information on grill equipment—where to get it, how to use it. There are also instructions for making the foil packets that so frequently appear throughout this book.

---

*Basics*

*Argument still rages over the origin of the word barbecue. Some find it in the French expression* barb à queue, *which mean "beard to tail"—referring to spit-roasting an entire animal over a fire. No one knows the etymology for sure, but most will agree that barbecuing is broader in concept today. It can mean cooking in and out of doors, over a wood or charcoal fire, using gas or electricity, and it is the name of a piece of equipment itself.*

---

## IMPORTANT SAFETY RULES

1. Never use charcoal for indoor cooking (or heating). Toxic carbon monoxide fumes may collect—with lethal consequences.

2. Alcohol, gasoline and kerosene are not to be used for lighting charcoal or other fuels. They can flash or explode when lit, resulting in serious burns.

3. Hot air and steam accumulate inside a covered grill. Open hood slowly and carefully to prevent burns.

# TYPES OF GRILLS

The units shown are good examples of the various types of equipment, but many other brands are available as well. Shop around to find the model with the features you prefer.

The BRAZIER, also known as an open grill, consists of a firebowl, usually made of heavy steel, with a screw-type mechanism that raises and lowers the grill to control the heat during cooking. The firebowl rests on long legs for waist-height barbecuing; the legs usually have wheels. On some models there is a half-hood or windscreen that can hold a spit at one side. Braziers are inexpensive and of varying quality. Check legs for stability, and check the thickness of the firebox metal.

CHARCOAL OVENS are designed to hold in heat and smoke, which circulate around the food. In other words, they cook like ovens. The units have hinged or door-opening hoods, which may be either open or closed during cooking. The better models have a height-adjustable firebox and heat deflectors that rest on the firebox. Direct, indirect and rotisserie cooking, as well as smoking, are possible with these units.

The CHARCOAL WATER SMOKER is a tall cylinder with a fuel grate, a grid (which converts to an open grill), a water pan with a food rack above, and often a second grid. Smokers create the ideal heat for smoking, 150°F to 200°F. Most have openings to add more water and coals. A Japanese smoker, the "Kamado" of heavy earthenware with a hinged lid, can function as an open grill. It is inexpensive but neither the cooking grid nor the charcoal pan adjusts.

CHARCOAL WATER SMOKER—Has double grid. Moisture from water pan mixes with heat from charcoal (or from optional electric element) and smoke from aromatic wood chips to baste food continuously during cooking. By Meco.

CHARCOAL OVEN—Stainless steel hood with window; two separate stainless steel work tables. Has V-shaped grid (for improved grease drainage), adjustable firebox, heat indicator and ash pan. By Hasty-Bake.

The ELECTRIC SMOKER first "cures" the meat or fish, then applies warm, dry air. The food is loaded on grids and slipped into the smoker through either the top or front. A pan is filled with the desired fuel (and sometimes has to be refilled, depending on the recipe). Though the drying time may be up to 20 hours, the units are practical and efficient for most recipes.

because charcoal isn't handled, but they do need a fuel canister (for outdoors) or a natural gas hookup (for indoors). Temperatures reach 700°F to 900°F. On both indoor and outdoor models hot coals produce smoke as fat and juices hit them, and they can take wood chips but not chunks. Models for indoor home use, requiring special venting, are growing fast in popularity. Many restaurants already use large gas-fired grills.

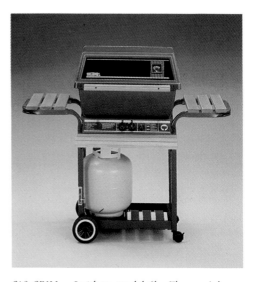

*ELECTRIC SMOKER—Can be used on porch or patio, in carport or in any other well-ventilated area where electric outlet is available. Will smoke meat, fish, game, cheese and other foods. Choice of top- or side-loading models with capacity of up to 20 pounds. By Luhr-Jensen.*

*GAS GRILL—Outdoor model (by Thermos) has a 40,000-BTU double burner with two-piece porcelain-coated steel cooking grid. Full-length tempered glass window, heat indicator, foldaway warming rack. Wooden cart is on casters.*

The GAS-FIRED FLATTOP usually comes as an option with commercial-type indoor ranges. Varying from about a foot square to 4' x 3', it is a highly polished sheet of metal that is set over gas jets and becomes intensely hot.

GAS GRILLS provide gas-heated, briquette-shaped rocks or lava stones as a substitute for charcoal. They are covered, with square or rectangular designs based on hooded grills. Gas grills heat up quickly and are neat

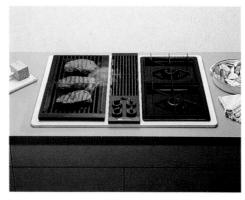

*Indoor gas cooktop grill (by Jenn-Air) has stainless steel or porcelain enamel perimeter, total 16,000 BTUs.*

The HIBACHI and other portable grills are simple vented units with one or two grates. The grids have several brackets to adjust the height of the rack from the fire. Coals are placed on the grate to allow air flow underneath, which is controlled by the vents. Hibachis are small, efficient, transportable and inexpensive. Recently there has been a swarm of new portables to hit the market. Many come with folding legs or windscreens. They are inexpensive but check for sturdiness before you buy.

The HOODED GRILL is a square or rectangular version of the kettle cooker. If the hood is open, it cooks like an open grill. Closed, it creates smoke and heat faster. As a rule, fuel grates and cooking racks or grids are adjustable, and some units have temperature gauges built into the hood. Optional appointments such as rotisseries, side shelves and rib racks are available. Models range from inexpensive to high-priced; most are attractively designed.

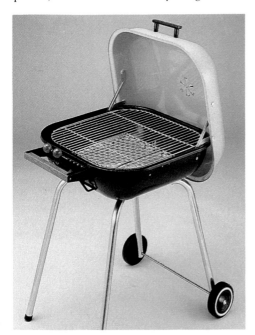

HOODED GRILL—Charcoal fueled; four-position adjustable cooking height. Removable grid is 21½ inches square, vented hood is adjustable. Some models feature rotating spit and foldaway side tables. By Meco.

The INDOOR ELECTRIC GRILL is usually a small unit with an electric element set in an attractive ceramic base for tabletop use. These are smokeless, so foods should be marinated or "mopped" for full flavor.

BUILT-IN ELECTRIC GRILL—Firebox holds lava stones. This indoor model features 12 heat settings, deep fryer, stainless steel lid to cover grill when not in use. By Gaggenau.

INDOOR ELECTRIC GRILL—Tabletop models have removable drip pans, detachable cords. By Maxim (12 × 9-inch rectangular model) and (see next page)

*Contempra (12-inch round). Heavy-duty model by U.S. Range has ceramic coals, adjustable top grate: available in 24- to 60-inch width.*

The TIN REFLECTING OVEN, an antique piece of equipment that is undergoing revival, is a box with one side open to the fire. Outfitted with a spit, the box is placed right up to the fire on an indoor hearth.

The KETTLE GRILL is similar to the brazier but has a cover, vents and a stationary rack that doesn't move up or down. It comes with a rotisserie, electric or battery operated. This is probably the most popular charcoal barbecue unit in the country, because grilling food under a cover reduces cooking time and increases the smoked flavor. The kettle is an oven, a smoker and a grill all in one. It cooks food more quickly and evenly than the open grill.

The OUTDOOR ELECTRIC GRILL is a cousin of the indoor type, but larger, sturdier and with exterior-grade wiring and plug.

The ROTISSERIE BARBECUE is similar to the kettle and hooded grill. The rack can be raised and lowered, but the rotisserie's main feature is the rotating spit. It allows an entirely different cooking method; the meat is basted with its own juices to insure a moist result.

*KETTLE GRILL—A popular charcoal-fueled model with adjustable vents. Bottom can be opened for ash removal. Made of heavy-gauge steel coated with porcelain enamel to resist rust. Available in several sizes and colors. By Weber-Stephen.*

# THE IMPORTANT TOOLS

Quality is the most important consideration in selecting cooking tools: imagine a spatula separating from its handle just as you are ready to turn a delicate piece of fish! Grilling tools must be sturdy and long-handled. All the following tools are important—some more than others, so don't be misled by the alphabetical order. Check the section at the end of the book for good sources.

BASTING BRUSHES—Consider long handles offset at a 45-degree angle. Buy several, for different marinades and bastes require individual brushes if you are grilling more than one item.

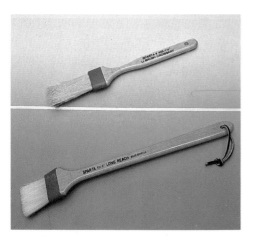

*BASTING BRUSH—Angled 12-inch wooden handle with bleached, sterilized boar bristles. By Sparta Brush.*

CARVING BOARDS—All kinds are available, but consider one with "canals" or troughs to catch juices. A porcelain or ceramic platter is unsuitable for carving. Cut on the board first, then transfer the meat to plates or a platter and spoon on the juices.

CHARCOAL STARTER—The chimney-type starter lights charcoal quickly and efficiently without fluids. Only a match and a few pieces of newspaper are needed for foolproof fire every time.

*CHARCOAL STARTER—Wooden handle has safety heat shield; chimney is sheet aluminum. By Easy Embers.*

*ELECTRIC CHARCOAL LIGHTER—Has heating element that starts charcoal fire in about 8 minutes. By Meteor of Nu-Rod.*

DRIP PANS—Make your own or buy them in various sizes. Disposable and inexpensive, they are available in almost every food shop. If you make your own, use double heavy foil—but use store-bought ones for water pans.

FLASHLIGHT—I couldn't survive without two of them as I never know when the battery will give out. I'm uncomfortable juggling the flashlight in one hand and cooking tools in the other, but what can I do? I like to grill in the dark.

FOIL—As indispensable as plastic wrap, but for a different reason: It creates a unique form of cookery (cooking *en papillote*) and it shields foods on the grid from intense heat. Purchase heavy-duty foil.

FORKS AND SPOONS—Long, heat-resistant handles are essential—made of wood or thermoplastic. The wood handles are more expensive and worth it.

HINGED WIRE BASKET—These thin grills are made of cross-hatched wire. Anyone who thinks they're superfluous hasn't spent much time at the grill. They help cook whole fish and are virtually essential for small pieces of fish—fillets and steaks—if you're cooking more than three or four. A hinged grill is perfect for any small foods that are not skewered.

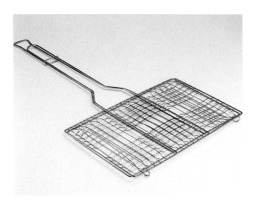

*HINGED WIRE BASKET—Available in various sizes and shapes, including one type in a fish contour for grilling whole fish without risk of it falling apart. Model shown by Thermos.*

KEBAB RESTS—These may fall into the category of extracurricular equipment, but they can come in very handy. To wit: try the sirloin on skewers on page 133, with and without a kebab rest, and you'll know what I mean. With the rest, the sirloin cubes will sit ½ inch or so above the grid, preventing the food from sticking.

KNIVES—An obvious need, but good ones are necessary for slicing all kinds of food—especially for cutting into a steak to check for doneness.

MARINADE PANS—Fortunately, oversized glass and porcelain dishes are readily available. Do not use aluminum because acidic liquids react to the metal and the food can end up with a metallic taste. Stainless steel, however, is fine.

MEAT THERMOMETER—Only useful for foods at least 1 inch thick; it may be more precise than one's eye or finger. Instant-reading thermometers register internal temperatures right away; regular ones take a few minutes longer.

MITTS—Must be insulated. They will become your hands, they are needed so often.

PLASTIC WRAP—This is obvious, yet one of the most important "tools." Its airtight and see-through qualities make it indispensable. Foil is fine on the grid, but it's plastic wrap for pre-grid work.

SKEWERS—Long, thin wooden ones are excellent and inexpensive. Soak them in water for 30 minutes or so to keep them from burning on the grill. They're ideal for individual servings and they do little damage to food, whereas gaping holes from large metal skewers are not particularly attractive. But metal skewers are necessary for such grills as pork satay, page 136, because the weight of the meat requires a strong support. Beware of plain round metal skewers, as they cause food to spin (you'll note that the same side of the food is being cooked over and over again). And learn to use double wooden skewers as described in the salmon recipe on page 62.

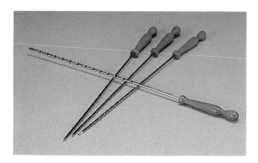

*SKEWERS—Have easily grasped wooden handles and notched blades to hold meat and fish pieces firmly in place. By Thermos.*

SPATULAS—As important as tongs, this tool should be "offset"—which means with a blade set lower than the handle—and about 8 inches long by 2½ to 3 inches wide. There's no other way to flip fish fillets or other delicate foods except with this and the hinged wire grill.

SPRAY BOTTLES—A water sprayer is sometimes needed more for the wild, rocketing spark than for a flareup—in either case as an extinguisher. But be careful; I once saw someone put out his fire with overspritzing.

STORAGE CONTAINERS FOR COAL—All grill cooks have had the experience of burning charcoal that isn't quite right. The cause usu-

ally is dampness. Use an airtight container to store coal; even a pail with a lid is better than nothing. The idea is to keep moisture from creeping in.

TABLES—There is never enough space on grills, even with ultra-deluxe models. Keep a table nearby for plates, platters and grill paraphernalia. I use an old marble-top, iron-based café table that can stay outdoors all year long.

TONGS—They should be stainless steel and spring-loaded. Some have cupped ends and can be used as a spoon to pour marinade over whatever is being grilled. Consider owning two pairs.

WIRE BRUSH—Without one, cleaning the grid is drudgery. With one, the task is minimal and sometimes, I think, I get a psychological lift from the ease of scraping grime off the grid. For three dollars or so, it is a lifesaver.

*WIRE BRUSH—Has brass bristles and steel wool pad for cleaning barbecue grill. By Thermos.*

# GRILL GUIDELINES

## EASY STEPS TO STARTING A FIRE IN A KETTLE-TYPE GRILL

1. Open all the vents and the hood and remove the cooking grid.

2. To get a good fire, use a high-quality hardwood charcoal or wood such as mesquite. Charcoal made from birch, elm, hickory, maple or oak will burn clean, with no unpleasant odors.

3. Use an easy fire-starter appliance, such as "Easy Embers," or an electric starter. Coal should burn 15 to 20 minutes, until it is covered with a light gray ash.

4. Arrange coals for grilling by spacing them ½ inch apart. This helps prevent flareups from drippings, as some of the drippings will fall between coals.

## CHARCOAL OVENS

Most of these units have a ventless hood that creates an enclosed oven. Many accommodate rotating spits. The firebox may be mechanically adjusted up or down with an outside crank. The units also include a heat deflector plate, which rests on the firebox and distributes heat evenly throughout the cooking area; the food is not exposed directly to the fire. There are usually two draft vents below the hood to control the fire.

One unique feature of the charcoal oven is the V-shaped grid that allows grease to drain into a foil grease catcher attached to the outside of the unit.

## GAS GRILLS

### GENERAL RULES:

1. Read and study the manufacturer's manual. Know your particular equipment; understand how to light your grill safely. This is as important for safety as it is for better grilling.

2. Consider the elements—temperature and wind in particular—at the time of grilling. Cooking temperatures and times will be affected by outside conditions.

3. Gas grills require preheating, which may take up to 20 minutes. Do not bypass this important step.

4. Be sure to coat the grid with vegetable oil.

5. Clean the grid often to avoid giving an off-taste to later meals.

## WAYS TO AVOID FLAREUPS

1. Remove excess fat (which will also improve your diet).

2. Use a drip pan, especially with fatty foods (like chicken and hamburgers).

3. Move food away from flareup area and allow grease to burn off.

4. Don't use water to put out flareups; the grill will be damaged if this becomes a steady practice. Some advise sprinkling baking soda on the flames, but this is unnecessary if you follow the other suggestsions here.

5. Sear both sides of chops, steaks and hamburgers over high heat to seal in juices; then raise the grid (or lower the flame) to complete grilling.

6. Keep grid and grill clean.

## CLEANING LAVA ROCK AND CERAMIC BRIQUETTES

Cut a piece of heavy-duty foil to fit over the lava rock or briquettes and place it right on top of them. Be sure to leave about 1 inch of space all around the inside of the grill—that is, the foil should not touch any side of the grill. This will provide for proper ventilation. Any buildup of food or grease will burn off the rock if the grill is turned to high and kept that way for about 10 minutes, or whatever time is specified in the manufacturer's manual.

## CLEANING THE BURNERS AND VENTURI

Brush with stiff wire brush every six months or so to unclog port holes. For persistent clogged holes, use a wire or thin metal skewer. Insects and especially spiders are known to build nests or webs in Venturi tubes, creating a potential hazard. Clean the tubes with an old coffee percolator brush or toothbrush.

## WOOD AND WATER SMOKERS FOR GAS GRILLS

1. Wood smoker—This is a heavy cast iron box with lid that fits on the fire grate of any gas grill. Holes in the lid let in just enough air to allow wood chips to smolder but not flame. The box is about 2 inches thick, 4 inches wide and 8 inches long. A foil log may be substituted; see page 00.

2. Water smoker—an additional unit that contains water, allowing for slow smoking of meats and fish. Is is best suited to a gas grill with dual burners; fire up one side of the grill and place the food on the other side. The water smoker achieves moist smoked foods if you don't have a regular smoker.

# GAS GRILL COOKING GUIDES FOR VEGETABLES, BEEF, PORK, POULTRY, SAUSAGE AND SMOKING

The following Cooking Guides were developed by Preway Industries, Evansville, Indiana, and are printed with permission.

*See page 18.
**If your grill has two burners, cook and preheat over one burner only.
***For a reduced calorie dish, substitute water for butter.

## VEGETABLE COOKING GUIDE

In each case, grill is preheated for 10 minutes; heat setting and time is with hood closed.

ACORN SQUASH, two to one and one half pounds each, 4 servings:
Method: Cut in half. Remove seeds. Combine ½ cup firmly packed brown sugar, 4 tablespoons butter, 1 teaspoon cinnamon, ½ teaspoon freshly ground pepper, ¼ teaspoon nutmeg. Place ¼ of mixture in each half. Bundle wrap* individually.
Heat setting & cooking time: MEDIUM**, 25 to 35 minutes.

ASPARAGUS, 1 pound, 4 to 6 servings
Method: Remove tough ends. Drugstore wrap* or place in covered casserole with 2 tablespoons butter and 2 ice cubes.
Heat setting & cooking time: MEDIUM**, 15 to 20 minutes.

CARROTS, 1 to 1½ pounds, 4 to 6 servings
Method: Cut into 2-inch pieces. Drugstore wrap* or place in covered casserole with 2 tablespoons butter, ½ teaspoon dried dillweed and 2 ice cubes.
Heat setting & cooking time: MEDIUM**, 20 to 25 minutes.

CAULIFLOWER, whole, 2 pounds, 4 to 6 servings

Method: Trim outer leaves. Bundle wrap* with 4 ice cubes. After grilling, top with 1 slice of American processed cheese, if desired and let stand, covered, for 2 minutes.
Heat setting & cooking time: MEDIUM**, 30 to 35 minutes.

CORN ON THE COB, 4 ears
Method: Peel back husks but do not detach. Remove silks. Replace husks over ears. Use string to tie husks in place at end of each ear. Soak in cold water for 10 to 15 minutes.
Heat setting & cooking time: MEDIUM**, 20 to 25 minutes (turn 2 or 3 times).

GREEN BEANS, 1 pound, 4 to 6 servings
Method: Remove ends. Drugstore wrap* or place in covered casserole with 2 tablespoons butter, ¼ cup slivered almonds and 4 ice cubes.
Heat setting & cooking time: MEDIUM**, 20 to 25 minutes.

MUSHROOMS, 8 ounces sliced or whole, 3 or 4 servings
Method: Drugstore wrap* or place in covered casserole with 1 tablespoon butter, 2 teaspoons dry red wine, pinch each of freshly ground pepper and salt.
Heat setting & cooking time: MEDIUM**, 8 to 10 minutes.

ONIONS, Two, 8 ounces each, 4 servings
Method: Peel and cut in half. Sprinkle with pinch each of seasoned salt and fennel seed. Top each with 1 tablespoon butter. Bundle wrap* individually.
Heat setting & cooking time: MEDIUM**, 20 to 25 minutes (rearrange once).

POTATOES, BAKED, four, 8 ounces each, 4 servings

Method: Lightly brush with vegetable oil, if desired. Prick several times with a fork. Wrap each in single thickness of aluminum foil. Bake on upper cooking rack.
Heat setting & cooking time: MEDIUM**, 45 to 60 minutes (omit foil wrap for crisper potatoes).

POTATOES, BOILED, 2 pounds, 4 to 6 servings
Method: Peel potatoes. In grill-safe casserole, combine potatoes, 2 teaspoons salt and enough water to cover potatoes. Cover. Remove cooking grid. Place casserole directly on lava rock grate, arranging rocks around dish.**
Heat setting & cooking time: HIGH until water boils, then LOW for 15 to 20 minutes.

YAMS, four, 8 to 12 ounces each, 4 servings
Method: Prick several times with fork. Wrap each in single thickness of aluminum foil. Bake on upper cooking rack.
Heat setting & cooking time: MEDIUM**, 45 to 60 minutes.

### BEEF COOKING GUIDE
Cooking time for medium doneness Hamburgers, 4 ounces each ½ inch thick
Heat setting: MEDIUM
Cooking time: 12 to 14 minutes.
Method: Preheat grill for 10 minutes. Grill burgers with hood closed. Turn once.

### STEAKS
T-BONE OR PORTERHOUSE, 1 to 1½ pounds each, 1 inch thick; 1½ inches thick
Heat setting: MEDIUM
Cooking time: 8 to 10 minutes; 25 to 30 minutes.
Method: Preheat grill for 10 minutes. Trim excess fat from steaks. Grill with hood closed. Turn steaks once. Sirloin, 2 to 3 pounds, 1½ inches thick, 4 to 6 servings
Heat setting: MEDIUM
Cooking time: 18 to 20 minutes

Method: Preheat grill for 10 minutes. Trim excess fat from steak. Grill with hood closed. Turn steak once.

TOP ROUND, 2 to 3 pounds, 1½ inches thick, 4 to 6 servings
Heat setting: MEDIUM
Cooking time: 20 to 25 minutes.
Method: Marinate. Preheat grill for 10 minutes. Grill steak with hood closed. Turn once.

FLANK, 1½ pounds, ¾ inches thick, 4 servings
Heat setting: HIGH
Cooking time: 12 to 15 minutes
Method: Marinate. Preheat grill for 10 minutes. Score steak with diamond patterns. Grill with hood closed. Turn steak once.

### ROASTS
POT ROAST OR CHUCK ROAST, 3 pounds, 1½ inches thick, 6 to 8 servings
Heat setting: MEDIUM
Cooking time: 20 minutes to sear, 1 to 1½ hours to cook Method: Marinate. Preheat grill for 10 minutes. Sear roast, turning once. Place in grill-safe baking dish or on double thickness of heavy-duty aluminum foil. Cover or wrap tightly. Grill using indirect heat with hood closed.

SIRLION TIP, 4 to 5 pounds, 8 to 10 servings
Heat setting: MEDIUM
Cooking time: 1 to 1½ hours to cook
Method: Remove cooking grid. Center drip pan directly on lava rocks. Spit-roast with hood closed. (Roast should reach internal temperature of 150°F).

### RIBS
BEEF SHORT RIBS, 4 pounds, 4 servings
Heat setting: MEDIUM
Cooking time: 20 to 30 minutes to sear, 1 to 1½ hours to cook.

Method: Preheat grill for 10 minutes. Sear ribs, turning several times. Place in grill-safe baking dish or on double thickness of heavy-duty aluminum foil. Add 2 cups barbecue sauce. Cover or wrap tightly. Grill using indirect heat with hood closed.

## PORK COOKING GUIDE

BACON, 4 slices
Heat setting: HIGH
Cooking time: 5 to 9 minutes.
Method: Preheat grill for 5 minutes.* Place seasoned griddle on cooking grid. Preheat for 5 minutes longer. Place bacon on griddle. Cook with hood open. Turn bacon once.
*If your grill has two burners, preheat and cook over one burner only.

CANADIAN BACON, 6 to 8 slices
Heat setting: HIGH
Cooking time: 2 minutes
Method: Same as above.

PORK CHOPS, 4, 4 to 8 ounces each, ½ inch thick; 1 inch thick
Heat setting: LOW
Cooking time: 15 to 20 minutes; 25 to 30 minutes.
Method: Season cooking grid with vegetable oil. Preheat grill for 5 minutes. Grill chops with hood closed. Turn and rearrange once.

PORK ROAST (boneless), 5 pounds, 8 to 10 servings
Heat setting: LOW
Cooking time: 2¼ to 3 hours.
Method: Remove cooking grid. Center drip pan on lava rocks. Skewer and balance roast on spit. Roast until internal temperature of roast reaches 170°F.

SMOKED PORK CHOPS, 4 (fully cooked), 7 to 8 ounces each, ½ inch thick
Heat setting: MEDIUM
Cooking time: 10 to 15 minutes

Method: Season cooking grid with vegetable oil. Preheat grill for 10 minutes. Grill chops with hood closed. Turn once.

SPARE RIBS, 4 pounds, 4 servings
Heat setting: LOW
Cooking time: 1 to 1¼ hours
Method: Preheat grill for 5 minutes. Grill ribs with hood closed. Turn once. Brush with sauce during last 20 minutes, if desired.

COUNTRY-STYLE RIBS, 4 pounds, 4 servings
Heat setting: LOW
Cooking time: 30 to 45 minutes
Method: Parboil ribs for 20 minutes. Preheat grill for 5 minutes. Grill ribs with hood closed. Turn once. Brush with sauce during last 20 minutes, if desired.

## POULTRY COOKING GUIDE

CHICKEN PIECES, 2½ to 5 pounds, 4 to 8 servings
Heat setting: LOW
Cooking time: 35 to 45 minutes
Method: Preheat grill for 10 minutes. Grill chicken until juices run clear, turning several times. Brush with sauce during last 15 minutes, if desired.

WHOLE CHICKEN (BROILER-FRYER), 2½ to 3 pounds, 3 to 4 servings
Heat setting: MEDIUM
Cooking time: 1 to 1½ hours.
Method: Remove cooking grid. Center drip pan on lava rocks. Skewer and balance chicken on spit. With string, tie legs and wings close to body. Spit-roast until internal temperature of chicken reaches 185°F. Let stand for 10 minutes before carving.

WHOLE DUCKLING, 4½ to 5 pounds, 3 to 4 servings
Heat setting: MEDIUM
Cooking time: 1½ to 2½ hours.
Method: Remove cooking grid. Center drip pan on lava rocks. Skewer and balance duckling on

spit. With string, tie legs and wings close to body. Spit-roast until internal temperature of duckling reaches 185°F. Let stand for 10 minutes before carving.

WHOLE TURKEY, 9 to 10 pounds, 8 to 10 servings
Heat setting: MEDIUM
Cooking time: 3 to 4 hours.
Method: Remove cooking grid. Place drip pan filled with 1 to 2 inches water directly on lava rocks on one half of grate. Replace cooking grid. Preheat grill for 10 minutes. Place turkey, breast side up, on grid above drip pan. Roast using indirect heat with hood closed until internal temperature of turkey reaches 185°F, rotating turkey once. Let stand for 10 minutes before carving.

### SMOKE COOKING GUIDE
WHOLE FISH, 4 to 5 pounds
Cooking time: 1 to 1½ hours.

PORK SPARERIBS, 4 pounds
Cooking time: 1 to 2 hours.

BEEF CHUCK ROAST, 2 to 3 pounds, 1¼ inch thick
Cooking time: 45 minutes to 1½ hours.

### SAUSAGE COOKING GUIDE
SAUSAGE LINKS (fully cooked), 3 to 4 ounces each
Heat setting: HIGH
Cooking time: 5 to 7 minutes
Method: Preheat grill for 10 minutes. Score sausages in 2 or 3 places. Grill with hood open. Turn sausages several times.

SAUSAGE LINKS (UNCOOKED), 2 ounces each, ½ inch thick
Heat setting: MEDIUM
Cooking time: 15 to 20 minutes
Method: Preheat grill for 10 minutes. Grill with hood closed. Turn sausages and rearrange several times.

SAUSAGE PATTIES (UNCOOKED), 2 ounces each, ½ inch thick
Heat setting: MEDIUM
Cooking time: 5 to 7 minutes
Method: Preheat grill for 5 minutes.* Place seasoned griddle on cooking grid. Preheat for 5 minutes longer. Place sausages on griddle. Grill with hood open. Turn patties once.
*If your grill has two burners, preheat and cook over one burner only.

WIENERS
Heat setting: HIGH
Cooking time: 3 to 5 minutes
Method: Preheat grill for 10 minutes. Grill with hood open. Turn wieners several times.

# ELECTRIC GRILLS

The electric grill sears food from its underside, not from above as with oven broilers. The reason for this is to seal in the juices on the underside as quickly as possible before losing them. An open rack is employed instead of a griddle. Many outdoor electric grills use a special heat-absorbing bed, such as lava stone or iron stone, which causes juices and fats hitting it to smoke and vaporize, flavoring the food. Because of the open area at the base and the position of the reflectors, the outer bowl never gets too hot; natural air convection keeps it cool enough to carry to the table, usually without potholders. There are easy-to-clean drip trays. The heating element reflector systems are designed to heat up quickly and barbecue or grill evenly. The reflector systems, including the trays, are easy to take out and wash.

Most electric grills are small and portable, using approximately 1500 watts, 12.5 amps or less (limited by the 120-volt plug-in outlet). This is comparable to a toaster or hair dryer. They are energy efficient and cost pennies to operate—less than 5 cents per hour for units without lava stones and 12 cents per hour for lava stone units, based on national average data by the Edison Electric Institute Residential Service as of this printing.

## SOME ADVANTAGES

1. These grills fill a need for those people who want a safe alternative to charcoal, wood or gas grills, both indoors and out.

2. Many electric grills, both indoor and outdoor models, are available at reasonable cost—from below $50 to several hundred dollars. The outdoor grills are compact and plug into any 120-volt outlet. This can be most convenient for those who live in highrises or townhouses where open-flame grills are not recommended.

3. Indoor electric grills are just about smoke-free, so they make it possible to grill year-round in apartments where balconies or patios are nonexistent.

## ELECTRIC GRILL GUIDELINES

Although most manufacturers provide important and detailed guidelines with their products, here are some essential points to keep in mind if you plan to use an electric grill/barbecue.

1. Meat should be at room temperature to speed cooking time and facilitate fat dripping. Meats should be trimmed of excess fat and scored at the edges to keep curling to a minimum.

2. Grills must be preheated to create faster sizzling. As a general rule, foods should be turned only once to encourage browning and create grill marks.

3. If meat has not been marinated, be sure to oil the grill to prevent sticking. If using sauces containing sugar (or other sweeteners) or tomatoes, baste only during the last 5 minutes' cooking time on each side.

**4.** Food to be grilled should be as flat as possible. For example, in grilling chicken it is best to remove the wings so that the breast quarter or half can lie flat on the grill for even cooking. The wings, of course, may be grilled along with the other parts.

SPECIAL NOTE There is available a Japanese-style flattop electric grill. It is unique in that it has three distinct heat zones. The drip tray is concealed and traps any excess fat below the cooking surface; the surface is very thick cast aluminum, which retains heat and is easy to clean (it slides out for washing). The heat control is thermostatic.

# ELECTRIC GRILL TIME CHART

(Provided courtesy of Maverick Industries, Inc., Union, New Jersey.)

All cooking times are for an indoor ventless electric grill without heat reflector hood, and for meats at room temperature. Additional time may be needed for cold meats. On lava stone and iron stone grills, times will be 20 percent shorter due to adjustable hood, even less if flareup occurs.

### FISH AND SEAFOOD
Swordfish and other firm steaks and fillets (1-1½ inches thick) Cooking time in minutes: cooked through, 20-30.

SHRIMP, skewered and grilled flat Cooking time in minutes: cooked through, 15-20.

SCALLOPS, skewered tightly together
Cooking time in minutes: cooked through, 20-25.
*Rare—seared outside with cool, red center
Medium rare—seared outside with warm, red center
Medium—seared outside with hot, pink center
Well—no traces of pink

### PORK
CHOPS: all types Thickness: ¾-1 inch
Cooking time in minutes: medium 30-35, well 35-40.

RIBS: country-style, Chinese and back (separated)
Thickness: ¾-2 inches
Cooking time in minutes: medium 35-40, well 40-45.

KNOCKWURST (whole) Cooking time in minutes: cooked through, 15-20.

BRATWURST (split, cooked flat) Cooking time in minutes: cooked through, 10-12.

FRANKFURTERS Cooking time in minutes: cooked through, 15-20.

### LAMB
CHOPS: Rib, Loin or Shoulder
Thickness: 1 inch
Cooking time in minutes: rare* 15-20, medium rare 17-23, medium 20-25.

RIBLETS (separated) Thickness: 1 inch
Cooking time in minutes: rare* 15-20, medium rare 17-23, medium 20-25.

## CHICKEN

Cut-up broiler (2 ⅓ to 3 pounds), wings removed from breasts
Cooking time in minutes: cooked through, 30-40.

## CHICKEN DRUMSTICKS

Cooking time in minutes: cooked through, 35-45.

## BEEF

RIB STEAKS
Thickness: ½-1 inch
Cooking time in minutes: rare* 10-15, medium rare 15-20, medium 20-25.

TENDERLOIN AND SIRLOIN STEAKS Thickness: 1-1½ inches
Cooking time in minutes: rare* 15-20, medium rare 20-25, medium 25-30.

LONDON BROIL (shoulder steak) Thickness: 1-1 ½ inches
Cooking time in minutes: rare* 20-25, medium rare 25-30, medium 30-35.

## KEBABS

BEEF AND LAMB Thickness: 1- 1½ inches
Cooking time in minutes: rare* 15-10, medium rare 20-25, medium 25-30.

SHORT RIBS Thickness: 2 inches
Cooking time in minutes: rare* 20-15, medium rare 25-30, medium 30-35.

BACK RIBS Thickness: 1 inch
Cooking time in minutes: rare* 15-20, medium rare 20-25, medium 25-30.

HAMBURGERS (5 ounces) Thickness: 1 inch
Cooking time in minutes: rare* 15-20, medium rare 17-23, medium 25-30, well 27-33.

# ELECTRIC SMOKERS

Electric smokers are designed to cure (and smoke) meats and fish. The main advantage is that no charcoal is necessary. Most electric smokers are simple in design, are relatively small and fall into one of two categories, top- or front-load.

One popular model has an aluminum exterior but is all steel inside. It operates on regular household current. The element maintains the heat chamber at 160°F, which is ideal for smoke curing. The unit is for outdoor use and is quite versatile; it can take aromatics such as apple, alder, cherry or hickory wood.

In choosing an electric smoker, it is important to understand the difference between the smoking and drying portions of the unit's processing cycle. For example, if a particular recipe calls for a total drying time of six to 12 hours or more but only two panfuls of aromatic wood, this means that the unit will be smoking for only two hours. Yet the food will need much more time to complete the full curing cycle. Of course you can use these units only to smoke, but if not eaten immediately the food will have to be refrigerated or frozen to preserve freshness.

# WRAPPING FOOD IN FOIL

$B$ecause some foods need turning on the grill and others do not, two methods of wrapping are used.

The *drugstore wrap* is best for foods that need to be turned, such as loose vegetables and flat cuts of meat. Because the wrap is sealed, it is more difficult to open and close (especially to check for doneness). To make this wrap,

1. Use heavy-duty foil large enough to enclose food and to allow for several folds on top and sides.

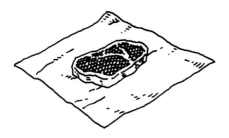

2. Place food to be wrapped in center of foil. Bring edge up over food and fold two or three times, leaving some air space in packet.

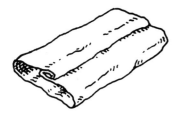

3. Fold ends tightly two or three times to avoid leaks.

The *bundle* wrap is best for foods that do not require turning, such as acorn squash halves, whole apples or a whole cauliflower. It is easier to open and close this type of packet. Here's how to do it:

1. Use heavy-duty foil three times the size of the food to be wrapped.

2. Center food on it. Bring the four corners together and fold tightly to seal, leaving some air space for steam inside packet. Fold under each of the four corners of the packet.

# BRINE CURING

Brine is basically a mixture of salt, saltpeter, sugar and water for preserving meat and fish. The brine mixture can be used two or three times and stored in the refrigerator for a week. Meat that is put into a brine is usually later smoked. Pickling or canning salt is not as costly as iodized table salt and may be used. The sugar can be brown or white, or in the form of maple syrup, molasses or honey.

Brines receive all kinds of seasonings and here the creative cook can realize his or her fancy. Garlic, onion, various peppers, syrups and so on can be added to a basic brine to create new flavors. Remember to stir the brine, even after the meat has been added; otherwise honey or molasses, for example, will settle to the bottom. Be sure to refrigerate brines.

Brine foods in a container made of a non-reactive material, such as glass, ceramic or plastic. It's important to immerse the food completely, adding a plate with a weight on top to accomplish this, if necessary.

## BASIC BRINE
makes enough for two 3-pound whole fish, one 6-pound brisket or six 1-pound Cornish hens
2 quarts water
1 cup salt
1 cup sugar
1 teaspoon saltpeter

## PICKLING SPICE BRINE

This and the herbed brine below make enough for three 3- to 4-pound whole fish, one 10- to 12-pound brisket or eight 1-pound Cornish hens
3 quarts water
½ cup salt
1 cup honey
1 teaspoon saltpeter
¼ cup mixed pickling spice
6 garlic cloves, peeled and cracked

## HERB BRINE

3 quarts water
1½ cups salt
1 cup firmly packed dark brown sugar
1 teaspoon saltpeter
22 sprigs fresh thyme
2 bay leaves
12 peppercorns, cracked
12 juniper berries, cracked

Bring water to boil. Add remaining ingredients and return to boil. Remove from heat and cool before using.

# FIRE AND FUEL

"Most grillers I know worry about the meat or fish they're going to grill," says Jim Price, a good friend and good cook. "I worry about the wood." As a youngster, Jim learned to grill foods with his grandfather on the expansive Long Island beaches. He explains, "We would dig a large hole in the sand and bank it with stones. Then we placed special hardwoods, such as birch, oak, hickory or ash, in criss-cross fashion with a teepee on top— and we never mixed woods. A grid would go right on top of that. The fish we caught was gutted right away and cooked immediately, but only when we knew we had the right kind of heat—at the embers stage. We'd grill mako (shark) and eat it with freshly made lime sauce. We never used lighter fluid—only wood chips and paper (but not newspaper). We might use brown paper bags or magazine paper."

Jim says to use wood that's aged at least one year, and he reminded me that American Indians used to throw pumpkin and other seeds on the fire to create aromatic smoke.

These days we are fortunate to have available a variety of fuels and fire materials. For years now, charcoal briquettes have been the main fuel for grilling foods and it's easy to understand why. Although they take longer to create a fire suitable for grilling, briquettes burn longer than most other materials. Reasonably priced, they are readily available and do a good job overall. I have found that, in addition to briquettes, lump charcoal (which now comes with hickory and other flavors) is an ideal fuel. It's easy to light and creates intense heat. Both briquettes and lump charcoal must burn down to gray ash—while still glowing red inside—to cook properly.

Many chefs like to add mesquite to a fire for the flavor it provides. Some prefer charcoal mesquite over chips or logs, because the charcoal burns at a much more intense heat— approximately 1000°F—and consequently sears in the flavors and juices of whatever is cooked over it.

Starting a fire is remarkably simple with one of the easy starters that have appeared on the market in recent years. The starter is in the form of a truncated cone made of sheet metal; it has a handle at the side and holes at the bottom. To use it, you fill the cone with charcoal and place twists of newspaper under the bottom grate. After the newspapers are ignited, they turn the charcoal red hot in only a few minutes.

Whether you choose briquettes or lump charcoal, you'll need a bed 2 inches thick and a little wider than the food you plan to grill. The coals will have to spread more if you plan to use a drip pan or spit, which is explained in other sections of this book.

Fires can also be started with a lit newspaper under a mound of coal, or with an electric starter—which seems to be gaining popularity among those who have an electric outlet near their grill. There are various other fire starters too. In any case, these days there is no reason in the world to use chemical starters and I advise strongly against their use.

Successful grilling depends on a good fire. It should be hot enough to maintain steady heat, but not so hot that it blackens food. There are two ways to tell whether the fire is ready: white ash must be evident and the coals must be at the proper grilling temperature. When the coals are gray or white, shake them gently to rearrange them, allowing ½ inch or so between coals. This moderates the heat and allows some of the drippings to fall in between, preventing flareups that would blacken food on the grill. To test for the right temperature, place your hand, palm down, about 6 inches directly over the fire. If you have to pull away in 2 or 3 seconds, it's time for adding food to the grill; this temperature is right for searing. Once the food is seared, the grid can be raised so the food cooks more slowly until done. If your hand can remain over the coals for 4 or 5 seconds, the fire is medium hot—ideal for normal grilling (cooking without searing).

Be aware of adjustable vents on the bottom or side of the grilling unit. Most hoods have vents also. They definitely influence the temperature of the coals—hotter if opened, cooler if closed. With some practice, you can learn to control flareups without using water (surely the sign of an amateur), and to speed up or slow down the burning rate.

Charcoal is not safe to use indoors—not even in a fireplace, and certainly not in a garage or barn (a location many resort to in inclement weather). When used indoors, charcoal produces carbon monoxide fumes, which are potentially lethal. I will never forget one Christmas Eve in Rome many years ago. After I requested some heat in my chilly *pensione* room, a chambermaid brought in a freshly lighted brazier of charcoal and I began to warm immediately by snuggling up to it. But were it not for a friend's tap on the door, I wouldn't be here today. As I got up to answer the knock, I keeled over. I remember being revived by a doctor's slaps—out on the balcony where he had moved me for the fresh air. A Roman holiday to remember.

Today, a wide variety of gas and electric grills are available for indoor and outdoor grilling. In fact, gas-fired grills with lava stones have become the *modus operandi* in many famous grill restaurants. There is a distinct advantage to these modern grills: they have no season and are not beholden to weather.

# GRILLING WITH WOOD CHIPS

Wood chips are a flavoring agent, not a fuel. Control the amount of flavor by the quantity of chips used.

| SUGGESTED CHIPS | SUGGESTED FOODS |
| --- | --- |
| Alder, hickory, mesquite, sassafras, grapevines | Chicken |
| Hickory, mesquite, oak, grapevines | Beef |
| Fruitwoods, hickory, oak, sassafras | Pork |
| Fruitwoods, mesquite | Lamb |
| Fruitwoods, grapevines | Veal |
| Alder, mesquite, sassafras, grapevines | Seafood |
| Mesquite | Vegetables |

1. Chips, wood chunks or vines must be soaked in water for at least 30 minutes.

2. For fires using charcoal briquettes or lump charcoal, sprinkle drained wood chips or chunks evenly over the fire.

3. For gas or electric grills, make an open-ended foil package or "log" of drained chips or chunks. Place log on lava rock.

4. Dried herbs and branches (and fresh ones, too) can be pre-soaked (as with wood chips and chunks) and added to charcoal fires. For gas grills, create a foil package, leaving ends open or make foil packet and puncture holes in foil to let aromatics escape and flavor the food.

# HOW TO MAKE A FOIL LOG

Presoaked wood chips or chunks may be thrown directly onto a charcoal fire, but they must be wrapped in foil, log fashion, for use with gas grills. Almost any aromatic wood may be made into a log—hickory, pecan, cherry, apple, walnut, alder, even grapevine cuttings. Smoking with foil logs works best on gas grills with two burners, but the technique is also useful on single units. Make several foil logs if the smoking is expected to last for several hours. It is to your advantage to keep chips soaking in the event you need to throw more on the fire or make another log

1. Put dried wood chips to soak in a pan of water well before you start grilling. Chips should soak a minimum of 30 minutes.

2. Cut a piece of heavy-duty foil 12 or 18 inches square. Fold in half to get a 12 × 6-inch or 18 × 9-inch rectangle.

3. Put about 2 cups drained wood chips in the center of the foil. Bring the short ends of the foil together, folding over several times to make a secure seam. Leave the ends of the log open to allow the smoke to escape from the ends.

4. Remove the cooking grid and move all the lava stone to one half of the grate.

5. Preheat the grill according to the manufacturer's instructions. Place the open log on the lava stones.

6. Place the filled water pan in the empty area of the grate. Replace the cooking grid over the water pan and close the hood. Heat setting should be on high until wood chips ignite.

7. Turn burner to low under the lava stones and off under the water pan. Place the food over the water pan, close hood and smoke food. Check to see if log needs replacing.

# BASIC MARINADES

One school of thought advocates grilling foods *au naturel*: in essence, a steak is grilled as is, and that's it. There is surely a place for simple grilled foods, and often I've tasted nothing better than a plain grilled porterhouse steak or hamburger. But most grilled food today is marinated with a "rub," a "mop" or one of the many wine-, vinegar- or lemon-and-oil-based marinades. And for a very important reason: as Brian Whitmer, a talented young chef at New York's Montrachet, puts it, "I marinate for flavor. The meats in this country are good and rarely do they need to be tenderized. But I marinate quail, duck and many meats for up to 48 hours, because only in this way do the flavors of the herbs, spices and even tomatillos come through."

Some cuts of meat — for example, beef flank or skirt steaks — may not be as tender as shell steaks or beef tenderloins, and marinating will tenderize them. But for most foods the goal of marination is to add flavor. Given the endless variety of ingredients that can be added to a marinade, there is no limit to the possible flavors. It's exciting and satisfying to create a marinade that is uniquely one's own; this is evident in the many talks I have had with working chefs across the country. Each has his or her special rub or mop for a particular fish or cut of meat.

A few thoughts about marinades:
- Use a glass, ceramic, stainless steel or other nonreactive container to hold marinade ingredients. The container should be large enough to hold the food in one layer. It doesn't have to be covered by the marinade; just be sure to turn it several times. As a rule, it is best to add salt after food is grilled, since salt tends to draw out juices, so omit it in the marinade.

- Most poultry and meat needs 1 to 3 hours marination at room temperature or overnight in the refrigerator. Bring refrigerated food to room temperature before adding it to the grill. Fish should be marinated for 15 to 30 minutes.

- Use marinades to baste food on the grill. If the marinade contains tomato or sugar, baste toward the end of the grilling time to avoid blackening the food. Oils and butter in marinades will cause flareups, so baste judiciously and learn to move meats around the grid or to lower the cover of the grill to tame flareups.

The marinades in this section are for application to food both before and during cooking, while sauces, relishes and chutneys (see page 312) are to be served with the food after it is grilled.

*Catsup*
*English catsup was made of vinegar with either mushrooms or oysters for flavor. This was the catsup, or "ketchup," used by the early settlers of Virginia and the Carolinas. It had no tomatoes because they were not eaten until later in the 18th century. As people moved West, tomatoes became a catsup ingredient. When sugar cane arrived from the Caribbean, it became an ingredient too.*

## BASIC BARBECUE SAUCE

Makes 4 cups

This is an all-purpose barbecue sauce, and a good one. Eventually many cooks become expert at devising sauces. This recipe serves as a good foundation.

### INGREDIENTS

2 tablespoons vegetable oil
1 medium onion, finely chopped
2 cups bottled chili sauce
1 cup water
¼ cup firmly packed brown sugar
2 tablespoons Worcestershire sauce
¼ cup red wine vinegar
juice of 2 lemons
1 tablespoon dry mustard
1 teaspoon paprika
salt and freshly ground pepper

1. Heat oil in a large stainless steel or enamel skillet over medium heat. Add onion and sauté until it begins to brown. Add all other ingredients and bring to boil. Lower heat and simmer for 20 minutes.

2. Use sauce right away or let cool, transfer to a tightly covered glass jar and refrigerate for up to 1 month.

> *Herbs*
> *While fresh herbs are preferable to dried, it is not always possible to grow them or find them in the markets. There is nothing wrong with using commercially dried herbs, but remember that they are stronger than fresh; when you substitute dried for fresh use ½ teaspoon crushed (or ¼ teaspoon powdered) for every tablespoon of the fresh. Dried herbs should be replaced at least once a year as their volatile oils evaporate. Buy your herbs and spices in small packages to avoid waste. Keep them in airtight containers in a dark, cool place. The flavor of dried herbs is intensified by crushing or rubbing them between your fingers.*

# BALSAMIC MARINADE

Makes about 1 cup

Balsamic vinegar, a trendy item these days in the United States, has been on the scene in Italy for generations; there it is considered a staple. Good balsamic vinegar is aged at least three years. In Modena, Italy, it has been packaged for hundreds of years, the ancient casks handed down from one generation to the next. The vinegar's distinct flavor not only enhances salad dressings but creates a fine base for a marinade.

### INGREDIENTS

¼ cup balsamic vinegar
⅔ cup olive oil
salt and freshly ground pepper
2 tablespoons finely chopped herbs such as thyme, tarragon, basil, oregano and/or others of your choice

Place the balsamic vinegar in a bowl and whisk in the oil. When combined, add the remaining ingredients.

*Olive Oil*

*Olive oil is a common ingredient in grilled foods, probably because both are so universal. Olive oil does not burn as fast as butter, and it is helpful to remember this when composing marinades and sauces, although you'll find that some in this book call for butter or oil and butter together. Many food authorities believe the best olive oil is Italian, specifically from Lucca in Tuscany. The oil is pressed from tree-ripened olives. The first pressing, "extra virgin," is considered the finest.*

*Look for clear, golden oil; the greener ones are fruitier and many prefer them. Store oil in a tightly covered container in a dark, cool place.*

*If you wonder why olive oil is used in so many recipes in this book, keep this in mind: it contains no cholesterol and is very digestible. Tests conducted by the American Heart Association's Nutrition Committee showed that using olive oil in place of saturated fats in the diet reduces blood cholesterol levels.*

# PRIMAVERA BARBECUE SAUCE

Makes 1 cup

In summer, when fresh herbs are abundant in the garden, combine them to add a light, fresh, summery Italian flavor to grilled fish, chicken and almost any cut of meat. Dried herbs may be substituted but the sauce will not be as fragrant.

### INGREDIENTS

⅔ cup fresh lemon juice
⅓ cup olive oil
2 garlic cloves, minced
1 tablespoon finely chopped fresh basil
1 tablespoon finely chopped fresh oregano
1 tablespoon finely chopped fresh Italian
    parsley
salt and a generous sprinkle of freshly ground
    pepper

Combine lemon juice and olive oil until well blended. Add other ingredients and mix well. Let stand at room temperature to allow flavors to develop.

# SESAME-CHILI MARINADE

Makes about ½ cup

This is a hot marinade, but you won't have to chop hot chili peppers and burn your fingers and eyes. Sesame-chili oil adds a distinctive, enjoyable flavor to grilled foods.

### INGREDIENTS

½ cup soy sauce
2 tablespoons sesame-chili oil (available at
    Oriental markets)
2 tablespoons olive oil
1 tablespoon chopped fresh ginger

Combine all ingredients and mix well.

---

### Basil

*In Genoa, the home of pesto, basil is forced in greenhouses in tropical heat and humidity. Picked when 6 inches tall, bunched in paper, green leaves or grass with roots intact, it is sold in markets everywhere.*

*I'm always asked how to preserve basil. It can be frozen in plastic bags and containers. But I prefer the Italian method of washing and drying the leaves, if necessary, and layering them tightly in a wide-mouth jar with a cover, salting the layers (not every leaf). When the jar is filled to the top with basil, slowly pour in olive oil until the basil is completely submerged. Close the cover tightly, refrigerate and use as needed. It will darken in time, but the flavor is second-best to fresh basil.*

*Always prized in Mediterranean countries, basil became popular here on pizza during the '50s and '60s, but now it's one of the trendiest herbs and fresh bundles of it sell out quickly. Basil sauces on meats and fish are considered haute cuisine.*

# SHERRY MARINADE

Makes about 2 cups

This is especially good on chicken, pork and some cuts of beef. To substitute dry sherry for cream sherry, increase the honey to ½ cup. Whenever honey is part of a marinade, it will require more frequent stirring.

### INGREDIENTS

½ cup cream sherry
½ cup soy sauce
1 cup water
⅓ cup honey
2 garlic cloves, minced
pinch of red pepper flakes, optional

Combine all ingredients until well blended. Before adding to the meat, stir well to be sure honey is combined with other ingredients and has not settled to bottom. It's a good idea to stir while marinating for the same reason.

# WINE AND OIL MARINADE

Makes 1¼ cups

Use red or white wine, depending on what will be marinated and on which you prefer. The carrot adds a touch of sweetness in addition to color.

### INGREDIENTS

1 cup red or white wine
¼ cup olive oil
2 green onions, thinly sliced
1 small carrot, cut into ¼-inch dice
3 fresh parsley sprigs, coarsely chopped
freshly ground pepper

Place the wine in a bowl and whisk in the oil. When they are combined, add remaining ingredients and mix well.

## CHILI AND FENNEL MOP FOR FISH

Makes enough for 6 pounds fish

INGREDIENTS

1 dry red chili, seeded and crumbled
1 tablespoon ground fennel seed
¼ teaspoon white peppercorns, cracked
2 tablespoons coarse salt
3 garlic cloves, minced
½ cup olive oil
juice of 1 lemon

1. In a mortar, combine chili, fennel, peppercorns, salt and garlic and grind until a paste is formed. Slowly incorporate oil and lemon juice; mix well.

2. Mop fish all over, inside and out.

## MARINADE FOR WHOLE FISH

Makes about ⅓ cup

INGREDIENTS

2 teaspoons coarse salt
1 tablespoon whole white peppercorns, finely cracked
¼ teaspoon red pepper flakes
2 tablespoon finely chopped fresh coriander
¼ cup olive oil

In a mortar or spice grinder combine salt, peppercorns and pepper flakes (if using a mortar, add coriander; if using a spice grinder, add coriander with oil) and grind until well combined. Add oil a little at a time, whisking until well incorporated.

# MARINADE
# FOR FISH STEAKS AND
# KEBABS

Makes about 1½ cups

INGREDIENTS

1 cup soy sauce
juice of 1 lemon
¼ cup dry sherry
2 tablespoons finely chopped or grated fresh
   ginger
¼ cup finely chopped green onion
1 garlic clove, minced
pinch of cayenne pepper
1 tablespoon freshly ground pepper

Combine all ingredients in a glass or ceramic
container and mix well.

# WHITE WINE-SAGE
# MARINADE FOR FISH

Makes about 1 cup

INGREDIENTS

½ cup dry white wine
⅓ cup olive or vegetable oil
2 teaspoons dried crushed sage
2 tablespoons finely chopped parsley
salt and freshly ground pepper

Combine all ingredients and mix well.

## MARINADE
## FOR BEEF STEAKS

Makes enough for four 1-pound steaks

### INGREDIENTS

¾ cup olive oil
¼ cup balsamic vinegar
2 tablespoons soy sauce
juice of 1 lemon
2 tablespoons Worcestershire sauce
2 garlic cloves, minced
1 tablespoon dry mustard
1 teaspoon chopped parsley
freshly ground pepper

Combine all ingredients and mix well. Marinate beef at room temperature for 1 to 2 hours before grilling.

## SPICE RUB
## FOR BEEF STEAKS

Makes enough for two 2-pound steaks

### INGREDIENTS

1½ tablespoons dry mustard
1½ tablespoons black peppercorns, cracked
1½ tablespoons ground coriander
1½ tablespoons paprika
1½ teaspoons cayenne pepper
2 large garlic cloves, minced
2 tablespoons peanut oil
3 tablespoons cognac

Grind dry spices and garlic in a mortar with pestle. When finely ground, work in oil and cognac. Rub over both sides of steak and let marinate for 1 to 2 hours at room temperature before grilling.

## GINGER, SOY AND SHERRY MARINADE FOR PORK

Makes about 2 cups

### INGREDIENTS

2 garlic cloves, finely chopped
2 tablespoons peeled and finely chopped fresh
  ginger
1 cup soy sauce
½ cup dry sherry
½ cup catsup

**1.** Combine all ingredients and mix well. Coat the meat liberally with the sauce and allow it to marinate for several hours.

**2.** During the last 10 to 15 minutes of grilling, baste the meat with the marinade.

---

*Juniper*
*Juniper berries grow on prickly waist-high bushes. They take several years to ripen; only the blue ones are selected for flavoring. The plants are easy to grow in a home garden, but remember that only female bushes produce berries.*

*Almost always crushed before use, the berries are used in venison and pork marinades, in pâtés, sauerkraut and conserves. They go well with many other herbs — bay, fennel, marjoram, parsley and thyme, to mention a few. They're excellent combined with garlic and spices, with brandies and many wines. Young chefs all over the country are popularizing the flavor of juniper.*

---

## HONEY AND PINEAPPLE MARINADE FOR PORK

Makes about 2 cups

### INGREDIENTS

½ cup honey
½ cup soy sauce
¼ cup white wine vinegar
1 cup finely chopped fresh pineapple
2 tablespoons grated fresh ginger or 1 teaspoon
  ground
2 garlic cloves, minced

Combine all ingredients and pour over pork. Let marinate overnight in refrigerator; remove 1 to 2 hours before grilling. Baste meat with marinade during last 5 to 10 minutes of grilling.

# BARBECUE SAUCE
# FOR PORK

Makes about 2 cups

Ann Couper grew up in Atlanta, Georgia, and was a friend of Margaret Mitchell, who wrote *Gone with the Wind*. She shared with me notes written by Miss Mitchell when they were school chums in their early teens. Here is her recipe for a sauce that she said had been used by her family for generations.

### INGREDIENTS

⅔ cup cider vinegar
½ cup peanut oil
juice of 1 lemon
⅓ cup firmly packed dark brown sugar
1 cup catsup
2 tablespoons Gulden's prepared mustard
¼ cup Worcestershire sauce
3 small to medium garlic cloves, very finely
   chopped
3 tablespoons bourbon, optional

Combine all ingredients in a nonaluminum saucepan and bring to boil. Lower heat immediately and simmer for 3 to 4 minutes.

# KENTUCKY
# BARBECUE SAUCE

Makes about 3 ½ cups

This recipe for a pork basting sauce comes from the Kentucky Home Pork Producers Association, which has been preparing barbecue for the Kentucky Colonels Derby barbecue since 1977.

### INGREDIENTS

2½ cups water
1 tablespoon sugar
3 tablespoons freshly ground black pepper
2 tablespoons butter
¼ cup vinegar
1 tablespoon salt
¼ cup chopped onion
1 garlic clove, minced
1 teaspoon cayenne pepper
1 teaspoon chili powder
1 teaspoon hot pepper sauce
1 teaspoon dry mustard
3 tablespoons Worcestershire sauce

1. Combine all ingredients in a nonaluminum saucepan and bring to boil. Reduce heat and simmer 5 minutes. Cool. Refrigerate overnight. Warm before using.

2. Start basting meat at beginning of cooking and continue until pork registers 170°F on meat thermometer.

## GINGER, MINT AND HONEY MARINADE for LAMB

Makes about 1½ cups

### INGREDIENTS

1 cup fresh orange juice (about 2 oranges)
¼ cup soy sauce
¼ cup honey
2 tablespoons chopped fresh mint or 1 teaspoon dried
2 tablespoons finely chopped fresh ginger or 1 teaspoon ground
3 garlic cloves, minced
salt and freshly ground pepper

Combine all ingredients and mix well. Pour over lamb. Marinate at room temperature for at least 2 hours or refrigerate overnight. Remove from refrigerator 1 hour before grilling.

## HERBED YOGURT MARINADE FOR LAMB

Makes about 1¼ cups

### INGREDIENTS

1 cup yogurt
3 tablespoons olive oil
2 small garlic cloves, finely chopped
1 teaspoon chopped fresh mint or ½ teaspoon dried
1 teaspoon chopped fresh tarragon or ½ teaspoon dried
generous sprinkling of freshly ground pepper

In a food processor, pulse the yogurt several times until smooth. Pour in the olive oil and pulse 2 or 3 times. Add remaining ingredients and pulse until blended.

---

*Ginger*
*Deeply rooted in history, ginger has known every civilization — Arabic, Chinese, Greek, Indian, Roman, Southeast Asian and so on. Resembling an iris root, its tuber has a paper-thin, light brown skin that can be easily peeled off with a parer. Ginger freezes well and slivers well. It's popular in gingerbread, cookies and marinades. It has an exciting flavor; use it often.*

---

*Barbecued Mutton*
*There are over 125 barbecue restaurants in Kentucky. In 1806 there appeared the first written reference to Kentucky barbecued mutton, which was prepared at the wedding of Tom Lincoln and Nancy Hanks. It was reported that "guests were served a sheep that two families barbecued whole over coals of wood burned in a pit with boughs to keep the juices in."*

## BARBECUE SAUCE WITH HORSERADISH

Makes enough for two 3-pound chickens or 4 to 5 pounds ribs

The noted food writer and critic, Bernie O'Brien, from Hollywood, Florida, thinks this is one of the best barbecue sauces, especially on chicken. He says it's excellent on pork, too, but not on fish.

### INGREDIENTS

1 cup (2 sticks) butter, melted
⅓ cup fresh lemon juice (about 2 lemons)
½ cup cider vinegar
½ cup catsup
2 teaspoons Worcestershire sauce
3 or 4 drops hot pepper sauce
2 tablespoons freshly grated or ⅓ cup prepared
    horseradish
salt and freshly ground pepper

Combine all ingredients in a nonaluminum saucepan and bring just to boil. Lower heat immediately and simmer for 15 minutes before using.

## MADEIRA WINE MARINADE FOR CHICKEN AND PORK

Makes about 1½ cups

### INGREDIENTS

½ cup Madeira
½ cup firmly packed brown sugar
1½ teaspoons finely chopped orange zest
½ cup fresh orange juice
salt and freshly ground pepper

Combine all ingredients in a nonaluminum saucepan and mix well. Cook over medium heat until sugar dissolves. Cool, pour over pork or chicken and let marinate overnight in refrigerator. Remove from refrigerator 1 to 2 hours before grilling. Use marinade for basting during last 5 to 10 minutes of grilling.

# SEAFOOD

Seafood is a natural for the grill and there are many ways to cook it. One of the best ways to grill a single whole fish is in a hinged wire basket. Wire grills come in several shapes; the wires are closer together for fish, farther apart for meat. If a wire basket is not available, be certain to oil the grid before placing the fish on it and always have two large spatulas ready to help turn the fish. It should only be turned once; it is fragile and can break or tear easily if handled too much.

If the fish is more than 1 ½ inches thick, grill it covered in order to cook it all the way through. Overcooking will ruin your fish. As a guide, a 1-inch fish steak rarely needs more than 10 minutes and sometimes less, provided it was at room temperature when put on the grill. Fragile fillets of sole and flounder are difficult to handle on an open grill and are better suited to foil cooking or "grilling" under a salamander (a type of broiling unit) or broiler.

There are two dependable tests for doneness: either insert a fork in the thickest part to check if the flesh is opaque white and just beginning to flake, or insert a wooden skewer to see if it meets no resistance. In either of these cases the fish is fully cooked.

Although most seafood bastes itself because of its oil content, it is best to use a flavored oil marinade (usually not for longer than 30 minutes) or a brushing of oil with lean fish such as sea bass. No other foods absorb the smoky flavors of the grill as quickly and easily as seafood.

Fresh, tender fish and shellfish require only brief cooking to firm their flesh and develop their natural flavor. They can be cooked in a variety of ways:

**Fish fillets** — plump, round fish such as snapper, trout, bluefish and striped bass make better fillets than those from flatfish (turbot, sole or fluke) for grilling directly on the grid. These plump fish yield fillets an inch or more thick, which do not dry out or disintegrate when grilled. Flatfish fillets are thinner and are easier to broil or to packet in foil for grilling.

Some people don't like to bother with skin and bones on their plates, so fillets are ideal for them. Fillets invite all kinds of sauces (one of the best is on page 307). Grill fillets in flat hinged wire baskets to simplify turning. Basting can easily be done right through the wire mesh.

**Steaks** — round fish can be cut into steaks; salmon, swordfish, halibut, tuna, sablefish, sturgeon and shark are some of the more popular choices. Thin steaks, about ½ inch thick, require fast grilling over high heat by searing both sides and removing the fish quickly before it dries out. Thicker steaks are better on a medium fire so the inside can cook without blackening the outside. Of course, there are exceptions to this general rule; see tuna steak on page 77.

**Kebabs** — pieces of one or more kinds of fish and shellfish, thick enough to be skewered with or without vegetables (and to remain on the skewer while cooking), creating different textures and tastes. The kebab pieces should be about 1 inch thick, cubed from a steak or fillet. Naturally fat fish like swordfish, salmon or trout make the best kebabs. Marination and basting will improve flavors and help keep the fish moist.

**Whole fish** — one of the wonders of the culinary world is a moist, tender, crisp whole grilled fish. They are easy to prepare and require little time to cook; the use of a hinged wire basket makes the task even simpler. For a perfect, never-fail, wonderfully grilled whole fish, try the recipe on page 38

**In and out of the halfshell** — clams and oysters can be delicious in and out of their shells. Take the normal precautions with them, such as discarding opened ones, removing sand and so on. Add butter, lemon, bacon, crumbs, herbs or spices and you can grill in the half-shells; if shucked, put them in a wire basket or thread on a skewer.

**Planked** — this is a simple arrangement of nailing unskinned fish fillets to a plank of wood and placing it upright, with the top of the plank at a slight angle away from the fire but immediately in front of it. The skin holds the fillets together while cooking. Planking can be done indoors as well as out; the fish is cooked by radiant heat. Use an old thin cutting board and aluminum or stainless steel nails, and always marinate the fillets in oil and aromatics.

I had an instructive experience cooking the same fish recipe twice, at the same time: one fish was done in a microwave oven and the other on an open grill. The microwave one was fine but the grilled fish was more flavorful.

More and more varieties of seafood are being prepared at home and in restaurants. The grill provides one of the most rewarding ways to prepare it, not just because it is healthful but because seafood tastes better cooked this way.

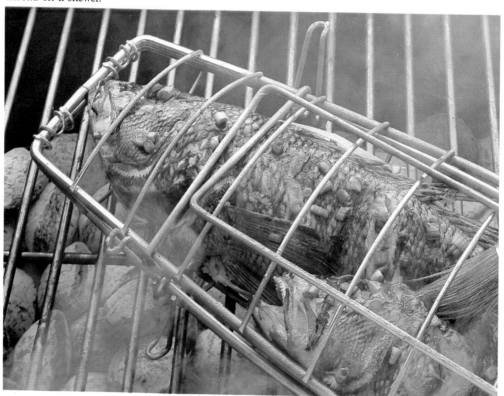

# FISH AND SEAFOOD SELECTION AND PORTION SIZE

Provide one small whole fish, such as rainbow trout, per person. If buying steaks or fillets, serve 8 ounces per person. The best lobsters are 1 to 2 pounds each. Purchase them alive, asking your fishmonger to split and clean them. Shrimp seem to go faster than anything else, so it is best to allow 8 ounces per person.

## FISH SUBSTITUTIONS

If you want to make a recipe but don't have the fish specified, other varieties can be substituted. According to the U.S. Department of Commerce and the National Marine Fisheries Service, the following are groups of fish varieties that are similar in flavor and type.

### WHITE MEAT; VERY LIGHT, DELICATE FLAVOR

| | |
|---|---|
| Cod | Rex Sole |
| Cusk | Southern Flounder |
| Dover Sole | Spotted Cabrilla |
| Haddock | Summer Flounder |
| Lake Whitefish | (Fluke) |
| Pacific Halibut | Witch Flounder |
| Pacific Sand Dab | Yellowtail Flounder |
| Petrale Sole | Yellowtail Snapper |

### WHITE MEAT; LIGHT TO MODERATE FLAVOR

| | |
|---|---|
| American Plaice/Dab | Rock Sole |
| Arrowtooth Flounder | Sauger |
| Butterfish | Snook |
| Catfish | Spotted Sea Trout |
| Cobia | Starry Flounder |
| English Sole | White King Salmon |
| Lingcod | White Sea Trout |
| Mahi Mahi | Whiting |
| Pacific Whiting | Winter Flounder |
| Red Snapper | Wolffish |

### LIGHT MEAT; VERY LIGHT, DELICATE FLAVOR

| | |
|---|---|
| Alaska Pollock | Rainbow Trout |
| Brook Trout | Smelt |
| Giant Sea Bass | Tautog |
| Grouper | Walleye |
| Pacific Ocean | White Crappie |
| Perch | White Sea Bass |

### LIGHT MEAT; LIGHT TO MODERATE FLAVOR

| | |
|---|---|
| Atlantic Ocean Perch | Monkfish |
| Atlantic Salmon | Mullet |
| Black Drum | Northern Pike |
| Buffalofish | Perch |
| Burbot | Pink Salmon |
| Carp | Pollock |
| Chum Salmon | Pompano |
| Crevalle Jack | Rockfish |
| Croaker | Sablefish |
| Eel | Sand Shark |
| Greenland Turbot | Sculpin |
| Jewfish | Scup/Porgie |
| King (Chinook) | Sheepshead |
| Salmon | Silver (Coho) Salmon |
| Lake Chub | Spot |
| Lake Herring | Striped Bass |
| Lake Sturgeon | Swordfish |
| Lake Trout | Vermilion Snapper |

### LIGHT MEAT; MORE PRONOUNCED FLAVOR

Atlantic Mackerel
King Mackerel
Spanish Mackerel

### DARKER MEAT; LIGHT TO MODERATE FLAVOR

Black Sea Bass
Bluefish
Ocean Pout
Sockeye (Red) Salmon

plete cooking on one side. Turn fish over and spoon on some of the marinade, including the coriander and green onions. Sear and cook second side; baste again when it is done, about 10 minutes total.

4. Set fish on large platters, pour any remaining marinade over and serve immediately.

## GRILLED SEA BASS IN A WIRE BASKET

Serves 4

If the bass is really fresh, this is an outstanding dish. It is easy to prepare and filled with honest smoky flavor. I believe it is one of the best dishes in this book.

### INGREDIENTS

2 whole sea bass (2 ¼ pounds each), cleaned, with head and tail on, rinsed and dried
4 garlic cloves, halved
2 tablespoons white wine vinegar
¼ cup sesame oil
⅓ cup tamari soy sauce
6 very thin slices fresh ginger, cut into thin strips
4 sprigs fresh coriander, cut in thirds
4 thinly sliced green onions

1. Make 2 slashes, about ½ inch deep, on each side of both fish. Place them in one or two glass or ceramic dishes.

2. Combine all other ingredients and pour over fish. Let marinate for about 30 minutes at room temperature, turning fish after 15 minutes.

3. Place each fish in a hinged wire grill basket and set them on the grill when the fire is ready. Sear about 3 inches from the heat, then raise grill 2 to 3 inches higher to com-

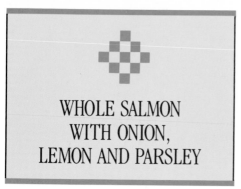

# WHOLE SALMON WITH ONION, LEMON AND PARSLEY

Serves 4 to 6

A whole salmon is excellent for the grill. It can be served warm or cold and is easy to prepare in a foil package. If you decide to keep the head on, cover the eye with a slice of lemon when you serve it.

### INGREDIENTS

1 whole salmon (3 pounds), cleaned, with
    head removed if desired
vegetable oil
juice of 1 lemon
coarse salt and freshly ground pepper
3 tablespoons butter
1 cup chopped fresh porcini mushrooms, or ¼
    cup dried, soaked in water for 30 minutes,
    drained, rinsed and chopped
⅓ cup dry white wine
6 fresh plum tomatoes or 3 large tomatoes,
    cored, peeled, seeded and chopped, or 6
    canned plum tomatoes, seeded and chopped
½ cup thinly sliced green onions
⅓ cup chopped parsley
1 lemon, thinly sliced and seeded
green onions and parsley sprigs for garnish
1½ cups salmon fumet (see below)

1. Wash and dry the salmon. Prepare a double thickness of heavy-duty foil large enough to envelop salmon in a drugstore wrap (see page 18). Brush foil and entire surface of fish with oil and place fish in center of foil.

Carefully brush lemon juice all over the salmon, inside and out, using all the juice.

2. In a skillet, melt butter over medium heat. Add mushrooms and wine and cook for 3 to 4 minutes. Add tomatoes, green onions, parsley, and salt and pepper and cook until sauce is slightly thickened, about 5 minutes. Reserve about ¼ of this mixture for sauce. Use remainder to stuff salmon. If cavity isn't large enough to receive stuffing, halve fish lengthwise and "sandwich" with mushroom mixture.

3. Secure package with drugstore wrap and place it on grid about 6 inches over heat source. Cover and grill salmon for 25 minutes, turning once and being careful not to puncture foil. Test for doneness by removing package from grill, opening it and inserting a wooden skewer into thickest part of fish. The skewer should meet no resistance, and the flesh should appear flaky. If it is still translucent, it needs more grilling; rewrap and grill a few minutes longer.

4. To serve, unwrap package and turn salmon onto large warmed platter. Garnish with lemon slices, green onions and parsley.

5. Heat salmon fumet and stir in reserved mushroom mixture. Serve with fish.

Note: Salmon can also be cooked on an open grill; add 10 to 15 minutes cooking time.

## SALMON FUMET

Makes about 4 cups

## GRILLED
## SALTED SEA TROUT
## OVER AN OPEN FIRE

Serves 4

### INGREDIENTS

2 pounds salmon head and bones
2½-inch piece of carrot, diced
1-inch piece of celery, leaves trimmed
white and green of 1 leek, cleaned
small bouquet garni (thyme, bay leaf and
    parsley stems)
5 black peppercorns
a few grains of salt
1 cup Chardonnay
3 to 4 cups water

**1.** Clean the fish carcass of tail fin, gills and any livery substances. Chop bones to fit a nonaluminum saucepan. Add vegetables, herbs, spices, wine and enough water to come 1 inch above the bones.

**2.** Bring to boil over medium flame. Lower heat and cook at the gentlest possible simmer for 30 minutes, crushing the bones midway through cooking. Turn off heat and let fumet stand for 10 minutes. Strain through a colander and then through a strainer lined with moistened cheesecloth into a tall, narrow container. Let cool until fat surfaces. Skim fat completely off; remove final drops of fat with a paper towel.

Best cooked over charcoal. Remove the grill so the fish cooks directly over the coals. If using a hibachi, remove the grill and anchor the skewered fish by letting the skewer ends rest against the hibachi's edge.

### INGREDIENTS

2 fresh sea trout (1½ pounds each), cleaned,
    with head and tail on, rinsed and dried
1 teaspoon soy sauce
2 tablespoons salt
2 tablespoons finely chopped preserved ginger
1 lemon, quartered lengthwise
2 green onions, finely chopped

**1.** Have fish at room temperature. Rub soy sauce onto skin and put ginger inside. Heavily salt heads and tails of both fish to prevent scorching; sprinkle some salt over the fish for seasoning.

**2.** Run a 12-inch skewer lengthwise through each fish. Use a second skewer if necessary to keep fish from rotating.

**3.** Grill one side, then the other, 6 inches above grayed charcoal. Transfer to a platter and carefully remove skewers. Add lemon wedges and sprinkle with green onions.

# GRILLED SEA BASS
# WITH SORREL SAUCE

Serves 2

Emilie and Dominique Chadelat own and operate Le Dauphin, a small inn 70 miles south of Paris in Villeneuve-sur-Yonne. It is an inn that perfectly distills anyone's dream of the French provinces. One enters the courtyard between the fluted pillars of a Renaissance archway; in the restaurant you'll find excellent food and service, and reasonable prices.

### INGREDIENTS

1 pound fresh sorrel
4 tablespoons unsalted butter
3 shallots, finely diced
¼ cup dry vermouth, chilled
2 tablespoons heavy cream
3 egg yolks
2 fresh sea bass (8 to 9 ounces each), cleaned
1 tablespoon olive or vegetable oil
salt and freshly ground pepper

1. Wash, trim and drain sorrel. In a stainless steel saucepan, combine 1 cup water with a pinch of salt and bring to boil. Add sorrel and cook 2 minutes. Drain well and mince.

2. In another saucepan, melt butter over medium heat and sauté the sorrel with the shallots for 4 to 5 minutes, stirring constantly with a wooden spoon. When shallots are browned, remove from heat. Add the chilled vermouth, stir vigorously and return pan to heat. Add heavy cream and bring to boil; remove from heat. Add yolks, one at a time, mixing well; keep warm.

3. Wash fish, pat dry and rub with oil. Broil or grill over high heat for about 4 minutes per side. Season with salt and pepper to taste.

4. To serve, distribute hot sauce over 2 plates and place a grilled bass on top of each.

# FRESH SEA BASS GRILLED WITH ORANGE MARMALADE MUSTARD

Serves 2 to 3

Other light-fleshed fish may be used here also. This is a simple preparation; the fish doesn't take long to grill, and it marinates no longer than 30 minutes.

### INGREDIENTS

1 fresh sea bass (2 ½ pounds) cleaned, with head and tail left on, rinsed and dried
coarse salt and freshly ground pepper
¼ cup freshly squeezed orange juice (peel reserved)
¼ cup orange marmalade
¼ cup Dijon mustard
2 tablespoons mustard seed

1. Sprinkle inside of fish with salt and pepper. Place the fish in a glass or ceramic dish and set aside.

2. Combine orange juice and marmalade in a small nonaluminum saucepan and heat just to melt the marmalade. Let cool slightly, then whisk in mustard, mustard seed, 1 teaspoon coarse salt and pepper to taste.

3. Spread orange marmalade over both sides of fish and let marinate at room temperature for 20 to 30 minutes. Transfer fish to a hinged wire basket.

4. When the fire is ready, cut reserved orange peel into small pieces and toss over the coals. Grill fish on one side for about 6 minutes, then turn and grill other side until done. Transfer fish to platter and serve.

*Note: Because it is sweetened, the orange marmalade will blacken the fish. Some charring is desired, but watch carefully to avoid burning.*

---

*Lean Fish*
*Sea bass is a lean fish and low in fat and cholesterol. It grills easily and adapts flavors of the marinade quickly and easily. It develops a smoky, grilled flavor even in the short time it is on the grill. Be sure your fish is at room temperature and don't overcook it.*

---

# GRILLED WHOLE STRIPED BASS WITH GINGER SAUCE

Serves 2 to 3

Other light-fleshed fish, such as red snapper, grouper and sea bass may be used.

### INGREDIENTS

4 tablespoons softened butter
1 tablespoon Dijon mustard
salt and freshly ground pepper
1 striped bass (about 2 pounds), cleaned, with
    head and tail on, rinsed and dried

### Sauce

½ cup fish stock or clam juice
1 teaspoon soy sauce
2 tablespoons grated fresh ginger
1 garlic clove, minced
1 tablespoon peanut oil
1 tablespoon finely chopped fresh coriander or
    flat parsley leaves

1. Combine the butter, mustard, salt and pepper. Brush half of mixture inside the fish, the remainder on the outside.

2. When the fire is ready, grill the fish in a hinged wire basket if you have one. If not, place the fish on an oiled grill; turn only once. This is a small fish and will take about 10 minutes total grilling time.

3. Combine all sauce ingredients except coriander or parsley in a small saucepan and bring to boil. Lower heat and simmer for about 10 minutes. Remove from heat, add coriander and parsley and serve with the fish. The sauce may be made ahead of time and kept warm, or refrigerated and reheated. Check the sauce for seasoning before serving, adding another dash of soy sauce if needed.

> *Fish Grill Tips*
> *1. Oil the grid before putting the fish on it.*
>
> *2. Use a wire basket and oil it. It will then not be necessary to oil grid.*
>
> *3. Small fish (e.g. a 2-pounder) cook fine on an open fire. If heavier, use a covered grill if you have one.*
>
> *4. Use long, wide spatulas to turn fish and turn only once.*

## GRILLED
## RED HOT SNAPPER

Serves 2 to 3

Other light-fleshed fish, such as striped bass or sea bass, may be substituted if fresh red snapper is not available in the markets.

### INGREDIENTS

1 tablespoon whole white peppercorns
¼ teaspoon red pepper flakes
2 teaspoons coarse salt
2 tablespoons finely chopped fresh fennel or 1 teaspoon dried
2 tablespoons finely chopped fresh coriander or 1 teaspoon dried
¼ cup olive oil
1 red snapper (about 2 pounds), cleaned, with head and tail on, rinsed and dried
4 tablespoons butter

1. With a mortar and pestle (or spice grinder), grind together the peppercorns, pepper flakes and salt. If using dried herbs, pulverize with peppers and salt. Transfer to a small bowl and work in the olive oil. If using fresh fennel and coriander, add them now.

2. Reserve about ⅓ of the herb mixture. Brush or rub remainder over the fish inside and out. Allow to marinate 30 to 60 minutes.

3. When the fire is ready, place the whole fish on an oiled grill and turn only once. Use a hinged wire grill if available; it will make turning the fish much easier. This is a small fish and will take about 10 minutes total grilling time.

4. While the snapper is grilling, melt the butter in a small saucepan and stir in the reserved herb seasoning. Serve 2 tablespoons butter sauce with each portion.

*Whole Fish in Wire Basket*
*A hinged wire basket is an indispensable tool for grilling a whole fish. Any size and almost any type of fish can be grilled whole and the basket helps keep the fish from breaking apart on the grid. Oil the basket and flip it once to turn the fish. Be sure the fire is ready for searing, as you want the fish to be crisp outside, tender and moist inside. Flavors can be enhanced by placing herbs inside the basket, between the fish skin and the wires. Baste fish frequently right through the wire mesh.*

*Fish and Herbs*
*Americans have known herbs such as parsley, rosemary, thyme and summer savory and use them in many foods. Lately, other herbs are gaining in popularity, such as coriander. Here is a recipe where both coriander and fennel are used with a light fish and the result is a new taste and a delicious one, too.*

# GRILLED RED SNAPPER
# WITH TWO SAUCES

Serves 2 to 4

From Del Mar, a superb fish restaurant in Rio de Janeiro.

### INGREDIENTS

2 red snapper (about 2 pounds each), cleaned
    with head and tail on, rinsed and dried
1 tablespoon finely chopped fresh oregano or
    ½ teaspoon dried
salt and freshly ground pepper
juice of 1 lemon
⅓ cup olive oil
1 garlic clove, cut into four pieces
snail butter (see below)
almond sauce (see below)

1. Sprinkle the inside of the fish with oregano, salt and pepper.

2. Combine lemon juice, olive oil and garlic, pressing down on the garlic pieces with a fork to release the juices. Discard the garlic. Brush the fish with marinade, place them in a grill basket and set it over the fire. Turn and baste the fish often; it will be done in less than 15 minutes. Serve immediately with the two sauces.

### SNAIL BUTTER

Makes about 1 cup

### INGREDIENTS

1 cup (2 sticks) butter
3 shallots, minced
2 garlic cloves, minced
1 tablespoon finely chopped parsley
salt and freshly ground pepper
pinch each of nutmeg, mace and dried thyme

Combine all ingredients in a saucepan and warm over low heat until butter is melted, stirring often.

### ALMOND SAUCE

Makes about 1 cup

### INGREDIENTS

4 tablespoons butter
½ cup olive oil
2 tablespoons small capers, drained and dried
⅓ cup toasted slivered almonds
salt and freshly ground pepper

Melt butter with oil. Add capers, almonds and seasonings. Serve hot.

# GRILLED RED SNAPPER
# WITH WILD FENNEL

Serves 4 to 6

Felipe Rojas-Lombardi created this recipe. He worked with James Beard and is now the chef/owner of the Ballroom Restaurant in New York.

### INGREDIENTS

1 red snapper (6 pounds), cleaned, with head and tail on, rinsed and dried

*Molido*
3 garlic cloves, chopped
1 dried hot red chili, seeded and crumbled
1 tablespoon ground fennel seeds
¾ teaspoon white peppercorns, cracked
2 tablespoons coarse salt
½ cup light rum
½ cup olive oil
1 pound dried fennel stalks, soaked in warm water for 1 hour*
½ cup dry white wine
4 tablespoons olive oil
3 large fresh fennel bulbs (about 2 pounds), quartered

1. Make shallow diagonal slashes, 2 inches apart, on both sides of the fish.
To prepare *molido*:

2. In a mortar, combine garlic, chili, fennel, peppercorns and salt and pound until a paste is formed. Stir in rum, then olive oil. (Or combine all ingredients in a blender and blend until smooth.)

3. Rub the fish inside and out with the *mol-ido*. Place half the soaked fennel stalks in a hinged wire grill for fish. Set the fish on top and place stalks in the cavity; cover with the remaining fennel stalks. Combine wine and 3 tablespoons of the oil and sprinkle over fish and fennel. Rub the remaining oil over the quartered fresh fennel pieces. Place one piece into the mouth of the fish and the others around the fish inside the wire grill. Close the grill.

4. When the fire is ready, grill the fish for about 45 minutes, turning it several times. To serve, open wire grill, remove top layer of sticks and transfer fish to warm platter.

*Dried fennel sticks may be purchased at Dean and DeLuca, 121 Prince Street, New York, N.Y. 10012 (800/221-7714 or 212/431-1691).*

# GRILLED SALMON MARINATED IN JUNIPER, SUGAR, SALT AND ORANGE

Serves 6

From Joyce Goldstein, the innovative chef at Square One in San Francisco. Serve with sautéed spinach or Swiss chard and garnish the plate with a lemon or orange wedge.

### INGREDIENTS

3 tablespoons coarse salt
6 tablespoons sugar
3 tablespoons juniper berries, ground
1 teaspoon freshly ground pepper
1 tablespoon grated orange zest
6 boneless salmon fillets (6 ounces each)
olive oil

1. Combine salt, sugar, juniper, pepper and orange zest. Rub the spice mixture over the fish fillets, cover and refrigerate for 4 to 12 hours.

2. Bring the fish to room temperature before grilling. Prepare barbecue grill or preheat broiler to high heat. Brush the fish lightly with olive oil. Grill 2 to 3 minutes per side.

# SEA BASS BROILED IN SMOKED TROUT AND DILL BUTTER

Serves 4

Steve Mellina of Manhattan Ocean Club Restaurant serves this with several interesting side dishes. In the summer he adds a salad of cold roasted peppers with capers. At other times he surrounds the fish with a few fried oysters and tomato coulis (see page 312).

### INGREDIENTS

1 cup (2 sticks) softened butter
4 ounces smoked trout, skinned and boned
1 tablespoon finely chopped fresh dill
1 tablespoon fresh lemon juice
3 twists of a peppermill
4 sea bass fillets (8 to 10 ounces each)

1. Combine all ingredients except fish in a food processor or blend by hand until well mixed but not overprocessed. Shape 4 walnut-size balls of butter for garnish and set aside.

2. Preheat broiler. Place fillets on individual heatproof plates and broil until half-cooked, about 2 minutes. Coat thickly with butter mixture. Return to broiler until cooked through, about 2 more minutes; top should be golden and crisp.

3. Transfer fish to warmed serving plates and add butter noisettes. Serve immediately.

## PARCHMENT-STEAMED BLACK BASS WITH LIME AND SESAME

Serves 4

Use striped bass, flounder, sole, grouper or white perch if you can't get black bass. When you butter the parchment, do it roughly; don't try to cover the entire sheet. The reason for buttering is to develop some color in the paper.

### INGREDIENTS

4 black sea bass fillets (7 to 8 ounces each)
4 tablespoons butter, melted
2 tablespoons sesame oil
1 tablespoon sesame seeds
3 tablespoons fresh lime juice
1 garlic clove, minced
¼ cup thinly sliced green onions
2 tablespoons finely chopped flat parsley leaves
salt and freshly ground pepper

1. Wash and dry the fillets; put each one on a sheet of buttered parchment paper large enough to envelop and secure it, providing for some air space in the envelope.

2. Combine all the remaining ingredients and stir well. Distribute over fish fillets.

3. Fold up and secure the parchment packages using a bundle wrap (see page 18). When the fire is medium-hot, put a double fold of heavy-duty foil on top of the grid; it should be 2 inches larger all around than the 4 parchment packets placed side by side. Put fish pack-ets on top of the foil, close cover and cook for about 20 minutes. The heat gauge in the dome should register around 450°F; if hotter, reduce cooking time to about 15 minutes.

4. Serve each packet on an individual plate and allow guests to open their own.

# CODFISH AND CAPERS WITH GREEN ONIONS, ENOKI MUSHROOMS AND DILL

Serves 6

An unusual combination of ingredients make this cod a very special presentation and so easy to prepare.

### INGREDIENTS

6 codfish fillets
4 tablespoons butter
salt and freshly ground pepper
½ red bell pepper, stem, ribs and seeds
    removed, thinly sliced lengthwise
1 packet (4 ounces) enoki mushrooms,
    trimmed
6 green onions, thinly sliced diagonally
¼ cup drained and rinsed capers
¾ cup half and half
⅓ cup chopped fresh dill or 1 tablespoon dried

1. Run fillets under cool water and pat dry. Use 1 tablespoon butter to smear centers of 2 heavy-duty foil sheets, each 18 x 18 inches. Season fish on both sides with salt and pepper. Place 3 fillets in center of each foil sheet.

2. Arrange red bell pepper slivers, mushrooms, onions and capers over fish. Top each fillet with ½ tablespoon butter. Spoon half and half over and sprinkle with dill.

3. Secure package by bundling as directed on page 18 (this package will not be turned).

4. When fire is ready, place packets 6 inches over heat source and cook for about 15 minutes, or until fish is white and just beginning to flake. Remove from foil before serving.

*Codfish*

*Most of us know that Cape Cod got its name from the fish—an important food item in New England for many years—a long time ago, because of its economic value. Today, it is available all year long, especially on the Atlantic side of the United States.*

*Cod is lean, white-fleshed and low in fat. In this recipe it remains moist as it grills in a foil packet. The combination of bell peppers, enoki mushrooms, capers and dill is unusual! This is one sure way to appreciate cod as a main dish.*

# SOUTHEAST ASIAN CURRIED FISH FILLETS IN COCONUT SAUCE (*OTAK-OTAK*)

Serves 6

In Singapore and Malaysia, this dish is prepared by wrapping individual portions in banana leaves. Since the leaves are unavailable for most of us, the recipe is adapted for a foil packet on a grill. This dish can be kept uncooked in the refrigerator overnight and brought to room temperature before grilling.

### INGREDIENTS

2 cups unsweetened packaged coconut
1 cup heavy cream, heated just to boiling point
2 garlic cloves, coarsely chopped
½ teaspoon curry powder
½ teaspoon red pepper flakes
½ teaspoon salt
1 pound medium shrimp, shelled, deveined and halved lengthwise
¼ cup (about) peanut or vegetable oil
6 medium fillets of sole or flounder
juice of ½ lemon or 2 tablespoons tamarind water*

1. Toast 1 cup coconut in a dry heavy skillet over low heat until light brown, stirring very frequently. Set aside.

2. Blend remaining cup untoasted coconut and the heavy cream in a blender until smooth. Drain through 2 layers of dampened cheesecloth or strain through a fine sieve to make 1 cup coconut cream. Set liquid aside; discard solids.

3. In a blender, puree the garlic, curry powder, pepper flakes, salt and toasted coconut. Transfer to a double boiler, add the coconut cream and cook over moderate heat until the sauce thickens. Remove from heat and let cool. Combine the sauce and shrimp.

4. Cut 6 pieces of heavy-duty foil, each about 12 inches square. Brush some peanut or vegetable oil on one side of each foil sheet.

5. Divide the shrimp and sauce mixture into 6 parts and mound on the center of oiled side of each foil sheet. Coat the fish fillets with lemon juice or tamarind water and arrange on top of the shrimp and sauce, folding as necessary. Wrap in bundles as directed on page 18.

6. Place packets on grid about 6 inches over heat source. Cook for 10 minutes, or until shrimp are pink and fish is white and just beginning to flake. Serve immediately in packets.

*To make tamarind water, soak 1 tablespoon packaged tamarind pulp in ¼ cup hot water for at least 2 hours or overnight; strain.*

Makes about ½ cup

Indian curry powder does not include fennel, which is usually included in Southeast Asian curry. To grind a supply of curry powder for *Otak-Otak* and other Singaporean recipes, sauté the following whole seeds in a lightly oiled skillet until you can smell their aromas.

### INGREDIENTS

3 ounces (6 tablespoons) coriander seed
2 ounces (¼ cup) cumin seed
½ ounce (1 tablespoon) fenugreek seed
½ ounce (1 tablespoon) fennel seed
½ ounce (1 tablespoon) mustard seed

After the sautéed seeds are cooled, add 2 tablespoons coarsely chopped fresh or 1 teaspoon powdered lemon grass and grind to a powder. Store the curry powder in a tightly covered jar. The Dutch condiment firm Conimex sells powdered lemon grass, called *sereh* powder. If lemon grass is not available, use ½ teaspoon finely chopped lemon zest.

# GRILLED SHRIMP AND SCALLOPS WITH GINGER AND BUTTER

Serves 6

Spoon some sauce onto warm plates and lay grilled fish on top.

### INGREDIENTS

1 pound large shrimp, shelled
1 pound sea scallops
1 red bell pepper
1 yellow bell pepper
8 tablespoons butter
2 tablespoons vegetable oil
salt and freshly ground pepper
2 green onions, finely chopped
2 tablespoons white wine vinegar
2 teaspoons freshly ground ginger
2 tablespoons heavy cream

1. Rinse and dry shrimp and scallops. Stem and seed peppers and cut into 1¼-inch squares. Cover shrimp, scallops and peppers with 2 tablespoons melted butter and the oil. Add salt and pepper. Toss and set aside.

2. In a saucepan, sauté onions in 1 tablespoon butter for 2 minutes. Add vinegar and ginger and boil until vinegar is reduced by half. Add cream and reduce by half. Add remaining butter. When melted, remove from heat and keep warm.

3. Skewer shrimp, scallops and peppers. Grill for several minutes per side, until shrimp are pink and scallops are opaque. Serve with sauce.

# GRILLED
# FLOUNDER FILLETS
# WITH PROVENCAL SAUCE

Serves 4

### INGREDIENTS

4 thick flounder fillets (8 ounces each)
3 tablespoons olive oil
3 tablespoons butter
1 small eggplant with skin on, cut into small
   dice (1 cup)
1 red bell pepper, stem, ribs and seeds removed,
   cut into small dice
1 small onion, finely chopped
2 garlic cloves, minced
1 cup finely chopped ripe tomatoes
½ cup white wine
salt and freshly ground pepper
1 lemon
1 teaspoon chopped parsley


1. Wash and thoroughly dry the fillets. Heat
   1 tablespoon each oil and butter just until
butter melts. Cool and brush over fillets, coating all sides thoroughly. Set aside.


2. In a large skillet, heat remaining 2 tablespoons each oil and butter. Add eggplant
and red pepper and sauté over medium heat
for 3 to 4 minutes. Add the onion and sauté
about 2 minutes. Add garlic, tomatoes and
wine and bring to boil. Lower heat and simmer
for 10 minutes. Add salt and pepper to taste.
Keep warm.

3. Arrange fillets in an oiled hinged wire
   basket and grill over medium fire for 4 to
5 minutes per side; do not overcook.

4. Cut 4 very thin slices from lemon and
   squeeze juice from remainder. Stir lemon
juice into sauce. Spoon sauce onto 4 warmed
plates. With a spatula, place grilled fillets on
top of sauce. Garnish each fillet with 1 lemon
slice and sprinkle parsley over lemon and fish.

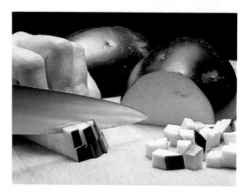

# GROUPER GRILLED IN CRUSHED MUSTARD SEEDS AND PEPPERCORNS WITH MUSSEL-SAFFRON SAUCE

Serves 4

Everyone who knows Steve Mellina — the inventor of this recipe — recognizes him as a Renaissance man. He speaks French, Spanish, Italian and English and has studied and worked here and abroad. A master chef, he is in his early thirties and heads the staff at New York's Manhattan Ocean Club.

### INGREDIENTS

4 grouper fillets, 8 ounces each and ½ to ¾ inch thick (see step 1)
1 tablespoon olive oil
mustard seed and peppercorn compound butter (see below)
mussel-saffron sauce (see below)

1. Ask your fishmonger to cut the fillets about the size of a dollar bill. Place them in individual broilerproof dishes and brush with oil. Broil for about 2 minutes or until half-cooked. Top fillets thickly with mustard seed butter, covering completely. Continue broiling until top is golden and crisp, about 4 minutes total.

2. Coat the bottom of each serving plate with saffron sauce. Place grouper in the center and garnish with 6 mussels (reserved from sauce), 3 to each side of the fillet. Serve immediately.

## MUSTARD SEED AND PEPPERCORN COMPOUND BUTTER

Makes about ¾ cup

### INGREDIENTS

¾ cup (1 ½ sticks) softened butter
¼ teaspoon white peppercorns, crushed
¼ teaspoon black peppercorns, crushed
½ teaspoon mustard seeds, crushed
1 teaspoon Dijon mustard
1 teaspoon Pomméry or other coarse-grained mustard
1 teaspoon chopped chives
1 teaspoon chopped parsley
1 teaspoon fresh lemon juice

Blend all ingredients in a processor or by hand using a rubber spatula.

Note: This amount is more than will be needed for the grilled grouper recipe serving 4; it is enough for 8 fillets. It will keep well in the refrigerator for several days.

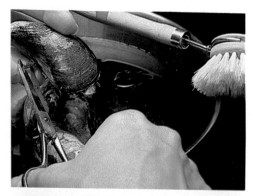

## MUSSEL-SAFFRON SAUCE

Makes 1 cup

This delicious sauce may also be used with other fish: lobster, lotte (monkfish), turbot, halibut, sole, flounder, John Dory, and so on.

### INGREDIENTS

24 mussels
1 cup dry white wine
½ cup water
3 or 4 parsley stems (leaves will discolor the sauce)
5 shallots, thinly sliced
freshly ground pepper
2 cups heavy cream
a generous pinch of saffron threads or ½ teaspoon ground saffron
8 tablespoons (1 stick) unsalted butter
salt, if needed

1. Scrub and debeard mussels; set aside.

2. Combine wine, water, parsley stems, shallot and several twists of a peppermill in a nonaluminum saucepan and bring to boil. Continue boiling until reduced by half. Add mussels, cover and cook just until mussels open.

3. Remove mussels and cover with a damp cloth; set aside for garnish. Strain the mussel broth through several layers of dampened cheesecloth. Return to a clean saucepan, add saffron and boil until reduced to a light syrup consistency.

4. Add cream and reduce by half. Whisk in butter a tablespoon at a time. Taste for seasoning. (Salt may not be needed as mussels are salty.)

3. Brush pike fillets with the olive oil and season with salt and pepper. Place them on an ultra-hot grill for about 90 seconds per side. Transfer quickly to warm plates, top with sauce and serve immediately.

# FRESH PIKE
# WITH RED PEPPER BUTTER

Serves 4 to 6

Zachary Bruell, owner of Z Contemporary Cuisine in Shaker Heights, Ohio is one of the country's leading young chefs. His talent with grilled fish is outstanding, as this recipe demonstrates.

### INGREDIENTS

2 large red bell peppers
juice of 1 lime
1 tablespoon cold water
1 cup (2 sticks) cold butter, cut into ½-inch
    cubes
1 teaspoon finely chopped fresh thyme
salt and freshly cracked black pepper
2 pounds pike fillets, bones removed
2 tablespoons extra virgin olive oil

1. Place whole peppers over the grill. As the skins turn black, rotate them until completely blistered. Place in ice water to cool, then remove the skins. Cut off the tops and remove seeds. Place the peppers in a food processor and puree, then force through a sieve. (Everything up to this point may be done ahead of time. Refrigerate puree if not using within an hour or so, but return to room temperature before preparing sauce.)

2. To make sauce, combine pepper puree, lime juice and water in a small nonaluminum saucepan. Whisk in the butter over

## GINGER-GLAZED SALMON

Serves 6

$S$erve with thinly sliced boiled potatoes, buttered and seasoned, and with asparagus spears topped with homemade dill mayonnaise.

### INGREDIENTS

6 salmon fillets with skin, 5 to 6 ounces each
    (see step 1)
¼ cup soy sauce
¼ cup cream sherry
2 teaspoons sugar
1 tablespoon grated fresh ginger
2 garlic cloves, finely chopped
oil
lemon wedges

1. Ask your fishmonger to slice salmon fillets so each is about 2 inches wide, 5 to 6 inches long, and ¾ to 1 inch thick at the midpoint.

2. Combine soy sauce, sherry and sugar in a small saucepan and heat only until sugar is dissolved. Add ginger and garlic and pour over salmon. Marinate in refrigerator for 2 to 3 hours or at room temperature for 30 minutes.

3. Remove salmon from marinade and transfer to a plate. Brush oil on both sides. Thread each fillet lengthwise on 2 long skewers.

4. Grill fish flesh side down first, basting with marinade. Turn and grill skin side, basting again; do not overcook. Any leftover marinade may be heated and served with fish. Garnish with lemon wedges.

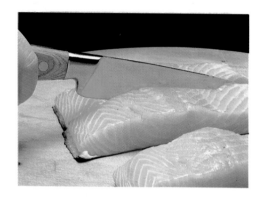

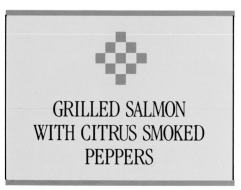

# GRILLED SALMON WITH CITRUS SMOKED PEPPERS

Serves 6

The Washington Square Bar & Grill, in San Francisco's North Beach, is surely one of the most cheerful and energetic restaurants in the United States. Chef Mary Etta Moose serves this with steamed baby potatoes.

### INGREDIENTS

salt and freshly ground pepper
6 salmon fillets (6 ounces each), cut 1 inch
    thick and bevel-edged
all-purpose flour
corn oil
citrus smoked pepper sauce (see below)

1. Sprinkle work surface with salt and pepper. Lay fish atop seasonings. Repeat on other side. Lightly flour both sides and shake off all excess.

2. Heat clean flattop grill slowly to medium heat (325°F to 350°F). Brush with corn oil. When oil is hot, lay the salmon fillets on the grill without touching.

3. Raise grill heat only long enough to bring the surface back to 325°F, about a minute. Cook fillets 3½ minutes. Turn and cook another 3½ minutes, or until flesh is just firm.

Serves 6

### INGREDIENTS

1 tablespoon chopped shallots
1 cup salmon fumet (see page 42)
½ cup white wine vinegar
1½ cups Chardonnay
½ cup heavy cream
1 pound unsalted butter, cubed, brought to
    room temperature
½ large smoked pepper, (see below), cut into
    ⅜-inch dice

1. Combine first 4 ingredients in a non-aluminum saucepan and boil over high heat until reduced to ¼ cup.

2. Add the cream and bring to boil. Remove from heat.

3. Working quickly, whip in butter one cube at a time, in fast succession. Return pan to heat after the first cube or two, and continue to adjust the heat so the temperature of the butter in the pan does not exceed 130°F. The volume of 1 pound of butter should keep butter temperature low enough that you will end up using a medium-high flame just to keep it at 130°F, and achieve a smooth emulsion.

4. Add smoked pepper and hold the sauce in a covered container in a warm, draft-free location.

## CITRUS SMOKED PEPPERS

I always smoke more peppers than needed for the grilled salmon recipe. They have excellent keeping properties (3 to 4 weeks, covered, in the refrigerator), and are a fine way to introduce a delicate smoke flavor into many dishes. Try some in potato salad, or combined with mushrooms, shallots and cream to sauce fettuccine.

### SMOKING MIXTURE

1 tablespoon lemon zest slivers
1 tablespoon orange zest slivers
1 teaspoon whole coriander seeds
1 teaspoon black peppercorns
5 allspice berries
1 cinnamon stick, broken up
1 teaspoon anise seeds
2 tablespoons black tea leaves
¼ cup firmly packed brown sugar

½ cup raw rice
1 to 4 red or yellow bell peppers

The smoking apparatus:
a deep pan with domed cover, such as a
    roasting pan or wok
heavy-duty foil
2 cans with tops and bottoms removed, to form
    metal rings 3 inches high
wire rack to fit inside pan, atop metal rings

1. Combine smoking mixture ingredients in a bowl and set aside until needed.

2. Line the pan and its lid with a double layer of foil, leaving a 3-inch overlap at edges. Spread rice thickly in the center of the pan. Pile the smoking mixture on top of the rice. Set the metal rings on either side of the smoking mixture, and the rack atop the rings. Set the peppers on the rack, a good inch above the smoking mixture. Place the foil-lined cover on the pan and fold the top and bottom overlaps tightly to contain all the smoke. Place over highest gas flame for 6 minutes. Immediately lower flame to medium high and smoke the peppers for 5 minutes. Turn off the heat and leave pan undisturbed for 10 minutes. Transfer peppers to cutting board. Seed and devein. Use what is needed and store remaining peppers in a covered container in the refrigerator.

---

*Allspice Berries*
*Allspice is versatile and this seems to be the first time it appears in a "smoking mixture." We usually see this spice in soups, stews, sauerbraten, pickled beets, preserves, stewed fruit and so on. Native to the Western Hemisphere, it was discovered by Columbus in 1494. The fruit or berries are sun dried until dark reddish-brown in color. It is also available in ground form.*

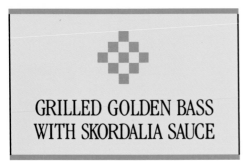

# GRILLED GOLDEN BASS WITH SKORDALIA SAUCE

Serves 8

Selma Nemer, the chef/owner of Eartha's Kitchen in Saratoga Springs, New York, is also a well-known cooking teacher. Her approach is both international and practical. For example, she suggests changing the character of the skordalia by adding just one different herb, such as tarragon. Note that Selma uses cold oils in making skordalia; she believes this helps keep it from separating. This sauce holds up well in the refrigerator for about a week. It is as good on grilled meats as it is on fish.

### INGREDIENTS

8 golden bass fillets (6 to 8 ounces each)
1 cup extra virgin olive oil
juice of 1 lime
2 teaspoons mushroom soy sauce or light soy
    sauce
Skordalia sauce (see below)

1. Wash and dry fillets and place them in a glass or ceramic dish.

2. Combine remaining ingredients and pour over the fillets. Let marinate for 30 to 60 minutes.

3. Prepare a fire of glowing coals with mesquite, cherry or applewood. Grill bass over medium heat 5 minutes per side, basting frequently with marinade; do not overcook.

4. Transfer to warm plates and serve with a generous dollop of skordalia sauce.

### SKORDALIA SAUCE

Makes 1 ½ cups

### INGREDIENTS

2 egg yolks
1 tablespoon Dijon mustard
3 tablespoons fresh lemon juice
1 cup cold corn oil
½ cup cold olive oil
salt and freshly ground pepper
dash of hot pepper sauce
pinch of cayenne pepper
1 cup mashed potatoes (without milk)
4 garlic cloves, minced
2 tablespoons each chopped fresh tarragon,
    parsley and chives

1. Combine egg yolks, mustard and 1 tablespoon lemon juice in food processor and pulse 2 or 3 times. With machine running, slowly add oils; continue processing to mayonnaise consistency. Taste for seasoning and add salt, pepper, hot pepper sauce and cayenne.

2. Add potatoes, garlic, remaining lemon juice and herbs and pulse until skordalia is light and fluffy. If sauce is too thick, thin with a bit more corn or olive oil.

# GRILLED RED SNAPPER WITH SAUCE ANTIBOISE

Serves 4

This recipe is from Gérard Pangaud, chef at New York's Aurora. A fillet of red snapper or other white-fleshed fish is grilled and placed on three croutons, each with a different spread. The sauce Antiboise is placed on one side, a garnish of ratatouille on the other. At Aurora's, a final touch of garlic quenelles are arranged around the ratatouille.

## INGREDIENTS

4 fillets of red snapper, 7 ounces each, skin on
½ cup olive oil
3 tablespoons fresh lemon juice
20 Spanish olives, each cut into 6 wedges
20 Niçoise olives, each cut into 6 wedges
3 medium size tomatoes, cored, peeled, seeded and cut into small dice
10 large basil leaves
croutons (see below)

1. Ask the fishmonger to scale and bone the snapper fillets, leaving the skin intact.

2. Whisk olive oil into lemon juice in a non-aluminum saucepan over low heat. Add olives, tomatoes and basil; keep warm.

3. When the fire is ready, grill the snapper skin side down until well colored. Turn carefully and grill skin side up. Keep warm in a low oven.

4. Center 3 croutons, one with each spread such as garlic paste, on each plate. Place the grilled fish on top. Sauce one side of the fish and add a vegetable, or ratatouille, (see page 317) as they do at Aurora's.

CROUTONS WITH THREE PUREES:

1 whole garlic bulb
olive oil
1 bunch parsley
1 bunch spinach
12 thin slices French bread
1 jar (4 ounces) olive tapenade

1. Break the garlic into cloves leaving the skin on. Drizzle with 1 tablespoon olive oil and roast in a preheated 350°F oven until tender, about 1 hour. Press flesh through fine sieve.

2. Blanch parsley and spinach in boiling salted water until tender. Refresh in cold water and drain well. Puree in a blender or processor.

3. Brush bread lightly with olive oil. Grill until golden.

4. Spread 4 bread slices with garlic puree, 4 with parsley-spinach puree and 4 with the olive tapenade.

## GRILLED SALMON STEAKS WITH VODKA AND ORANGE JUICE

Serves 4

This is a simple and never-fail recipe from my good friend Jim Price and his wife, Warrie. They prepare it on an indoor gas-fired grill under a properly vented hood. Jim says "The fire should be so hot that my hand can't stay here beyond a count of three." Jim's final piece of advice: "Once the fish is on the grill, baste, baste, and keep basting."

### INGREDIENTS

4 salmon steaks (about 1 inch thick)
½ cup vodka
¼ cup fresh orange juice
juice of 1 lemon
2 tablespoons coarse-grained mustard
¼ cup chopped fresh dill

1. Wash and dry steaks, then arrange in one layer in a glass or ceramic dish. With a fork, lightly puncture the outer edges of the steaks, on both sides, so they can absorb the marinade.

2. Combine remaining ingredients. Pour over fish, coating all sides. Marinate 20 minutes.

3. Over high heat, grill the steaks, basting frequently. Serve immediately.

## SWORDFISH WITH WHITE WINE AND SAGE

Serves 4

Americans are learning to use sage as Europeans in stuffing, stews, sausages, and fish. This is a simple and wonderful preparation.

### INGREDIENTS

2 swordfish steaks (1 pound each)
½ cup dry white wine
⅓ cup olive or vegetable oil
2 teaspoons crushed dried sage
2 tablespoons finely chopped parsley
freshly ground pepper
salt

1. Combine all ingredients except salt in a large shallow glass or ceramic dish or platter and marinate at room temperature for 1 to 2 hours. (Or marinate longer in the refrigerator but not overnight. If refrigerated, allow fish to return to room temperature, about 1 hour.)

2. Grill fish on one side by searing close to heat and then raising grill farther from heat to complete cooking. Turn and grill the other side, searing first as before. Total cooking time will be about 10 minutes. Remove from grill and salt to taste.

# GRILLED SWORDFISH WITH DICED VEGETABLES AND A LIGHTLY CREAMED MINT BROTH

**Serves 4**

It's worth a short ride, even a long one for that matter, to dine at Jillyflowers in Harrison, New York. Mark Filippo, its talented young chef, combines classic French cooking techniques with light American and international touches. This grilled swordfish is one of Mark's outstanding dishes.

### INGREDIENTS

2 large zucchini
4 swordfish steaks (7 ounces each), all skin, fat and red meat removed, cut ½ inch thick
2 tablespoons olive oil
coarse sea salt and freshly ground white pepper
2 large carrots, finely diced
1½ cups mint fumet (see below)
1 large tomato, peeled, seeded and diced
24 perfect mint leaves
6 tablespoons heavy cream

**1.** Trim ends from zucchini. Stand zucchini vertically and slice off the 4 sides — skin and ¼ inch of flesh. Discard squared-off core. Finely dice skin and attached flesh.

**2.** Rub the fish with olive oil and season with salt and pepper. Place on hot grill and cook about 3 minutes per side.

**3.** While fish is cooking, combine zucchini, carrots and mint fumet in a 2-quart saucepan and boil for 1 minute. Add tomato, 20 mint leaves, and cream and boil 2 minutes longer. Taste and adjust seasoning.

**4.** Ladle sauce with vegetables onto 4 deep plates. Place a piece of swordfish in the center of each plate and garnish with a mint leaf.

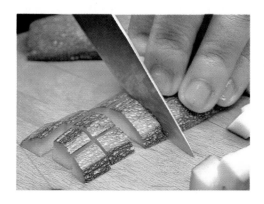

## MINT FUMET

Makes about 2 cups

This can be prepared in the morning and refrigerated, but don't make it farther ahead.

### INGREDIENTS

2 tablespoons unsalted butter
1 large onion, thinly sliced
20 large shallots, thinly sliced
2 firm white mushrooms, thinly sliced
¾ cup white vermouth
1 quart fish stock
2 bunches fresh mint
1 teaspoon coarse sea salt

1. Melt butter in a 2-quart saucepan over low heat. Add onion, shallots and mushrooms and cook 5 minutes, stirring often; do not let vegetables color.

2. Add vermouth and boil until almost completely evaporated. Add fish stock and bring to boil. Add one bunch of mint and ½ teaspoon salt and cook at a low boil for 10 minutes. Strain into another saucepan, add the second bunch of mint and cook 10 minutes longer. Taste to see if the remaining ½ teaspoon salt is needed. Strain into a stainless steel bowl. Keep in cool area of kitchen until ready to use.

# SWORDFISH STEAKS MARINATED IN TERIYAKI AND GRILLED WITH BUTTER AND BACON

Serves 4

Grill four large mushrooms, rubbed with oil and lemon juice, as you grill the steaks. Add one mushroom to each plate. A side dish of orzo with currants and zucchini goes well with this.

### INGREDIENTS

4 swordfish steaks (about 8 ounces each)
¼ cup saké or white wine
¼ cup soy sauce
2 tablespoons sesame-chili oil (available at Oriental markets)
6 tablespoons butter, melted
2 tablespoons sugar
1 tablespoon grated fresh ginger
2 garlic cloves, minced
4 strips bacon
¼ cup cream sherry
juice of 1 lemon

1. Wash and dry the steaks. Place in a large glass or ceramic dish in one layer. Combine wine, soy sauce, oil, 2 tablespoons butter, sugar, ginger and garlic and pour over steaks, turning to be sure they are well coated. Marinate for at least 30 minutes at room temperature or in the refrigerator for 2 hours, but bring to room temperature before grilling.

2. To grill, remove steaks from marinade and wrap a bacon slice around each one; stretch the bacon, if needed, to fit all the way around. Secure with toothpicks and set aside.

3. Stir remaining 4 tablespoons butter and lemon into marinade. Place steaks in a hinged wire basket or directly on an oiled grill. Cook on each side 6 to 8 minutes, basting frequently.

4. Heat the remaining marinade. To serve, divide steaks among warmed plates and spoon 2 tablespoons warm marinade over each.

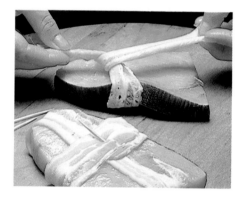

2. Preheat grill for 15 minutes or until it is as hot as possible. Grill tuna approximately 1 to 2 minutes on all 4 sides, or until outside is charred brown and center is barely cooked.

3. Place several shavings of pickled ginger on top of grilled steaks as a garnish. Spoon remaining marinade over steaks to taste.

## GRILLED MARINATED FILET MIGNON OF TUNA

Serves 2

Chef Ali Barker, of The Union Square Cafe in New York, says that the freshness of the tuna is of utmost importance to the success of this dish (which is the restaurant's most popular item). It should be cooked rare — "crusty on the outside, blue inside." If you find the marinade too salty, use less soy sauce and more lemon to your taste. Grilled zucchini or baby eggplant, rubbed with olive oil, makes a wonderful accompaniment to this dish.

### INGREDIENTS

1 cup soy or teriyaki sauce
juice of 1 lemon
¼ cup dry sherry
2 tablespoons finely chopped fresh ginger
¼ cup chopped green onions
1 garlic clove, finely chopped
pinch of cayenne pepper
2 tablespoons freshly ground pepper
1 pound prime yellowfin tuna (deep red in color), cut into 2 steaks, each 2 to 2½ inches thick
shaved pickled ginger for garnish

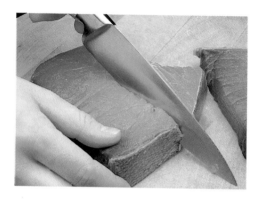

1. Combine soy sauce, lemon juice, sherry, fresh ginger, green onion, garlic, cayenne and pepper in a large glass or ceramic dish. Add tuna and marinate at least 5 hours or overnight in the refrigerator, turning periodically. Bring to room temperature before grilling.

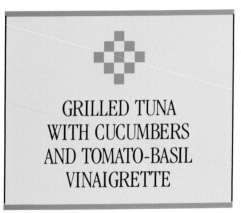

# GRILLED TUNA
# WITH CUCUMBERS
# AND TOMATO-BASIL
# VINAIGRETTE

Serves 2

This unusual combination of foods has been brought together by Petita Lago, a young New York chef.

INGREDIENTS

1/4 cup olive oil
juice of 1 lime
salt and freshly ground pepper
2 yellowfin tuna steaks (8 ounces each), at
    room temperature
6 red radishes, scrubbed and julienned
1 bunch fresh chives, sliced
4 tablespoons softened unsalted butter
2 hothouse cucumbers, washed and julienned
tomato-basil vinaigrette (see below)

1. Combine oil, lime juice, salt and pepper in a large glass or ceramic dish. Add tuna and marinate for at least 10 minutes before grilling. Grill until medium rare, turning twice.

2. In a mixing bowl, combine radishes, chives, butter, and salt and pepper to taste. Blanch the cucumbers in boiling salted water for 15 to 20 seconds; drain. Shake to remove excess water and add immediately to the mixture. Stir until the butter melts.

3. Divide cucumber mixture among serving plates, forming a small nest. Place the grilled tuna on top and spoon vinaigrette over the tuna. Garnish with basil or parsley.

TOMATO-BASIL VINAIGRETTE

Makes about 1¾ cups

INGREDIENTS

2 ripe tomatoes, cored, seeded and chopped
½ cup extra virgin olive oil
¼ cup balsamic vinegar
1 teaspoon sugar
2 tablespoons chopped fresh basil (do not use
    dried)
salt and freshly ground pepper
fresh basil or parsley for garnish

Combine all ingredients and adjust seasoning.

## ALBACORE TUNA WITH MUSHROOM-CAPER SAUCE

Serves 2

This is a good example of innovative grilling by so many new American chefs; this one was created by Sergio J. Abramoff.

### INGREDIENTS

2 tuna steaks (6 ounces each)
2 tablespoons vegetable oil
salt and freshly ground pepper
2 tablespoons olive oil
1 cup sliced shiitake mushrooms
1 tablespoon chopped garlic
¼ cup dry white wine
¼ cup fish or chicken stock
2 tablespoons capers
2 tablespoons butter, rolled in flour to coat
1 tomato, seeded and julienned
1 tablespoon chopped flat parsley leaves

1. Brush tuna with vegetable oil, season with salt and pepper and set aside.

2. Heat olive oil in a sauté pan over medium heat. Add mushrooms and sauté for 2 minutes. Add garlic and continue cooking until garlic begins to brown. Add wine and bring to boil, scraping up browned bits. Add stock and capers and return to boil, then reduce heat, add butter rolled in flour and simmer until slightly thickened. Add tomato and season with salt and pepper. Set aside in a warm place.

3. Grill tuna over high heat, being careful not to overcook. Arrange on a serving platter. Spoon sauce over and sprinkle with chopped parsley. Serve at once.

## CHARRED TUNA WITH GINGER AND ORANGE VINAIGRETTE

Serves 2

Elka Gilmore, until recently the chef at Camelions in Santa Monica, California, has achieved considerable renown for her adroit contemporary cooking.

### INGREDIENTS

2 tablespoons peanut oil
1 teaspoon chopped fresh ginger
1 teaspoon soy sauce
1 cup fresh orange juice
1 teaspoon finely chopped chives
pinch of cayenne pepper
pinch of freshly ground white pepper
1 pound fresh tuna steak, 1 inch thick
1 cucumber, peeled, seeded and finely julienned

1. Mix all ingredients except tuna and cucumber; set aside.

2. Cook tuna on a hot grill about 30 seconds, just long enough to char one side. Let rest for a minute, then carve into very thin slices.

3. Arrange slices of tuna on a plate and drizzle with vinaigrette. Garnish with cucumber julienne.

using a gas grill, make a foil log of chips and lay it on the lava stones; see page 22.) Baste with remaining marinade while shrimp are grilling.

## GRILLED MESQUITE-FLAVORED SHRIMP WITH TOMATILLO SALSA

Serves 4 to 6

The shrimp take only a minute or so per side to grill. They should be crisp on the outside and tender on the inside. Use large shrimp, about 12 to 14 count per pound.

### INGREDIENTS

2 pounds large shrimp
6 tablespoons butter
⅓ cup vegetable or safflower oil
3 tablespoons chili powder
juice of 1 lemon
tomatillo salsa (see below)

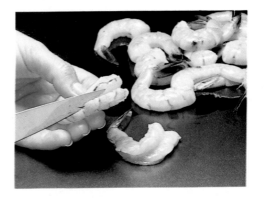

1 Wash, peel and devein the shrimp, leaving tails on. Dry well and place in a glass or ceramic dish large enough to hold shrimp in one layer.

2. Combine remaining ingredients, except the tomatillo salsa, in a saucepan and heat just until the butter is melted. Pour over shrimp and allow to marinate at least 30 minutes.

3. Skewer shrimp and grill over high heat for 1 to 2 minutes per side, using mesquite charcoal or regular charcoal briquettes with soaked mesquite chips added for flavor. (If

TOMATILLO SALSA

Makes about 1 cup

4 tomatillos, stemmed and coarsely chopped
2 garlic cloves, minced
1 jalapeño pepper, seeded and finely chopped
4 sprigs fresh coriander, stemmed
2 tablespoons fresh lemon juice
1 avocado, pitted, peeled and coarsely chopped
salt

1. Combine tomatillos and garlic in a small saucepan and bring just to boil. Lower heat and simmer slowly for 4 to 5 minutes, stirring frequently. Transfer to food processor.

2. Add jalapeño, coriander and lemon juice and pulse several time to combine. Add avocado and pulse again just until finely chopped; do not puree. Add salt to taste. Serve at room temperature.

# SPICY BLUE CORNMEAL GULF SHRIMP WITH MARINATED TOMATOES

Serves 4 as appetizer

This is a good example of Clive DuVal's creative cooking at his Houston restaurant, Tila's Cantina & Taqueria. To serve four as an entree, use 2 pounds shrimp and 1 ½ times the other ingredients.

### INGREDIENTS

1 pound large Gulf shrimp (8 to 12 count)
1 cup all-purpose flour
1 cup blue cornmeal
1 tablespoon chopped fresh parsley
1 tablespoon chopped fresh chervil
1 teaspoon cayenne pepper
1 teaspoon Cavender's seasoning (available at
    specialty markets) or seasoned salt
3 tablespoons olive oil
tomatoes in marinade (see below)
¼ cup grated Fontina cheese
2 tablespoons crumbled Gorgonzola cheese
2 tablespoons ricotta cheese
paprika and chopped fresh chives for garnish
4 hot flour tortillas

1. Wash, peel and drain shrimp; set aside. Place flour in a small bowl; have a second small bowl of water beside it.

2. Combine cornmeal, parsley, chervil, cayenne and seasoning powder in a third small bowl.

3. Heat olive oil in a sauté pan until smoking. Quickly roll shrimp in flour, dip in water and roll in cornmeal mixture. Sauté shrimp until golden; remove from pan and drain on paper towels.

4. Remove tomatoes from marinade with a slotted spoon and gently press out marinade. Toss tomatoes with shrimp and place on a baking sheet. Combine cheeses and spread over the shrimp. Broil until cheeses are melted. Sprinkle with paprika and chives. Serve with hot tortillas.

## TOMATOES IN MARINADE

Makes 1 cup marinade

### INGREDIENTS

½ cup red rice vinegar (available at Oriental
    markets)
1 teaspoon brown sugar
1 green onion, chopped
1 teaspoon cracked black pepper
½ teaspoon celery salt
¼ teaspoon ground allspice
1 teaspoon Dijon mustard
½ cup olive oil
4 ripe tomatoes

**1.** Combine all ingredients except oil and tomatoes. Slowly whisk in oil until fully incorporated. Set aside.

**2.** Core, peel and slice tomatoes. Pour marinade over and let stand at room temperature for 30 minutes.

# GRILLED SHRIMP
# WITH BROCCOLI
# AND SPICY LIME DRESSING
# ON CELLOPHANE NOODLES

Serves 8 as appetizer or 4 as main course

This international shrimp dish was originated by Selma Nemer.

### INGREDIENTS

16 jumbo shrimp
2 tablespoons olive oil
2 tablespoons heavy soy sauce
16 broccoli florets
1 package (6 ounces) cellophane noodles
3 tablespoons sesame oil
lettuce leaves
8 thin cucumber slices
8 radishes, cut into florets
spicy lime peanut dressing (see below)
½ cup toasted peanuts

1. Wash, peel and devein shrimp, leaving tails on. Place in a bowl with olive oil and soy sauce and toss to coat well. Set aside.

2. Cook broccoli in boiling water until crisp-tender. Drain and set aside.

3. Place noodles in a large bowl and pour boiling water over. Let stand for 3 minutes. Drain and toss well with sesame oil.

4. Grill shrimp over a charcoal/mesquite fire about 3 minutes per side, basting frequently with oil/soy marinade.

5. Arrange a lettuce leaf on a plate with a bed of cellophane noodles in the center. Add 2 broccoli florets, 2 grilled shrimp, a cucumber slice and a radish flower to each plate. Spoon dressing over, sprinkle with peanuts and serve.

### SPICY LIME PEANUT DRESSING

Makes ½ cup

### INGREDIENTS

2 garlic cloves, minced
6 tablespoons fresh lime juice
¼ cup mushroom soy sauce or light soy sauce
3 tablespoons peanut oil
3 tablespoons sesame-chili oil (available at Oriental markets)
1 tablespoon red pepper flakes or to taste

Combine garlic, lime juice, soy sauce, peanut oil and chili oil and mix well. Add red pepper flakes a little at a time and taste; the sauce should be fiery hot, but you may wish to add less red pepper.

# RED PEPPER SHRIMP

Serves 4

**W**hat becomes a legend? The answer is this shrimp preparation as done by Eileen Weinberg at Carolina's in New York.

### INGREDIENTS

1½ pounds medium shrimp (about 24), tails left on
4 garlic cloves, minced
1 teaspoon salt
4 dried red peppers, crushed
1 cup olive oil
1 tablespoon hot pepper sauce
3 lemons, cut into 8 wedges each
12 large bay leaves, halved, or 24 small bay leaves

1. Wash and dry shrimp, leaving shells and tails intact. Place in a large ceramic or glass bowl.

2. In a small bowl, combine garlic, salt, red pepper, ½ cup olive oil and the hot pepper sauce and mix well. Blend in remaining oil and pour over shrimp, turning to coat all sides. Marinate for 4 hours in refrigerator; remove 1 hour before grilling. Drain, reserving marinade.

3. Thread lemon wedges, bay leaves and shrimp alternately on 4 skewers.

4. When the fire is ready, grill the shrimp for about 3 minutes on each side, brushing with reserved marinade. Serve on the skewers.

# FISH STOCK

Makes about 2 quarts

### INGREDIENTS

3 tablespoons butter
3 tablespoons vegetable oil
2 leeks (including green parts), washed carefully and coarsely chopped
2 medium onions, washed but not peeled, coarsely chopped
2 stalks celery with leaves, washed and coarsely chopped
2 large carrots, scrubbed clean but not peeled, coarsely chopped
4 cups dry white wine
3 quarts water
4 pounds fish heads and bones
2 bay leaves
¼ teaspoon fennel seed
6 parsley sprigs
12 peppercorns
1 teaspoon salt

1. Heat butter and oil in a large stockpot. Add the leeks, onions, celery, and carrots and cook for about 10 minutes, or until the onions are pale yellow.

2. Add the wine, water, and fish heads and bones, and bring the liquid to a boil, skimming foam as it accumulates on the surface. Add the bay leaves, fennel, parsley, peppercorns, and salt. Stir all the ingredients well and simmer the stock, partially covered, for about 2 hours, or until liquid is reduced by half. Strain, refrigerate, and defat. This may be frozen for several months.

# PREPARING LOBSTER FOR GRILL

**1.** To kill a lobster humanely kill it instantly. Put the lobster on a cutting board and plunge the tip of a large, sharp knife between the eyes.

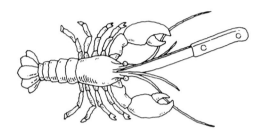

**2.** Immediately cut down sharply in the direction of the tail, splitting the whole lobster in half. (The lobster is killed once the cut is made between the eyes.)

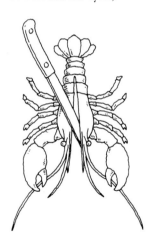

**3.** With a paring knife, remove the intestinal tract; it looks like a thin vein running the length of the lobster. Also remove the sandy sac just underneath the eyes.

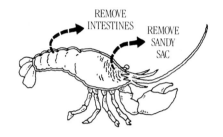

REMOVE INTESTINES

REMOVE SANDY SAC

**4.** The lobster is ready for grilling (see recipe on page 86).

# AN ALTERNATIVE METHOD

**1.** Bring water to boil in a very large pot to hold one or more lobsters. Plunge lobster(s) into boiling water head first and return water to boil.

**2.** Lower heat, cover pan immediately and let lobster simmer for 3 minutes or until it turns pink.

**3.** To avoid overcooking, immediately drain and plunge lobster into a pan of cold water. Drain well and cut in half lengthwise as above. Remove sandy sac near the eyes and the intestinal vein. Lobster halves are ready for the grill.

# GRILLED LOBSTER WITH BUTTER AND LEMON

Serves 6

Many supermarkets and fish stores sell live lobsters that are kept in water tanks. Other than catching your own, these are the freshest available.

### INGREDIENTS

6 live lobsters (about 1½ pounds each)
2 cups (4 sticks) butter, melted
juice of 2 lemons
1½ tablespoons Worcestershire sauce
4 to 6 drops hot pepper sauce or to taste
salt and freshly ground pepper

**1.** Prepare lobsters by splitting and cleaning as noted on page 85. Set aside.

**2.** In a bowl, combine all remaining ingredients.

**3.** When fire is ready, grill lobster halves shell side down, brushing sauce frequently into cavities. When shells turn bright red, 5 to 10 minutes, turn lobster halves meat side down and grill 4 to 5 minutes longer. Turn again, meat side up; when lobster meat is white, lobster is done.

**4.** Serve remaining sauce with lobster.

# GRILLED WHOLE LOBSTERS WITH GARLIC, GINGER, CHILI AND BUTTER SAUCE

Serves 4

A peppery accent adds to the grill flavor. Put sauce on the lobster as it grills and serve more sauce with it.

### INGREDIENTS

1 cup (2 sticks) butter
¼ cup dry sherry
¼ cup light soy sauce
2 garlic cloves, minced or pressed
1 small dried chili, seeded and crumbled, or a generous pinch of red pepper flakes
2 tablespoons grated fresh ginger
4 whole fresh lobsters (about 1¼ pounds each)

1. Bring water to boil in a very large pot to hold one or more lobsters. Plunge lobster(s) into boiling water head first and return water to boil.

2. Prepare lobsters by splitting and cleaning as shown on page 85.

3. When fire is ready, grill lobster halves shell side down, brushing sauce frequently into cavities. When shells turn bright red, 5 to 10 minutes, turn lobster halves meat side down and grill 4 to 5 minutes longer. Turn again, meat side up; when meat is white, lobster is done.

4. Serve remaining sauce with lobster.

## GRILLED CLAMS WITH A SPRINKLE OF FRESH VEGETABLES

These should be cooked in a covered grill. If using an open grill, cover securely with foil to create an "oven." Check your fishmonger or supermarket for clams in a tank with circulating water. These clams have already shed their sand and the three hours of soaking will not be necessary.

### INGREDIENTS

24 littleneck or 12 cherrystone clams
2 tablespoons chopped shallots
2 garlic cloves
1 celery stalk from heart
2 tablespoons chopped parsley
1 small carrot, sliced
¼ cup olive oil
3 tablespoons fresh lemon juice
salt and freshly ground pepper

1. Scrub clams well with a stiff brush and soak in cold salted water for about 3 hours. Shuck the clams; strain and reserve the juice. Place each clam on its lower shell, discarding top shells.

2. In a processor or by hand, finely chop the shallots, garlic, celery, parsley and carrot. Transfer to a mixing bowl. Add oil, lemon juice, salt and pepper and mix well. Spoon over clams.

3. When the fire is ready, carefully arrange the clams on the halfshell in a hinged wire basket. Close the basket and set it on the grid. Quickly add a teaspoon of clam juice to each through the wire basket. Grill for 3 to 5 minutes, or until juices boil. Serve immediately with any leftover clam juice on the side.

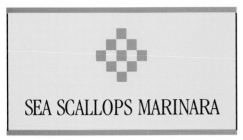

# SEA SCALLOPS MARINARA

Serves 4 to 6

This fresh, lovely sauce of Mediterranean flavors will surely enhance any fresh, white, light fish.

### INGREDIENTS

1½ to 2 pounds whole sea scallops
juice of 1 lemon
6 tablespoons olive oil
1 large onion, finely chopped
1 garlic clove, minced
2 cups cored, peeled, seeded and chopped
 fresh tomatoes, or canned plum tomatoes
 put through a food mill
¼ cup chopped fresh basil or ½ teaspoon
 dried
1 teaspoon sugar
salt and freshly ground pepper
4 to 6 slices homemade white sourdough or
 Italian or French bread

1. Wash the scallops, place them in a bowl with the lemon juice and toss to coat. Let stand at room temperature for 15 to 30 minutes. Drain, dry and set aside.

2. Heat 4 tablespoons olive oil in a skillet over medium-high heat and sauté the onion until translucent. Add the garlic. As soon as garlic begins to color, add tomatoes, 2 tablespoons fresh basil (or all the dried basil), sugar, salt and pepper. Bring to a boil and remove from heat. (This sauce can be prepared hours ahead of time and refrigerated. Reheat before grilling the bread and scallops in the following steps.)

3. Thread 6 to 8 scallops on each skewer. Brush both sides of bread slices with remaining 2 tablespoons olive oil. Grill the bread until there are grill marks on both sides. Move the bread to the side of the grill and keep warm. Place scallops on the grill and cook for a few minutes until opaque, rotating skewers for even grill marks.

4. To serve, place a piece of bread on each plate and top with 3 to 4 tablespoons marinara sauce. Remove scallops from skewers and rest on top of the marinara sauce. Sprinkle with remaining chopped basil.

---

*Scallops*
*There are two types of scallops. Bay scallops are tiny and available locally according to season and region, but almost always from October to April. They are preferred by many cognoscenti for their delicately sweet flavor. Sea scallops, much larger, are available all year long. They are succulent, tender and delicious when skewered and grilled.*

*The only edible part of a scallop is the muscle that opens and closes the shell. Like other seafood, scallops should not be overcooked or they will be tough and dry. To grill bay scallops, place them on a punctured sheet of foil on the grill and cook briefly with butter, lemon and any other desired flavoring.*

# SQUID A LA PLANCHA

Serves 6

This comes from Felipe Rojas-Lombardi, internationally known chef/owner of the Ballroom in New York. "In Spanish, *plancha* means grill," he explains. "The flavors of oil and garlic are the distinctive signature to this Spanish way of cooking — and remember, from start to finish they take barely two or three minutes to grill." If you don't have a flat-top gas grill, use an iron skillet and cook the seafood in several batches.

### INGREDIENTS

2½ pounds fresh or frozen small to medium squid (1¼ pounds squid bodies and ¼ pound tentacles after cleaning)
¼ cup olive oil
1½ teaspoon minced garlic
⅛ teaspoon coarse salt
1 tablespoon chopped flat parsley leaves
8 lemon or lime wedges

1. Prepare squid (see directions in box below). If using baby squid, leave them whole. If using medium squid, cut into ½-inch diagonal slices. Drain the squid in a colander. Just before grilling, dry completely with paper towels.

2. When the grill or skillet is very hot, coat lightly with olive oil. When almost smoking, add about ⅓ of the squid, allowing room for tossing. The bodies will change shape quickly, becoming somewhat puffed, and may ooze some liquid which should quickly evaporate. Toss until lightly browned, then transfer quickly to a warm platter; do not overcook.

3. Wipe the grill or skillet with a paper towel. Reheat, add a little oil and brown the remaining squid in two more batches. Wipe off the grill or skillet.

4. Combine the oil and garlic. Reheat the skillet and add the grilled squid, draining off any liquid on the platter. Immediately drizzle the oil/garlic mixture over the squid, tossing and turning until the squid glistens; do not let the garlic burn. Add salt and taste for seasoning.

5. Transfer the squid to serving plates, top with parsley and serve immediately with lemon or lime wedges.

---

*How to Dress a Squid*
*Lay the squid on a flat surface in front of you and stretch it lengthwise from left to right, tentacles to your right. With a sharp knife, cut just below the eyes; this will free the tentacles. There are 10 tentacles, and in the center of them is the mouth; pull or cut it off and discard it. Pull off whatever skin you can from the tentacles, but don't be concerned if you don't get much off. Squeeze the body and pull the head out; the viscera will come out of the body easily. Discard all this. Now pull out the transparent center quill. What remains of the squid is a sac. Wash this well and peel off the outer skin, which is purplish-gray and membranelike; it pulls off easily.*

# SEA SCALLOPS AND BACON WITH MUSHROOMS, SNOW PEAS AND CARROTS

**Serves 4**

This pleasant combination of foods is brought together by Kay Baumhefner, chef at the Opera House Cafe in Petaluma, California. Kay cooked her first dish at age 7.

### INGREDIENTS

MARINADE
½ cup dry vermouth
¼ cup Pernod
¼ cup olive oil
peel of 1 large orange, cut into strips
3 large garlic cloves, pounded or pressed
1 bunch green onions, minced
½ teaspoon freshly ground pepper
2 tablespoons chopped parsley
1 pound sea scallops
poaching liquid:
    1 cup water, ½ teaspoon salt, 2 tablespoons
    fresh lemon juice, 3 tablespoons butter
1 pound button mushrooms, trimmed and
    washed
1 cup rice
8 ounces bacon strips, ¼ inch thick, cut into
    1½-inch lengths
2 tablespoons olive oil
2 tablespoons butter
2 large carrots, peeled and cut into ⅛-inch
    diagonal slices the size of snow peas
1 pound snow peas, trimmed, strings removed
1 lemon, cut into slices or wedges, or chopped
    parsley (garnish)

1. Combine marinade ingredients in a large dish. Add scallops and marinate at least 1 hour, preferably overnight. Bring to room temperature before cooking.

2. In an enameled or stainless steel saucepan, bring the poaching liquid to a boil. Add the mushrooms, cover and simmer briskly for 5 minutes. Uncover, stir and set aside.

3. Preheat the broiler and cook the rice.

4. Place the bacon on a rimmed baking sheet about 5 inches from the broiler. Cook until browned, 2 to 3 minutes. Pour off fat. Turn the bacon and add scallops to pan. Return to the broiler for several minutes more just until scallops are opaque, turning once and removing the bacon if it starts to burn.

5. Meanwhile, in a large skillet, heat 2 tablespoons each olive oil and butter and sauté carrots for 2 minutes over high heat. Add the snow peas and toss rapidly for 1 to 2 minutes, or until they just turn bright green. Add the mushrooms and their poaching liquid and heat through.

6. Place the rice on a serving platter. Arrange the carrots and peas in a ring on top. Pour on the mushrooms and poaching liquid. Spoon the scallops and bacon in the center, then pour on their cooking juices. Garnish with lemon or chopped parsley.

# PASTA WITH GRILLED SCALLOPS, SHRIMP AND WESTPHALIAN HAM

Serves 4

This pasta is enhanced by grilled scallops and was created by Zachary Bruell.

½ cup plus 2 tablespoons olive oil
cracked black pepper
1 pound sea scallops, halved
1 pound shrimp, peeled and deveined, tails left
    on
1 cup fish stock
3 cups heavy cream
2 tablespoons chopped fresh tarragon salt
8 ounces angel-hair pasta
8 ounces Westphalian ham, julienned

1. Divide ½ cup olive oil and cracked black pepper between 2 bowls. Add scallops to one bowl and shrimp to the other; toss to coat. Marinate for 1 hour.

2. Bring a large pot of water to boil with 2 tablespoons olive oil.

3. Boil fish stock until reduced to a glaze. Add cream and reduce by ⅓, then keep warm over very low heat. Season with salt, pepper and tarragon.

4. Preheat oven to 200°F. Grill the seafood over high heat, using a hinged wire basket if available. Transfer to a pan or ovenproof dish and keep warm in the oven.

5. Add pasta to the boiling water and cook until al dente. If the pasta is fresh, it will take only a minute or two; if dried, it will take a little longer. In either case, do not overcook it. Drain the pasta.

6. Divide the sauce among 4 warm plates. Arrange the seafood on the plates but not in the sauce. Place the cooked pasta on the sauce and garnish with the julienned ham. Serve immediately, as pasta waits for no one.

# MIXED FISH
# EN BROCHETTE

Serves 4 to 6

This is delicious and one of the favorite recipes in this book. Brush marinade on the fish as it grills, but do not overcook it.

### INGREDIENTS

1 swordfish steak (10 ounces), about 1¼
   inches thick
1 tuna steak, (8 ounces), about 1¼ inches
   thick
8 sea scallops (about 8 ounces)
8 medium to large shrimp
2 teaspoons grated fresh ginger
1 tablespoon coarse-grained mustard
2 tablespoons fresh lemon juice
½ cup oil (part vegetable, part olive)
3 tablespoons finely chopped green onion
2 tablespoons finely chopped fresh coriander
salt and freshly ground pepper
1 cup mayonnaise
4 to 6 lemon wedges

1. Wash all the fish and scallops; peel and devein shrimp. Cut the swordfish and tuna into 1¼-inch cubes. Dry all the fish and arrange in one layer in a large glass or ceramic dish.

2. Combine ginger, mustard and lemon juice; gradually whisk in oil. Add green onion, coriander, salt and pepper. Pour over the fish and toss until all pieces are coated. Cover and let marinate for 30 minutes.

3. When the fire is almost ready, skewer the fish, alternating the various kinds. Thread 4 to 6 brochettes and grill about 10 minutes, turning the skewers so all sides are cooked and brushing frequently with remaining marinade.

4. Serve each skewer with a dollop of mayonnaise and a lemon wedge.

# SWORDFISH KEBABS WITH PEPPERS, LEMON AND BUTTER

Serves 4

The result is simple, colorful, wonderful food that is so easy to prepare. Lemon and butter beautifully complements the fish and peppers. This will be one of your favorites.

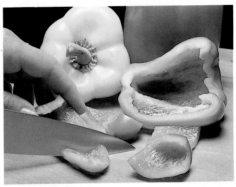

### INGREDIENTS

2 swordfish steaks (1 pound each), cut into
    1¼-inch cubes
1 each green, red and yellow bell pepper, cored,
    seeded and cut into 1¼-inch squares
juice of 2 lemons
8 tablespoons (1 stick) butter, melted
freshly ground pepper
salt

1. Place fish in one layer in a large shallow glass dish or platter. Combine bell peppers, lemon juice, butter and freshly ground pepper, pour over fish and marinate for 1 to 2 hours at room temperature.

2. Thread fish pieces on skewers, alternating with various colors of peppers. Grill, turning and basting frequently with remaining marinade, about 10 minutes. Season with salt to taste. Pour any remaining marinade over kebabs and serve.

---

*Fish Kebabs*
*Intermingle textures and tastes by grilling different kinds of fish on a skewer. Use good-sized cubes so they don't dry out. It's easiest to cut cubes from fish steaks or fillets at least 1 inch thick. Even if the cubes are marinated in oil before grilling, use naturally oily fish — salmon, swordfish, scallops — for extra moistness. As a rule, grilling time is about 10 minutes; rotate the skewer so all sides are evenly grilled.*

# GRILLED EEL
# WITH WHITE WINE,
# BRANDY AND THYME

Serves 6

Eels may be stewed or baked but they are especially flavorful when grilled. The flesh is sweet and firm, and it combines well with a variety of herbs, including bay leaves, rosemary, sage, or as in this recipe, basil. Eel must be freshly killed and skinned at once. The fishmonger will do this for you, or you can do it at home by making an incision in the skin near the head, holding the head with a towel and pulling the skin down smartly. Conger eel, also known as sea eel, is common on both coasts of the Atlantic. John Imperiale, my brother-in-law, created this recipe.

### INGREDIENTS

6 pieces of eel (each about 3 inches long)
juice of 1 lemon
1 cup semidry white wine
3 tablespoons brandy
1 tablespoon chopped fresh thyme or 1
    teaspoon dried
4 tablespoons olive oil
coarse salt and freshly ground pepper
2 tablespoons chopped fresh basil or 1
    tablespoon dried
⅓ teaspoon paprika

1. Ask your fishmonger to skin and cut the eel. He will remove the stomach and cut off the head and tail. Wash and dry the eel pieces and place them in a glass or ceramic dish in one layer.

2. Combine lemon juice, wine, brandy, thyme, 2 tablespoons olive oil, salt and pepper. Mix well and pour over fish. Marinate in refrigerator for 2 hours; bring to room temperature before grilling.

3. Split each piece of eel lengthwise and pat the basil in between the halves. Thread on skewers. When fire is ready, grill the eel for about 15 minutes, turning and basting frequently with a mixture of the remaining 2 tablespoons oil and the paprika. Eel is done when it turns white and a wooden skewer can be inserted with no resistance. Serve hot.

# GRILLED BEEF

Little else epitomizes the succulence of grill cooking like sizzling sirloin steaks, the aroma of rib eye or the marbled tenderness of tenderloin. It has been said that a crisp, molasses-colored steak may well be the exemplar of all grilled foods: it is, after all, the most typical request for a last meal!

Because most meats are seared first to retain their juices, they are exposed to very high temperatures. Therefore the cuts must be thick to prevent drying. And because steaks are flat, they cook evenly on the grill, in contrast to the larger, more irregular cuts that may be better suited for spit-roasting and smoke cookery.

Cuts from the tenderloin — filet mignon, tournedos and chateaubriand — are best for the grill, even though they are on the expensive side. The loin, which includes the tenderloin, provides more excellent meat for grilling: porterhouse, T-bone and shell steaks. In fact, many claim that these latter steaks are most flavorful of all. In either case, any one of them is perfect for the grill.

Like all meats, these cuts should be at room temperature before they are put on the fire. Steaks should be trimmed of most fat, leaving only a thin layer that should be scored every inch or so to prevent curling. It's a good idea to sear the meat first on an oiled grid, uncovered. After searing, thick steaks are usually grilled covered to complete cooking, but a cover is not always necessary if flareups can be controlled.

Rare meat will be soft to the touch. Medium is springy; press with the back of a fork and it springs back. Well-done meat is neither soft nor springy; it is rather rigid, with beads of juice on the outside. Any meat should rest for 5 to 10 minutes after it is taken off the grill, and then it is sliced thinly across the grain to serve.

Serve marinades, sauces and accompaniments to the side of the sliced meat, not on top. Sliced grilled meat that's juicy and pink inside is always a visual temptation — don't conceal it in sauce.

# BEEF SELECTION AND PORTION SIZE

HAMBURGER: Boned prime chuck, sirloin, filet mignon ends or any lean beef, ground to order, is best. If you have a food processor, you can grind your own at home. One and a half pounds will provide four adequate servings.

PORTERHOUSE OR T-BONE: Cut 1 ½ to 2 inches thick. Very flavorful but not as easy to cut as boned sirloin. Provide 12 ounces per person.

RIB ROAST, ROLLED: This is the same as a standing rib roast but without the bones. It is rolled, usually with a thin piece of fat, and tied. Four pounds serve four people.

RIB ROAST, STANDING: A two-rib roast will serve four; each additional rib serves two more people (there are seven ribs in this section of beef). Have butcher cut off short ribs and ask that he turn over and tie the flank.

SHELL STEAKS: Also known as club or Delmonico steaks. Usually boneless. Cut 1½ inches thick and one per person.

SIRLOIN STEAK: Buy from the round end, sometimes called wedge-bone sirloin. For grilling it should be 1 ½ to 2 inches thick. Provide 5 to 8 ounces per person.

TENDERLOIN (FILLET OF BEEF): The whole tenderloin is between 4 and 6 pounds. A 2-pound piece is the minimum for satisfactory grilling unless you use filet mignon steaks.

---

*Aging of Beef*
*It takes six to 10 days to transfer fresh meat from the packer to the butcher and then home. During this time, enzymes in the meat break down the fibers, tenderizing it. Loins and ribs get additional aging; this costs a little more, but it's why they're so tender. Meat can't be properly aged at home because humidity and temperature must be controlled at all times. Kosher meat is not aged at all; under orthodox Jewish custom, meat must be eaten within 72 hours of slaughtering.*

---

*Beef*
*These six cuts are low on the calorie and fat charts. Figures are for 3-ounce servings, cooked and trimmed.\**

*1. Eye of round: 5.5 g total fat (2.1 g saturated fat) — 155 calories*

*2. Top round: 5.3 g total fat (1.8 g saturated fat) — 162 calories*

*3. Round tip: 6.4 g total fat, (2.3 g saturated fat) — 162 calories*

*4. Top loin: 7.6 g total fat (3.0 g saturated fat) — 172 calories*

*5. Tenderloin: 7.9 g total fat (3.1 g saturated fat) — 174 calories*

*6. Sirloin: 7.4 g total fat (3.0 g saturated fat) — 177 calories*

*\*Source: USDA, Handbook No. 8-13*

---

*Ground Beef*
*The signs in a butcher shop read "ground chuck," "ground round," "ground sirloin" and so on, and naturally prices go up for the better-quality meat. If you can be sure of what you're getting at the butcher, buy ground beef. Otherwise, grind your own in the food processor.*

*Grinding tenderizes meat, yet the tenderness of ground beef has to do more with the ratio of fat to lean. For juiciness and good flavor, ground beef should be approximately 85 percent lean and 15 percent fat. More fat than that will cook away at the grill.*

---

*Beef*
*According to the USDA, 3 ounces of lean beef supplies less than 200 calories, but about 3 of its 8 grams of fat are saturated. Therefore, it's a good idea to trim all visible fat before cooking; this is one way to cut the fat and calorie counts.*

# GROUND SIRLOIN HAMBURGERS WITH SOY, SESAME AND GREEN ONIONS

Serves 4

INGREDIENTS

2 green onions, tender parts only, thinly sliced
⅓ cup soy sauce
1 tablespoon sesame-chili oil (available at Oriental markets)
2 tablespoons grated fresh ginger
1½ pounds ground sirloin
4 toasted, buttered sesame seed rolls
3 ounces chilled pickled ginger, shredded

1. Combine onions, soy sauce, oil and ginger in a small bowl and mix well.

2. Divide sirloin into 4 portions and add slightly less than 1 tablespoon soy mixture to each portion. Gently shape into burgers. Transfer burgers to a shallow glass or ceramic dish and pour the remaining soy mixture over. Let marinate 10 minutes (no longer), turning after 5 minutes.

3. When fire is ready, place burgers on oiled rack and grill to desired doneness: 4 minutes per side for rare, 6 minutes for medium and 7 to 8 minutes for well done. Baste with remaining marinade as meat is turned.

4. Serve on toasted rolls, topping each burger with a generous sprinkle of shredded ginger.

# GROUND PRIME CHUCK HAMBURGERS WITH BACON AND HERBS

Serves 4

## INGREDIENTS

1½ pounds ground prime chuck
¼ cup finely chopped parsley
¼ cup finely chopped fresh basil
salt and freshly ground pepper
¼ cup heavy cream
2 slices bacon, halved lengthwise
4 toasted buttered rolls or bread slices
4 slices red onion, ¼ inch thick
4 fresh tomato slices, ½ inch thick
4 teaspoons balsamic vinegar
4 fresh basil leaves

1. Lightly part meat with splayed fingers. Combine parsley, chopped basil, salt, pepper and cream in a small bowl and mix well. Pour slowly over meat, mixing lightly with hands. Gently form into 4 burgers.

2. In a skillet or on a flattop grill, half-cook bacon slices. Wrap a length around each burger and secure with a pick.

3. When fire is ready, grill burgers on oiled grid, each side 4 minutes for rare or longer for desired doneness. Six minutes will produce medium; 7 to 8 minutes, well done.

4. Serve on toasted buttered rolls. Add onion slice to side of the plate; place a tomato slice halfway overlapping the onion. Sprinkle a teaspoon of balsamic vinegar over tomato and onion. Set 1 basil leaf next to tomato.

# CHILI CHUCK BURGERS WITH BUTTER AND LIME SAUCE

Serves 4

This burger is not overpowered with chili. If you wish, add more chili powder, a sprinkle of red pepper flakes or 2 to 3 drops of hot pepper sauce to the onion mixture before adding it to the meat. Serve on a toasted roll or bread with pinto beans on the side.

### INGREDIENTS

1½ pounds ground prime chuck
2 tablespoons grated fresh onion with juice
1½ teaspoons red wine vinegar
1½ tablespoons olive oil
2 teaspoons chili powder
coarse salt
4 tablespoons butter, melted
¼ cup fresh lime juice
4 toasted, buttered rolls or bread slices
8 ripe tomato slices, about ½ inch thick, dressed with a lime, olive oil, salt and pepper vinaigrette

1. Lightly part meat with splayed fingers. Combine onion, vinegar, olive oil, chili powder and salt to taste in a small bowl and mix well. Pour slowly over meat, mixing with hands. Gently form into 4 burgers.

2. When fire is ready, place burgers on oiled grid. Grill each side about 4 minutes for rare or longer for desired doneness. Six minutes will produce medium; 7 to 8 minutes, well done.

3. Combine melted butter and lime juice. Baste burgers on grill with some of mixture, reserving the remainder for use as a sauce.

4. Serve toasted roll or bread on the side of the plate. Spoon butter/lime sauce over burgers. Add vinaigrette-dressed tomato slices.

# HUNGARIAN GRILLED MEAT CAKES

Serves 3 to 6

It's surprising how a few celery leaves can flavor this dish, says Mrs. Leskody who creates this dish for four or 40 people. Serve with fresh grilled corn, eggplant or onions and a green salad.

### INGREDIENTS

1 pound ground lean beef
1 hard roll, moistened with water and squeezed
   dry
1 egg
1 tablespoon finely chopped onion or green
   onion
2 tablespoons finely chopped celery leaves
1 tablespoon finely chopped parsley
¼ cup tomato juice
1 teaspoon salt
¼ teaspoon freshly ground pepper or a pinch
   of red pepper flakes

1. Combine all ingredients and mix well with splayed fingers. Shape into 6 patties.

2. Oil a hinged wire basket or the grid after the fire is ready. Sear one side of meat cakes, then raise grid to complete cooking the first side. Repeat on second side, first searing and then finishing off by raising meat higher above heat source.

---

*Early American Barbecues*
*Native Americans, followed by Colonial Americans, were already barbecuing hundreds of years ago. In one reference, a pig was cooked for a half day in a 4-foot pit, at a public gathering in what was to become the state of Virginia. Today we would call this an eastern Carolina-style barbecue. There are numerous identifiable styles, including North Carolina, South Carolina, Eastern Tennessee, Western Kentucky, Memphis, Arkansas, Georgia and Texas. They developed because of available fuels: mesquite in Texas, hickory in the South and East, and so on.*

# FILET MIGNON HAMBURGERS WITH THYME AND A SPRINKLE OF DEEP-FRIED LEEK CONFETTI

Serves 4

This will cost a little more than ground sirloin, or prime chuck, if you ask for the fillet ends. Surely this delicious meal is worth the extra cents.

### INGREDIENTS

1½ pounds filet mignon ends, ground
2 teaspoons finely chopped fresh thyme
salt and freshly ground pepper
3 leeks, 1 to 1½ inches thick and 3 to 4 inches
    long, white parts only
8 thin slices buttered Italian bread, grilled
4 tablespoons softened butter
vegetable oil for deep frying

1. Lightly break up meat with splayed fingers. Sprinkle 1½ teaspoons thyme, salt and pepper over it and mix lightly with hands. Gently form into 4 burgers.

2. Cut leeks in half lengthwise. Rinse carefully, removing sand lodged between layers; dry well. Cut into 1½- to 2-inch lengths, then into very fine julienne.

3. When fire is ready, place burgers on oiled grid. Grill each side about 4 minutes each for rare or longer for desired doneness. Six minutes will produce medium; 7 to 9 minutes, well done.

4. Meanwhile, heat deep frying oil to 350°F and fry leek "confetti" until browned. Remover burgers from grill and place each on one slice of bread; set the second slice next to it. Spread 1 tablespoon butter on each burger and sprinkle with remaining thyme. As soon as leeks are fried, place some on top of each burger with tongs. Serve immediately.

### Leeks

*Leeks are an important member of the onion family, but as a rule the leek is sweeter and milder. The leek is probably as old as the fig, historically speaking. No one seems able to determine its origin, although it was grown in ancient Egypt and Rome. The fact that it is more infinitely popular in Europe than in the United States is difficult to understand, because it is easy to grow, almost totally free of diseases and pests and unperturbed by frost. In Dutchess County, about 70 miles north of New York City, we leave leeks in the ground until Thanksgiving. They're easy to dig up, clean and freeze. Don't buy leeks with discolored tops or any that are very large. They must be washed very carefully, because sand is often lodged between the layers (much of the leek grows underground). Cut off the root end and slice the leek down the middle. This makes it easy to separate and wash.*

# GRILLED PRIME RIB ROLLS WITH VEGETABLES IN A JAPANESE SAUCE

Serves 4 to 6

It is as beautiful as it is tasty. Thin slices of prime rib will grill very quickly.

### INGREDIENTS

12 fresh asparagus spears, 5 to 6 inches long
12 carrot strips, about ½ inch thick and 5 to 6 inches long
1 pound beef prime rib, cut into 12 thin slices
cornstarch
2 tablespoons sugar
6 tablespoons water
3 tablespoons saké
3 tablespoons mirin
¼ cup soy sauce

1. Steam vegetables separately until crisp-tender; cool.

2. Arrange 2 slices of beef with lengths slightly overlapping to form a 6- x 6-inch sheet. Brush lightly with cornstarch. Place 2 asparagus spears and 2 carrot strips along edge nearest you and roll away from you; the roll should be fairly tight. Tie with string and place in a nonmetallic dish.

3. Combine all remaining ingredients to make marinade. Pour over beef rolls and marinate at room temperature for about 2 hours. Remove rolls from marinade and insert

2 skewers in each, one through each end of roll. Grill quickly on each side (meat is so tender that little grilling is required). Remove string and skewers and cut each roll into 1½-inch lengths. Arrange on individual warmed plates by standing cut rolls on edge to show vegetables.

4. Heat remaining marinade and spoon around rolls, not on top of them. Serve immediately.

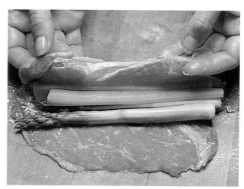

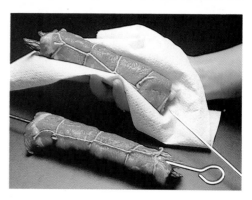

# HICKORY PORTERHOUSE STEAK WITH LEMON-MUSTARD BUTTER

Serves 4 to 6

$P$orterhouse steak is considered by some to be king of the grill. Seared and slow-cooked with hickory and stroked with a tangy lemon-mustard sauce, it qualifies for a regal place in the barbecue kingdom.

### INGREDIENTS

1 thick porterhouse steak (2½ to 3 pounds)
4 tablespoons softened butter
juice of ½ lemon
1½ tablespoons Dijon mustard
1 tablespoon finely chopped fresh thyme or ½
    teaspoon dried
salt and freshly ground pepper

1. Trim steak and score fat remaining around edges to prevent curling. Let steak reach room temperature before grilling. Soak 1 ½ cups hickory chips in water for 30 minutes.

2. Combine butter, lemon juice, mustard and thyme and mix well. Let stand at room temperature. Do not melt butter; it should be soft and pliable.

3. Prepare the fire and be sure the grid is clean. Drain hickory chips and add to fire. Place steak on it and sear quickly on both sides, as close to heat as possible. Raise meat from heat and continue to grill to desired doneness, about 20 minutes total.

4. Transfer steak to carving board and let rest for about 5 minutes. Spread lemon-mustard butter on top of steak. Slice diago-and serve immediately.

> *Porterhouse Steak*
> *This is considered the superior steak by many con-noisseurs. It is fairly expensive because only the porterhouse steaks can be cut from the beef short loin; each of the four will weigh a little under 3 pounds to a little over. The porterhouse contains a large part of the tenderloin (filet mignon) and the strip shell steak. T-bones, also cut from the short loin, are the same as porterhouse except that they have less tenderloin. Porterhouse seems to satisfy the American appetite more than anything else, except perhaps for hamburgers.*

# SPICE-RUBBED RIB STEAKS

Serves 6

The spices sound intimidating, but once the meat is grilled, the flavors soften. Grilled red onions make an excellent partner with this dish, as do asparagus with mustard vinaigrette.

### INGREDIENTS

2 prime rib steaks, 2 inches thick, bone in,
  (1¾ pounds each)
1½ tablespoons dry mustard
1½ tablespoons paprika
1½ tablespoons ground coriander
1½ tablespoons cracked Lampong black
  pepper*
1½ teaspoons cayenne pepper
2 large garlic cloves, minced
2 tablespoons peanut oil
3 tablespoons cognac
salt

1. Remove excess fat from steaks and score remaining fat to prevent curling. Wipe steaks and place in a large glass or ceramic dish. Bring to room temperature.

*(\*found in food specialty stores)*

2. Combine spices and garlic in a small bowl or mini-size food processor. Add oil and cognac and mix to a paste. With a rubber spatula, apply ⅔ of the paste to both sides of the steaks and allow to marinate 2 to 3 hours at room temperature. Keep remaining spice paste at room temperature.

3. Prepare a fire; when hot, sear steaks 3 inches above heat source on one side for 2 minutes. Raise rack to 6 inches above heat and continue cooking for 8 minutes. Turn meat over and brush some of the remaining paste on the cooked sides. Lower to 3 inches above heat and sear the second sides for 2 minutes. Raise the rack to 6 inches and continue cooking to desired doneness, about 8 more minutes (total grilling time is about 20 minutes). Smear remaining paste on second sides. Let meat rest for a couple of minutes. Season with salt.

4. Cut meat off bones and place bones on one side of large platter. Slice both steaks thinly, overlap slices on the same platter and serve.

# GRILLED RIB STEAK WITH HERB BUTTER, GRILLED ONIONS AND SAUTÉED SPINACH

Serves 4

Chef Ali Barker, of New York's Union Square Cafe, uses a 34-ounce rib steak — one huge chop — for two people. It looks spectacular and tastes wonderful.

### INGREDIENTS

8 tablespoons (1 stick) softened unsalted butter
2 sprigs each of 4 different fresh herbs
    (rosemary, thyme, parsley, mint, etc.),
    finely chopped
juice of 1 lemon
salt and freshly ground pepper
2 red onions, thickly sliced
½ cup (about) olive oil
2 double rib steaks (about 2 pounds each),
    bone in
peanut oil
2 bunches fresh spinach, stemmed
2 shallots, minced

1. Combine butter, chopped herbs and lemon juice. Season to taste with salt and pepper. Place the herb butter on a 12-inch piece of plastic wrap and roll into a 1-inch cylinder. Freeze until hard (herb butter can be made well in advance and kept frozen).

2. Place the onions on a baking sheet, coat lightly with olive oil and season with salt and pepper. Bake in a preheated 400°F oven for about 20 minutes or until soft. (This pre-cooking step makes the onions very sweet.)

3. To grill the steak, dry it well, season with plenty of salt and pepper and coat with peanut oil. Cook on a very hot grill, searing the outside. A cut of meat this thick will take approximately 30 minutes for medium rare. When the meat is done, remove it from the grill and allow it to rest about 5 minutes. Meanwhile, place the baked onions on the grill to mark them. Over high heat, sauté the spinach and shallots in 2 tablespoons olive oil until spinach is wilted, about 1 to 2 minutes. Season with salt and pepper.

4. To serve, slice the beef off the bone and top with slices of herb butter. Arrange the spinach and grilled onions around the meat on the platter.

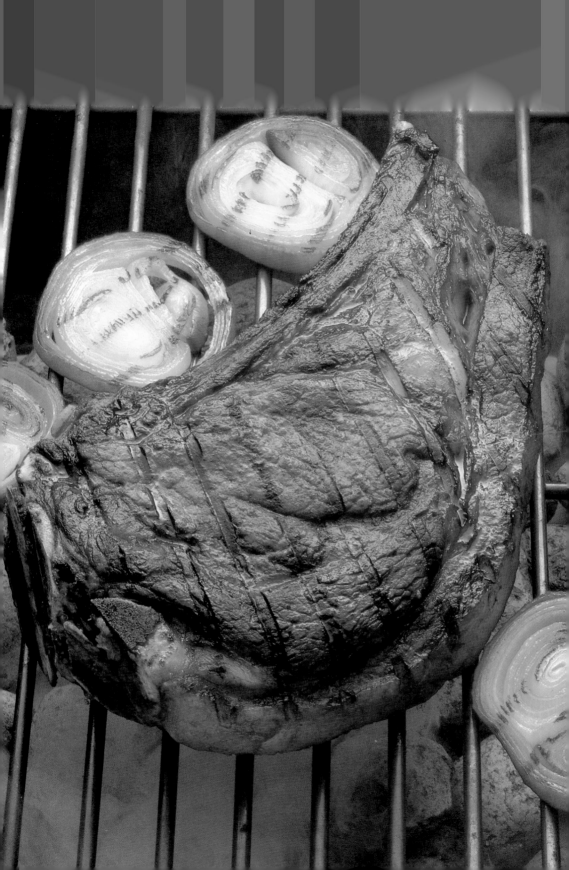

# MARINATED AND GRILLED SHELL STEAKS

Serves 4

It doesn't seem possible to improve a plain grilled shell steak, but this is a very special treatment. The marinade ingredients combine to enhance the flavor of this favorite dish, one that will be served often.

### INGREDIENTS

4 shell steaks, about 1½ inches thick (¾ to 1 pound each), at room temperature
¾ cup olive oil
¼ cup balsamic vinegar
2 tablespoons soy sauce
juice of 1 lemon
2 tablespoons Worcestershire sauce
2 garlic cloves, minced
1 tablespoon dry mustard
1 teaspoon chopped parsley, including stems
1 teaspoon freshly ground pepper
salt
butter

1. Arrange the steaks in one layer in one or more large glass dishes.

2. Combine all remaining ingredients except salt and butter and blend well. Pour over the meat. Allow to marinate 1 to 2 hours at room temperature.

3. Build a charcoal fire and allow it to reach the gray ash stage. Gently tap coals to shake off the ash. Move coals so they are about ½ inch apart to moderate heat.

4. Remove steaks from the marinade and place them on the grill. Lower it as close as possible to the heat source. Sear for 2 minutes, on one side only, to seal in the juices. Raise the grill about 4 inches from the coals and continue grilling until tiny bubbles of juice appear on top of the steak. Only then, turn steak with tongs; do not use a fork or other utensil that will pierce the meat. Turn only once.

5. Repeat grilling procedure as for first side; lower grid to sear second side for 2 minutes, raise grid to 4 inches above coals and continue grilling. Total cooking time will be 12 to 15 minutes. Remove from grill and spread some butter on each side of steak, adding salt to taste.

# GRILLED SIRLOIN STEAK

Serves 4

Sirloin steak needs only to be grilled. Its only enrichment is some butter added after it is grilled—a perfect touch!

INGREDIENTS

1 boned sirloin steak (2 pounds and 2 inches thick), at room temperature
2 tablespoons butter
salt and freshly ground pepper

1. Build a charcoal fire and allow it to reach the gray ash stage. Gently tap coals to shake off the ash. Move coals so they are about ½ inch apart to moderate heat.

2. Brush the grill with oil. Place the steak on it and lower it as close as possible to the heat source. Sear for 2 minutes, on one side only, to seal in the juices. Raise the grill about 4 inches from the coals and continue grilling until tiny bubbles of juice appear on top of the steak. Only then, turn steak with tongs; do not use a fork or other utensil that will pierce the meat. Turn only once.

3. Repeat grilling procedure as for first side; lower grid to sear second side for 2 minutes, raise grid to 4 inches above coals and continue grilling. Total cooking time will be 20 to 30 minutes. To test for doneness, insert a small knife into the meat.

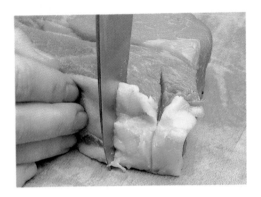

# GRILLED SIRLOIN OF BEEF WITH ROQUEFORT-NAPA CABBAGE SALAD

Serves 4

A wonderful beef dish created by the talented chef, Mark Filippo.

### INGREDIENTS

1 2-inch-thick sirloin or shell steak (1 pound)
salt and freshly ground pepper
Roquefort napa cabbage salad (see below)
oven-dried tomatoes (see below)
4 raw spinach leaves
balsamic vinaigrette (see below)
1 teaspoon finely chopped chives

1. Trim steaks, leaving a thin layer of fat. Season meat with salt and pepper. When the fire is ready, grill fat side down for 2 minutes. Then turn and grill remaining 3 sides, 2 minutes per side; steak will be rare. Allow to rest a few minutes. Trim away all fat and slice meat thinly, allowing 2 slices per serving.

2. Overlap slices at the bottom of the plate. Mound cabbage salad at top right. Place 2 oven-dried tomatoes on a spinach leaf to the left of the cabbage. Nap the beef with ½ tablespoon vinaigrette and sprinkle with chives.

### BALSAMIC VINAIGRETTE

Makes ½ cup

### INGREDIENTS

2 tablespoon balsamic vinegar
1 garlic clove
1 teaspoon chopped chives
¼ cup olive oil
2 tablespoons peanut oil
salt and freshly ground pepper

Combine all ingredients in a jar with tight-fitting lid and shake well. Let stand at room temperature before using.

### ROQUEFORT NAPA CABBAGE SALAD

Makes about 1½ cups

### INGREDIENTS

1 cup napa cabbage sliced ¼ inch thick
3 ounces Roquefort cheese
½ cup mayonnaise (see page 309)
salt and freshly ground pepper

Mix all ingredients until well blended. Taste and adjust seasoning. Refrigerate for 2 to 8 hours before serving.

OVEN-DRIED TOMATOES

Makes 20

Make extra ones and hold in olive oil for up to one week.

### INGREDIENTS

10 fresh plum tomatoes, uniform size
1 tablespoon coarse salt
1 quart olive oil
2 garlic cloves, peeled
½ teaspoon red pepper flakes

1. Halve tomatoes lengthwise and sprinkle inside with salt. Place in a colander and let drain for at least 6 hours.

2. Arrange tomatoes skin side down on a baking sheet and place in a 200°F oven for 6 hours. Turn off oven and let tomatoes rest in oven overnight. They should be half their original size and have a slight bit of moisture remaining.

3. Let tomatoes cool 1 hour. Place in a clean jar with olive oil, garlic and red pepper flakes. Allow to marinate at least 1 day in a cool place.

# SIRLOIN STRIPS, GRILLED
# KOREAN STYLE

Simple to prepare and simple to grill — about 2 or 3 minutes per side over direct heat. The idea is to sear the slices quickly. One way to do this successfully, all at one time, is to lay the slices close together in a hinged wire basket — a thin one as used for hamburgers. This Korean dish was adapted from a recipe by Peter Hyun in Nika Hazelton's *Picnic Book*, published by Atheneum.

### INGREDIENTS

2 pounds sirloin steak, 1½ inches thick, fat
    and bones removed
⅓ cup soy sauce
3 tablespoons sesame-chili oil (available at
    Oriental markets)
2 tablespoons dry sherry
4 garlic cloves, minced or pressed
4 green onions very thinly sliced
¼ cup sugar
4 green onions, trimmed, for garnish

1. Cut the steak across the grain into slices no thicker than ¼ inch. Place in one or two layers in a glass or ceramic dish.

2. Combine soy sauce, sesame-chili oil and sherry and mix well. Blend in remaining ingredients except garnish. Pour over meat, being sure all sides are coated. Cover with plastic wrap and refrigerate for at least 2 hours. Bring meat to room temperature before grilling.

3. Drain the steak slices and arrange in a hinged wire basket just before grill time; reserve any remaining marinade. When fire is ready, place basket directly over coals for 2 to 3 minutes to sear; if flareup occurs, lower cover. Turn basket and baste seared side liberally. Sear second side 2 to 3 minutes, turn and baste. Turn meat out onto a large platter. Pour any remaining marinade over all. Garnish with green onions.

---

*Sherry*
*One of the great Spanish wines, sherry comes from Jerez de la Frontera and is used often in cooking. The alcohol content of the wine cooks off as it is heated and only the flavor is retained. The sherry in the recipe on this page adds a special flavor to the sirloin strips. The marinade recipe here can also be used with chicken; be sure to include the wine.*

---

# MARINATED GRILLED SKIRT STEAK WITH ONIONS, PEPPERS AND PAPAYA

Serves 2

Clive DuVal, the owner and chef of Tila's Cantina & Taqueria in Houston, borrows ingredients from the cuisines of Mexico, Central America and South America. He combines them with his classic French techniques to create a unique menu. To tenderize the skirt steak in this recipe, Clive pounds it with a mallet. The "slivered" onion and papaya should be cut into thin slices, a little larger than julienned.

### MEAT MARINADE

½ cup red wine
½ cup beer
½ cup safflower oil
2 tablespoons Szechuan peppercorns
2 tablespoons cracked black pepper
4 garlic cloves, chopped
2 jalapeño peppers, chopped
2 tablespoons dried basil, crushed
⅓ cup fresh lime juice
⅓ cup fresh orange juice
⅓ cup Oriental barbecue sauce
2 tablespoons coarse salt
1 well-marbled skirt steak (14 ounces), trimmed and pounded with a mallet to tenderize
flour and corn tortillas, warmed
freshly grated Parmesan and Muenster cheeses
*pico de gallo* (see page 00)

### VEGETABLE MARINADE

½ cup balsamic vinegar
½ cup olive oil
2 tablespoons cracked black pepper
2 garlic cloves, minced
2 tablespoons minced fresh mint
1 small white onion, slivered
½ red bell pepper, sliced
½ green bell pepper, sliced
⅓ small firm-ripe papaya, slivered

1. Prepare the vegetable marinade by blending the balsamic vinegar and olive oil. Whisk in cracked black pepper, minced garlic and mint. Pour over the slivered onions and bell peppers and let stand uncovered for 1 hour.

2. Prepare a mesquite charcoal.

3. Drain the marinade from the onions and peppers and reserve it. Grill the onions and peppers in a wire basket over mesquite charcoal until soft. Remove from basket and replace with papaya; grill until fruit takes on a smoky flavor. Transfer papaya to a nonaluminum sauté pan, add reserved marinade and simmer 1 minute.

4. Combine wine, beer, safflower oil, Szechuan pepper, black pepper, chopped garlic, jalapeños, basil, lime juice, orange juice, barbecue sauce and salt in a food processor and puree. Pour over the skirt steak and marinate, uncovered, for 10 minutes at room temperature.

5. Grill the skirt steak over hot mesquite charcoal until the flesh is firm but still rare inside. Transfer meat to a warm platter.

6. Using a slotted spoon, remove vegetables and papaya from simmering marinade and pour over the steak. Serve with hot tortillas, freshly grated cheeses and pico de gallo.

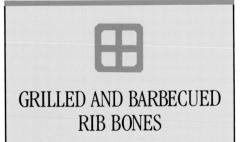

# GRILLED AND BARBECUED RIB BONES

Serves 4

The fat in the rib bones keeps them moist. The barbecue sauce is delicious but do not baste until the ribs are almost cooked. A simple Beaujolais Villages or other hearty red Burgundy will go well with this dish. A good vegetable accompaniment is turnips that have been parboiled whole, thickly sliced, buttered and put on the grill for score marks.

### INGREDIENTS

8 beef rib bones (about 4 pounds)
3 tablespoons peanut oil
2 garlic cloves, minced
1 onion, minced
½ cup tomato catsup
⅓ cup cider vinegar
2 tablespoons fresh lemon juice
2 tablespoons honey
1 tablespoon brown sugar
2 teaspoons dry mustard
1 teasoon ground ginger
salt

1. Wipe ribs and bring to room temperature before grilling.

2. Combine all remaining ingredients and pulse in food processor until well mixed, 8 to 10 times. Transfer to a bowl and set aside.

3. Grill ribs when the fire is ready. Any grill method (electric, charcoal, mesquite, etc.) will work but time will vary depending on heat and the thickness of the ribs. Grill the ribs plain; do not add salt, sauce or anything else. Turn to grill each side.

4. During last 5 to 10 minutes of grilling (rarely will these take more than 30 minutes in total grill time), baste with sauce.

5. When ribs are cooked, quickly bring remaining sauce to the boil. Spoon 2 tablespoons onto each plate, add 2 ribs and serve immediately.

---

*Short Ribs of Beef*
*Sometimes called "English ribs," these are flavorful but fatty. They are the ends of the rib bones; to serve four people, usually 3 to 4 pounds are needed. In kosher markets, short ribs are called flanken. They can be bought with the bone in or out. Short ribs may be used for the recipe on this page, although less fatty beef ribs may be preferred— i.e., the rib bones from roast beef cuts.*

# GRILLED SIRLOIN STEAK WITH MUSTARD SAUCE

Serves 4   (recipe for steak on p. 118)

Tawny port, which is so good with cheese and fruit, serves as the base for this rich, lusty sauce. It has a dark amber color and appealing fruity flavor, and it goes well with a crusty, grilled thick sirloin steak. Accompany with boiled new potatoes.

### INGREDIENTS

1 sirloin steak, 1½ inches thick (about 2 pounds)
1 cup tawny port
1 green onion, thinly sliced
1 cup beef stock
½ cup heavy cream
4 tablespoons butter
2 tablespoons coarse-grained mustard
salt
1 tablespoon freshly ground or cracked pink peppercorns

**1.** Trim steak of excess fat and score edge to prevent curling as it grills. Bring to room temperature.

**2.** Combine wine and green onion in a non-aluminum saucepan and boil until reduced by ⅔. Add stock and boil until thick enough to coat a spoon. Add cream and continue reducing until sauce begins to thicken. Whisk in butter a tablespoon at a time. Add mustard and salt and blend well. Keep sauce warm in the top of a double boiler over hot, not boiling, water.

**3.** Grill the steaks to desired doneness. Let rest briefly, then slice thinly across the grain. Spoon some of the sauce onto a warm plate and top with 2 or 3 steak slices. Sprinkle with crushed peppercorns.

> *Tawny Port*
> *Port is a wine made from the grapes grown in the valley of the upper Douro (Portugal), fortified at vintage time. Tawny port is not vintage port, the latter is made in one year and aged for many years to develop flavor. On the other hand, tawny port is a blend of wines of different years, aged in wood. It matures sooner than vintage, and can be used in a number of marinades and sauces.*

## MEXICAN FAJITAS (SKIRT STEAK IN TORTILLAS)

Serves 4

Two of the best home grill cooks I know, Gene and Jerry Ann Woodfin, put their heads together to produce this mouthwatering, totally satisfying garnished steak dish based on Mexican cuisine. The guacamole itself is worth several Texas stars.

### INGREDIENTS

1 skirt steak (2½ pounds)
1 cup Coca-Cola
2 teaspoons mesquite smoke seasoning
2 teaspoons fajita seasoning*
8 tortillas, warmed
¾ cup guacamole (see page 128)
½ cup *pico de gallo* (see page 234)

1. Marinate steak in Coca-Cola, mesquite smoke and fajita seasonings for 3 to 4 hours at room temperature.

2. Grill over a very hot fire until both sides are seared and meat is pink and juicy in the middle. This will take a couple of minutes per side, depending on the heat and grill height. Remove from grill and cut across the grain in finger-size slices.

*There are various fajita seasonings available; they can serve as marinades or mops. They tenderize the meat and provide a smoked flavor. One such marinade is bottled by The Figaro Co., Inc., Dallas, Texas 75207.

## GUACAMOLE

Makes ¾ cup

### INGREDIENTS

2 ripe avocados
juice of ½ lemon or 1 lime
1 garlic clove, pressed or minced
1 tablespoon grated onion
1 tomato, cored, peeled, seeded and chopped
1 tablespoon finely chopped fresh coriander
pinch of cayenne pepper or a few drops of hot
    pepper sauce
salt
1 or more serrano or jalapeño chilies, seeded
    and minced, optional

1. Cut avocados in half; discard pits and remove flesh. Transfer to mixing bowl. Add lemon or lime juice immediately or avocado will start to discolor. Mash it with a fork, keeping it a bit lumpy.

2. Add all other ingredients and mix well but do not puree.

3. Adjust seasoning, especially lemon or lime juice.

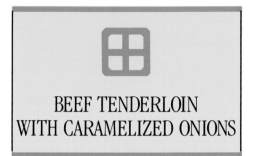

## BEEF TENDERLOIN WITH CARAMELIZED ONIONS

Serves 2

This excellent beef is prepared at Giovanni's in Beachwood, Ohio by its chef, Sergio J. Abramoff.

### INGREDIENTS

2 tablespoons vegetable oil
4 Spanish or Bermuda onions, cut into 1-inch
    dice
¼ cup brandy
1½ tablespoons coarse-grained mustard
1 tablespoon brown sugar
¼ cup beef stock
1 tablespoon butter
6 slices beef tenderloin, 3 ounces each
salt and freshly ground pepper
1 tablespoon chopped chives

**1.** Heat oil in a large saucepan over high heat. Add onions and stir until they begin to brown. Reduce heat to low and continue cooking and stirring for about 20 minutes, or until the onions caramelize. Add brandy and ignite, shaking pan until flames subside. Stir in mustard, sugar, stock and butter and simmer for 5 minutes. Set sauce aside and keep warm.

**2.** Season beef with salt and pepper and grill over high heat to desired doneness. Arrange slices on a serving platter. Spoon onion sauce over beef, sprinkle with chives and serve at once.

---

*Quality of Beef*
*It is generally agreed that the higher the degree of marbling, the higher the quality of the beef. Marbling is the lacing of fat in a piece of meat; its quantity is directly related to the meat's flavor and tenderness. Marbling is especially important in meats to be grilled. When buying beef, look for a bright red color with fat that is white to creamy white. The meat should be elastic to the touch. Prime beef is heavily marbled, more than Choice and other grades.*

---

# SKEWERED BEEF TENDERLOIN

Serves 4 to 6

$O$ne of the best recipes in this book. The meat is expensive but there is no waste or bone. Very easy preparation and delicious.

1½ pounds beef tenderloin, cut into 1½-inch
   cubes
3 tablespoons olive oil
8 tablespoons (1 stick) butter, melted
1 tablespoon chopped fresh thyme or ½
   teaspoon dried
1 tablespoon Dijon mustard
⅛ teaspoon red pepper flakes
salt and freshly ground pepper
6 tablespoons fresh lemon juice

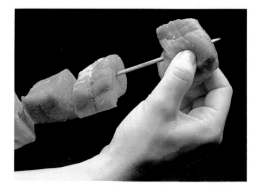

1. Divide the beef cubes between 2 long skewers.

2. Combine the oil, 4 tablespoons of the melted butter, thyme, mustard and red pepper flakes and mix well. Brush over all sides of the beef cubes. Season to taste with salt and pepper.

3. Grill for about 3 minutes per side, brushing with more of the oil mixture. Combine the remaining melted butter with the lemon juice. Heat quickly and pour over the skewered meat just before serving.

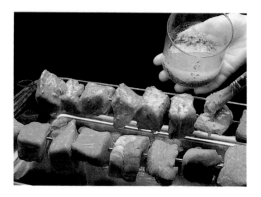

# GRILLED BEEF TENDERLOIN WITH TOMATILLOS

Serves 4

Jimmy Schmidt, co-owner of The Rattlesnake Club in Denver, Colorado, is a perfectionist who spends considerable time devising menu items that emphasize original combinations of flavors. He says, "Nothing is selected for effect. It has to work and be an integral part of the dish." The Rattlesnake Club is an architecturally stunning trilevel restaurant, but the main attraction is the food. Chef Schmidt knows how to handle color and texture: he smokes trout and combines it with blue corn blinis, sour cream and jalapeño peppers, and he grills pears and leeks to accompany duck.

### INGREDIENTS

¾ cup diced tomatillos
1 cup heavy cream
2 tablespoons unsalted butter
2 cups diced red onions
2 cups red wine
2 cups beef stock
1 tablespoon ground achiote (annatto) seed
   (available at Latin American markets)
salt
8 medallions of beef tenderloin (3 ounces each)
1 tablespoon ground cumin
½ cup roasted, peeled and diced red bell
   pepper
½ cup roasted, peeled and diced poblano
   pepper*

*found in food specialty stores

2 tablespoons finely chopped chives
2 tablespoons finely chopped fresh coriander
8 blue corn crêpes (see below)
fresh coriander sprigs for garnish

1. In a medium saucepan, combine ½ cup tomatillos and cream and bring to simmer over medium-high heat. Cook until thick enough to coat back of spoon, about 10 minutes. Strain.

2. In a heavy medium skillet, melt butter over high heat. Add onions and sauté until translucent, about 5 minutes. Add wine and boil until almost evaporated, 5 minutes. Transfer to food processor and puree. Strain.

3. Meanwhile, in a large saucepan, bring stock to simmer; continue to simmer until reduced to ¼ cup. Add red onion puree and cream mixture. Whisk in achiote until completely combined. Season to taste with salt.

4. Preheat grill or broiler. Rub surface of steaks with cumin. Grill to desired doneness (for a 1-inch-thick steak, about 3 minutes per side for medium rare).

5. Meanwhile, return sauce to simmer. Add remaining tomatillos, red pepper, poblano pepper, chives and coriander. Season to taste.

6. To serve, place blue corn crêpe on plate. On lower half, place 2 tenderloins slightly overlapping. Spoon sauce over. Fold top half of crêpe over the tenderloins. Garnish with coriander sprigs and serve.

## BLUE CORN CRÊPES

Makes 8 to 10

### INGREDIENTS

¼ cup all purpose flour
3 eggs
½ cup blue corn masa*
6 tablespoons milk
½ teaspoon salt
3 tablespoons (about) unsalted butter

1. In a medium bowl, whisk together flour and eggs. Mix blue corn masa and milk and add to flour mixture with salt. Let batter stand for 30 minutes before cooking.

2. In a 6-inch nonstick skillet, melt 1 tablespoon butter over high heat. Add enough crêpe batter just to cover bottom. Cook until browned, about 1 minute. Flip and cook second side. Repeat with remaining batter, buttering skillet as necessary. Stack finished crêpes on a plate; cover with a second plate and keep warm in low oven.

## SIRLOIN ON SKEWERS

Serves 4

Marinating is not necessary, but additional flavor may be picked up by adding the 1½" cubes of beef to the butter mixture for one to two hours before grilling.

### INGREDIENTS

8 tablespoons butter
2 garlic cloves, minced
1 teaspoon paprika
salt and freshly ground pepper
1½ to 2 pounds thick (1¼") beef sirloin, boneless
1 red bell pepper
8 large fresh mushrooms

1. In a small saucepan melt butter and add garlic, paprika, salt, and pepper. Simmer for one minute. Remove from heat.

2. Cut sirloin and pepper into 1½" pieces. Marinate, if you wish. Skewer beef, peppers, and mushrooms. Brush with the butter mixture. When the fire is ready, grill and baste. Turn over and brush with butter mixture as often as you can. May be grilled with cover down.

*found in food specialty stores

# SOUTHERN BARBECUED FILLET OF BEEF

Serves 6 to 8

My brother, Jerry, who has lived in the South for more than 40 years, says this is one of his favorite barbecues. Marination is short, as is the grilling time. The flavor is divine.

### INGREDIENTS

1 fillet of beef (4 to 6 pounds), trimmed
2 large garlic cloves, finely chopped
¼ cup red wine vinegar
½ cup catsup
2 tablespoons olive oil
2 tablespoons Worcestershire sauce
juice of 1 lemon
generous dash of hot pepper sauce
2 teaspoons sugar
2 teaspoons salt
10 tablespoons (1¼ sticks) butter

1. Wipe the fillet and place it in a glass or ceramic dish.

2. Combine all other ingredients except the butter in a saucepan and bring to boil. Lower the heat and add the butter 2 to 3 tablespoons at a time. When the butter is melted, remove from heat. Cool and pour mixture over the meat. Let marinate for at least 1 hour; the marinade will thicken as the butter cools.

3. When the fire is ready, drain the fillet and set it on the grill 2 or 3 inches above the heat source. Sear 3 to 4 minutes on each of the four sides. Raise the grill and cook meat to desired doneness, 20 to 30 minutes longer.

4. Slice fillet thinly. For each serving, overlap 3 slices on a warmed plate. Reheat the remaining marinade and serve as a sauce with the fillet, spooning it on the side of the plate.

> *Recipe Thought*
> *Almost everything cooked over coals, including this beef fillet, will benefit from marination. The marinade ingredients enhance the flavor of the beef and make a delicious sauce. Most of the marinade ingredients are on one's pantry shelf or in the refrigerator.*

# GRILLED PORK

The pork sold today is younger, leaner and more tender than it used to be, and may be bought fresh, pickled or cured, cured and smoked, even canned. For top flavor and juiciness, I prefer fresh pork cooked to an internal temperature of 170°F, although some claim it can be as low as 155°F.

The best cuts for grilling are the center-cut loin, rib chops and spareribs. The center-cut loin is the tenderloin of the hog and weighs 3 to 4 pounds. It is excellent grilled, spit-roasted and smoked in a variety of ways, as are pork chops. Thin pork chops tend to dry out on the grill, so choose thick ones. Spareribs are at their best when they have been marinated in any one of a variety of mixtures made with soy sauce, honey, fruit juices and/or barbecue sauces, and grilled.

One trick in grilling pork is to sear it first, then cook it in a covered grill; this helps retain moisture. Avoid the cheaper cuts of pork, such as blade pork chops. For a few cents more, buy center-cut chops and ask your butcher to cut them to order. The precut ones are too thin, usually about ¾ inch, and, if prepacked, they may be even thinner. For the grill, use chops about 1¼ inches thick. A little pinkness inside after cooking is fine, since the pork continues to cook after it is removed from the grill.

- Selection of the meat is of utmost importance. Only fresh Boston butts are used because they are the leanest. They weigh 6 to 8 pounds each.

- The fire is from a combination of pure charcoal and hickory. No briquettes are used. Fire is in an open pit that holds 60 butts.

- Fire must be started out high in one end and very low in the other end of the pit.

- Butts are started over the high fire to sear. Fire is doused as necessary with water to keep it from flaming out of control.

- After 2 hours, the meat is rotated and moved to the low fire at the other end.

- When moving and rotating butts to the other end, a long-handled fork is used but the meat is only turned from the ends to that juices will not escape. A fireproof long glove may also be used to turn butts.

- Cooking time is 6 to 7 hours.

- Meat is sliced for serving. It is never chopped in small pieces nor is it pulled apart like strings.

# THAI SATAY WITH PEANUT BUTTER SAUCE

Makes 16 appetizers

Victor Sodsook, who created this recipe, says it can be cooked indoors or out, using a broiler, salamander, gas or charcoal grill or what have you.

### INGREDIENTS

1 pound long, flat slices of chicken breast, lean pork, beef or lamb
3 garlic cloves, minced
½ onion, finely chopped
2 teaspoons minced fresh coriander, including root
1 tablespoon brown sugar
juice of 1 lime
1 tablespoon Thai fish sauce
1 tablespoon vegetable oil
peanut butter sauce (see below)

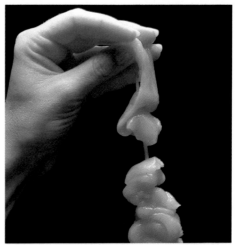

1. Thread the meat on sixteen 12-inch bamboo skewers. Combine the garlic, onion, coriander, brown sugar, lime juice, fish sauce and oil in a bowl. Pour over the skewers and marinate for 1 hour.

2. When the fire is ready, place the skewers on the grill and cook to desired doneness. Cooking time will be brief, so watch them carefully. Serve immediately with sauce for dipping.

## PEANUT BUTTER SAUCE

Makes 1½ cups

½ cup crunchy peanut butter
1 onion, minced
1 stalk lemon grass, minced*
1 cup coconut milk*
1 tablespoon brown sugar
1 teaspoon chili powder
1 tablespoon Thai fish sauce
1 tablespoon soy sauce

Combine all ingredients in a saucepan and bring to boil. Remove from the heat and pour into small bowls to serve.

*found in Oriental food markets

---

### Coriander

*Coriander has been used since ancient times in Europe, China and India, for both cooking and medicine. The fresh leaves are used extensively in Mexico and South America, and the herb's popularity is growing in this country owing to our interest in Chinese, Japanese and Mexican cuisines.*

*To keep a bunch of coriander leaves fresh, place it in a jar, immerse the roots in water, cover loosely with plastic wrap and refrigerate. For longer storage, the leaves may be frozen or preserved in salt or oil, as for basil. The seed is used for spicing sausages (see Churrasco, page 288), pork (see Pork Satay, page 150), lamb and fish, and it is one of the basic spices for curry.*

# PORK LOIN CUBES GRILLED OVER MESQUITE AND SERVED ON A BED OF APPLES AND CREAM

Serves 6 to 8

### INGREDIENTS

1 center-cut pork loin (4 to 5 pounds)
4 tablespoon butter
2 garlic cloves, finely chopped
1 cup white wine
salt and freshly ground pepper
1 tablespoon finely chopped fresh oregano or 1
    teaspoon dried
6 to 8 tart apples (such as Granny Smith),
    peeled, cored, and sliced
⅓ cup firmly packed brown sugar
½ cup heavy cream
6 to 8 green onions
1 cup chutney (see page 313)

**1.** Cut pork loin into 1½-inch cubes. Arrange in a glass or ceramic dish in one layer.

**2.** Heat 2 tablespoons butter in a skillet and lightly sauté the garlic. Add wine, salt and pepper. Remove from heat, add oregano and pour over pork. Marinate overnight in refrigerator or at room temperature for 3 hours, turning meat several times. Drain meat, reserving marinade.

**3.** Skewer meat cubes and grill until slightly charred at edges. The meat should be pink at the center.

**4.** Strain reserved marinade into a small saucepan and boil over high heat until syrupy. Heat remaining butter in a large, deep skillet and sauté apple slices until soft, about 10 minutes. Add brown sugar and cream and reduce marinade; cook until sugar is dissolved. Distribute among 6 to 8 warm plates. Place several pork cubes on top. Add a green onion and a tablespoon of chutney to each plate.

# MEDITERRANEAN PORK LOIN WITH EGGPLANT AND CHEESE

Serves 4

Many make the 40-mile trip from San Francisco to Petaluma, California, to enjoy Kay Baumhefner's cooking at the Opera House Cafe. This pork dish, she says, "is probably the most popular dish at the restaurant." Serve it with a green salad and with basil-buttered corn on the cob.

### INGREDIENTS

1½ pounds boned pork loin, trimmed (about 3 pounds with bone)

### MARINADE

salt
¼ teaspoon freshly ground pepper
zest of 1 lemon, cut into strips
¼ cup fresh lemon juice
¼ cup olive oil
2 tablespoons chopped parsley
½ teaspoon dried thyme
1 bay leaf
2 garlic cloves, crushed or pressed
1 large or 2 small eggplants

### CRUMB MIXTURE

½ cup fresh French breadcrumbs
½ cup freshly grated Romano cheese
1 teaspoon each dried basil, thyme, oregano and marjoram
¼ cup chopped parsley
¼ cup olive oil
8 ounces Teleme or Fontina cheese, cut into 8 slices
2 large ripe tomatoes, each cut into 4 thick slices

1. Cut the pork into eight 3-ounce slices. Pound each slice to ¼-inch thickness between two pieces of oiled parchment or waxed paper.

2. Combine marinade ingredients in a glass or ceramic dish. Add pork and marinate for at least 1 hour, or preferably overnight in the refrigerator. Bring to room temperature before grilling.

3. Preheat oven to 400°F. Peel the eggplant and cut into 8 thick slices. Sprinkle with salt and let stand for 30 minutes. Drain and pat dry. Arrange the eggplant slices on a baking sheet and brush both sides with olive oil. Bake on top oven rack for about 15 minutes, or until tender but not lifeless. Set aside.

4. Combine ingredients for crumb mixture and toss lightly. Set aside.

5. Preheat broiler. On an oiled baking sheet, broil the pork loin 5 inches from the heat until seared, about 2 minutes per side. Layer pork with eggplant and sliced cheese so that about half of each slice is covered by the next. Broil again until pork is almost done — springy to the touch — and the cheese is melting. Sprinkle the crumb mixture down the center and broil again just until crumbs are golden brown. Serve with the tomato slices.

# GRILLED PORK TENDERLOIN WITH CHILI RED AND GARLIC MUSTARD SAUCES

Serves 6 to 8

The sauces are tangy and the tenderloin is the quintessential cut of the pork family, ideal for the grill.

## INGREDIENTS

1½ cups soy sauce
3 tablespoons dark molasses
½ cup firmly packed brown sugar
¼ cup bourbon
3 pounds pork tenderloins (4 to 5), left whole, each about 1½ to 2 inches thick and 12 inches long
chili red sauce (see below)
garlic mustard sauce (see below)

1. Combine soy sauce, molasses, brown sugar and bourbon and mix well. Place tenderloins in a glass or ceramic dish and pour marinade over. Marinate overnight in refrigerator but bring to room temperature before grilling.

2. When the fire is ready, place the tenderloins on the grill and sear as quickly as you can on all sides, basting with marinade. Close cover on grill and cook for 20 to 30 minutes until pork is done; do not overcook.

3. When the pork is done, let it rest for a minute or two and then carve into thin slices on the diagonal. Arrange 3 or 4 pieces on each plate and add a tablespoon or two of each sauce at either side of the pork.

## CHILI RED SAUCE

Makes about 2½ cups

¼ cup vegetable, corn or peanut oil
1 medium onion, finely chopped
2 cups fresh ripe tomatoes, peeled and seeded, or 2 cups canned plum tomatoes put through a food mill
2 dried chilies, stemmed and chopped
2 garlic cloves, finely chopped
2 tablespoons dry mustard
2 tablespoons sugar
1 tablespoon red wine vinegar
salt

Heat oil in a saucepan over medium heat and sauté onion for 5 minutes; do not brown. Add all remaining ingredients, bring to a boil, lower heat and simmer about 10 minutes or until slightly thickened.

GARLIC MUSTARD SAUCE

Makes about 1½ cups

¾ cup white wine vinegar
2 tablespoons dry mustard
2 garlic cloves, pressed
2 eggs, room temperature
¾ cup sugar

1. Combine vinegar, dry mustard and garlic in a nonaluminum bowl and let stand at room temperature overnight.

2. The next day, beat eggs until frothy. Beat in sugar a tablespoon at a time until incorporated.

3. Combine both mixtures in the top of a double boiler and cook over simmering water until thick enough to coat a spoon, about 5 minutes.

# PHILIPPINE PORK INIHAW

Serves 6

Ateacher, lecturer, archivist and professional chef, Reynaldo Alejandro learned the rudiments of Filipino cookery as a child from his grandmother in the Philippines. He is considered by many to be the leading exponent of Philippine cuisine in America.

### INGREDIENTS

12 thick pork chops or pork spareribs
3 cups white wine vinegar
5 tablespoons minced garlic
¾ cup sugar
1½ tablespoons salt
¾ cup soy sauce
3 tablespoons hot pepper sauce

1. Trim the pork of excess fat and wipe clean. Arrange in one layer in a glass or ceramic dish.

2. Combine 2 cups vinegar, 4 tablespoons garlic, sugar, salt and soy sauce and mix well. Pour over the pork, cover tightly and marinate overnight in the refrigerator. Bring to room temperature before grilling.

3. Drain pork, reserving marinade. Grill over hot coals, browning all sides and basting as frequently as you can with the marinade; do not char.

4. Combine remaining 1 cup vinegar, 1 tablespoon garlic and hot pepper sauce. Serve as a dip.

# HICKORY-GRILLED COUNTRY PORK RIBS

Serves 4 to 6

Country pork ribs are the quintessential grilled food, a real classic. Meaty "country-style" ribs come from the back. They are often sold as individual ribs, but the butcher can cut them as you wish.

### INGREDIENTS

4 pounds country-style pork ribs, cut into 3- or
    4-rib sections
¾ cup peanut oil
¾ cup soy sauce
½ cup cider vinegar
¼ cup Worcestershire sauce
¼ cup orange juice
4 slivers of orange zest, 3 × ½ inch
¼ cup dry mustard
¼ cup chopped parsley
3 garlic cloves, minced or pressed
salt and freshly ground pepper

1. Wipe off ribs and place them in one or more glass or ceramic containers in one layer.

2. Combine all other ingredients, mix well and pour over ribs, coating them completely. Cover and refrigerate for at least 24 hours, turning ribs several times. Allow to reach room temperature before placing on grill.

3. Soak 2 cups hickory chips in water for 1 hour. Start fire and, when ready, add drained chips to it. Drain ribs, wiping off marinade with rubber spatula or with hands; reserve marinade. Place ribs on oiled rack about 6 inches above coals and grill 1 to 1½ hours, basting every 10 minutes or so with marinade.

SPARERIBS: Provide about 1 pound per person. Best left in slabs for spit-roasting or regular grilling. May be cut in pieces if a wire grill basket is used, but this is really not necessary.

HAM: For barbecuing buy mild-cured, ready-to-eat ham. If the bone is in, half a ham is about the minimum. Small whole hams, bone in, can be bought at 6 pounds (1 to 2 pounds less with bone out).

# GRILLED SPARERIBS WITH BIRMINGHAM BARBECUE SAUCE

Serves 6

Jack Burson, a friend from Birmingham, Alabama, has told me that his hometown offers some of the best barbecue he has eaten. Now that he's a neighbor in New York, we cook together frequently. Here is our version of one of the best-ever barbecue sauces.

INGREDIENTS

5 to 6 pounds pork spareribs
3 tablespoons peanut oil
2 garlic cloves, minced
1 medium onion, minced
⅔ cup tomato catsup
½ cup cider vinegar
¼ cup Worcestershire sauce
2 tablespoons fresh lemon juice
2 teaspoons dry mustard
1 teaspoon ground ginger
1½ teaspoons salt
¼ cup honey
2 tablespoons brown sugar

1. Trim the ribs, including fat and membrane, leaving the rack of ribs whole and at room temperature.

2. Combine all other ingredients except the honey and brown sugar. Lay ribs flat in a glass or ceramic dish and pour marinade over them. Allow to marinate at least 4 hours; bet-ter still, refrigerate overnight to gain maximum flavor. Bring to room temperature before grilling.

3. Remove ribs from marinade. Scrape marinade from ribs with a rubber spatula and reserve. Grill ribs over a slow fire for about 40 minutes, turning frequently; fire should not flare up and burn them.

4. Place reserved marinade in a saucepan and add sugar and honey. Heat only until the sugar is dissolved. Brush on ribs and continue grilling about 20 minutes more, basting as often as necessary to keep ribs moist.

5. Slice ribs just before serving. To serve, put 2 to 3 tablespoons of sauce on a plate and lay 2 or 3 ribs on top.

# OPEN-FACE SANDWICH OF GRILLED APPLEWOOD-SMOKED BACON WITH LEEK CONFIT AND MELTED GRUYERE

Makes 1 sandwich

At San Francisco's Washington Square Bar & Grill the chef, Mary Etta Moose, serves this with Sam's Cole Slaw (see page 147). She grills the bacon over applewood.

### INGREDIENTS

5 slices best-quality bacon
2 tablespoons leek confit (see below)
grated or shredded Gruyère cheese
2 slices sourdough sandwich bread, lightly toasted
freshly ground pepper

1. Grill bacon until not quite crisp. Drain on paper towels.

2. Spread confit on both slices of bread almost to the edge.

3. Lay the bacon on the confit. Cover with cheese and grind pepper over it. Melt cheese under the broiler flame. Crusts will overbrown during broiling; reach under the bacon to trim off browned crusts. Serve immediately.

Serves 6 to 8

3 leeks, 1½ inches in diameter
1 tablespoon extra virgin olive oil
1 tablespoon butter
3 garlic cloves, slivered
1 medium-size red bell pepper, stem, ribs and seeds removed, finely julienned
salt and freshly ground pepper
pinch of red pepper flakes
½ cup chicken stock

1. Trim leeks to 4 inches long. Wash well and slice thinly.

2. Place sauté pan over low heat. Add oil and butter. When they are hot, add leeks, garlic, bell pepper, salt, pepper and red pepper flakes. Toss.

3. Add just enough chicken stock to sweat the vegetables. Lay a sheet of waxed paper on the vegetables. Cover the pan and cook very slowly on a grill or over lowest possible heat until caramelized, about 10 minutes. Drain any remaining liquid.

Makes about 4 cups

Sam Deitsch, of the Washington Square Bar & Grill in San Francisco, is a purist about cole slaw. "It should be white, none of that multi-colored boutique stuff," he says. His marinated slaw is full of flavor, and goes well with many barbecued, smoked and grilled foods.

### INGREDIENTS

1 small white cabbage
½ cup cider vinegar
¾ cup mayonnaise
¾ cup sour cream
1½ tablespoons sugar
1 tablespoon coarse salt
1 teaspoon freshly ground black pepper
½ teaspoon mustard seeds
½ teaspoon celery seeds
½ teaspoon caraway seeds
juice of ½ lemon
2 tablespoons extra virgin olive oil

1. Remove outer leaves and core of cabbage; shred cabbage (you should have about 4 cups).

2. Combine all remaining ingredients, toss with cabbage and marinate in refrigerator overnight.

3. Serve as is in a large bowl with a slotted spoon, or drain in a colander before serving.

# SWEET GINGER PORK CHOPS

Serves 4

These are best when cooked in a covered grill.

### INGREDIENTS

4 center cut pork chops, 1½ inches thick
1 teaspoon ground ginger
2 garlic cloves, minced
3 tablespoons soy sauce
½ cup honey
2 tablespoons butter, melted

1. Prick chops with fork after trimming off fat. Rub each chop with ginger and garlic.

2. Combine soy sauce, honey and butter. Mix well. Marinate chops in this overnight and bring to room temperature before grilling.

3. Remove grid from grill, place drip pan in center on coals, and replace grid. Grill chops over drip pan, lid closed for about ½ hour. Chops should be basted with leftover marinade and turned 3 times.

## GRILLED HAM STEAK
## WITH CITRUS FLAVORS

Serves 6

Like beef steaks, ham steaks are easy to grill. They're especially delicious when combined with fruit flavors. Here we join the ham with grapefruit, orange and lemon. Accompany it with orange and grapefruit sections that have been tossed in a mint or basil vinaigrette.

### INGREDIENTS

1 ham steak, 1½ inches thick, about 2 to 3 pounds
1 tablespoon each finely chopped grapefruit, orange and lemon zest
½ cup fresh grapefruit juice
½ cup fresh orange juice
juice of ½ lemon
2 tablespoons corn oil
¼ cup light soy sauce
2 tablespoons brown sugar
3 green onions, tender parts only, finely chopped
salt and freshly ground pepper

1. Wipe ham and place in a large glass or ceramic container.

2. Combine all other ingredients and mix well. Pour over ham, coating both sides. Marinate at room temperature for 2 hours or in the refrigerator for 4 to 8 hours. Bring to room temperature before grilling.

3. When fire has reached gray ash stage, place ham steak on oiled rack, 5 to 6 inches over coals, and grill for about 15 minutes before turning. The second side will be done in a little less time than the first; total cooking time should not exceed 30 minutes.

4. Slice thinly across the grain and serve immediately.

# GRILLED PORK SATAY

Serves 4 to 6

These are not tidbit satays on tiny skewers for appetizers. Instead, they are man-sized hunks of pork that are crisp on the outside, juicy on the inside. Serve them hot — but they are also delicious cold the next day. The skewers are cooked over direct heat, but if there are flareups the cover can be let down. The pork should be slightly charred at the edges.

INGREDIENTS

2 pounds lean center-cut pork loin, in one
   piece
12 Brazil nuts, shelled
1 small onion, coarsely chopped
2 garlic cloves, coarsely chopped
2 heaping tablespoons ground coriander seed
1½ tablespoons brown sugar
pinch of red pepper flakes
⅓ to ½ cup soy sauce
juice of 1 lemon
salt and freshly ground pepper

1. Cut loin crosswise into 1½- to 2-inch-thick slices; cut the slices into cubes (you'll average 2 or 3 cubes per slice). Trim away fat. Arrange cubes in one layer in a glass or ceramic dish; set aside.

2. In a processor, chop nuts to texture of breadcrumbs; do not overprocess or they will become oily. Transfer to a large bowl.

3. Add onion and garlic to processor and chop finely, adding the coriander and brown sugar. Stir into nuts with remaining ingredients, using only ⅓ cup soy sauce. Marinade should be thick but pliable; if it is too thick, add more soy sauce. Pour over pork cubes and turn to coat evenly. Cover with plastic wrap. Marinate in refrigerator at least 3 hours, preferably overnight. Bring to room temperature before grilling.

4. Arrange cubes on long metal skewers with any fat on outside of skewer. Grill over a hot charcoal fire for about 20 minutes, or until pork is light pink inside, turning as each side is browned.

---

*Brazil Nuts*
*One of the largest trees in the Amazon forest is the* castanha *(Brazil nut). The nuts, about a dozen of them, grow in a pod that resembles a coconut. Inside, the nuts are segmented as in a grapefruit. The pod, when ripe, can weigh about 4 pounds and fall 100 feet. The nuts are indispensable in this recipe—one of my favorites.*

# GRILLED LAMB

As with beef and pork, the most tender cuts of lamb come from the loin and rib sections. But lamb also offers a flavorful leg, which can be grilled in many ways — including spit-roasting and smoking. In fact, many prefer grilled leg of lamb over any other meat. Bone in, bone out or butterflied, leg of lamb offers a vast variety of grill recipes, always mouthwatering.

Lamb is almost always marinated; when it is not, it's mopped and mopped some more on the spit. Chops are always thick, or should be — about 2 inches — yet they take only 6 minutes or so to grill on each side. Cooked over indirect heat, the leg will take about 20 minutes per pound; if butterflied, less time is needed.

Lamb chops should be seared first and then completed with slower cooking. Simple oil marinades are best to keep the meat moist. The chops should be trimmed of fat (in fact, all lamb should be), and the edges of the remaining fat scored. The flap end, called "the apron" by some butchers, should be skewered or tied to the body of the chop; this helps keep them moist.

If a leg is properly trimmed and butterflied, there's no waste at all. Because of its uneven thickness, it offers slices of meat at various stages of doneness to suit everyone's taste. Sear the butterflied leg and follow up with slower cooking, which will rarely exceed 30 to 40 minutes in total cooking time. Let grilled lamb rest before carving.

## LAMB SELECTION AND PORTION SIZE

To barbecue, at least a half-leg is needed; a leg is 6 to 8 pounds. Spring lamb is the best, and it is now available all year. A boned and butterflied leg of lamb will grill beautifully.

With chops, provide two per person, 1½ to 2 inches thick. For 1-inch-thick lamb steaks, cut from the leg, one per person is needed.

# GRILLED THICK LAMB CHOPS WITH BASIL BUTTER SAUCE

serves 4

### INGREDIENTS

⅓ cup olive oil
½ cup finely chopped fresh basil
2 tablespoons finely chopped fresh thyme
½ teaspoon pink peppercorns, cracked
8 lamb chops, trimmed of fat, each about 2
   inches thick

### SAUCE

2 cups veal or chicken stock
½ cup firmly packed fresh basil leaves
6 tablespoons softened butter
juice of 1 lemon
salt, optional
basil leaves for garnish

1. Combine the oil, chopped basil, thyme and peppercorns and mix well. Arrange the chops in a glass or ceramic dish and pour the oil mixture over them. Turn the chops over two or three times to be sure they are well coated. Marinate for at least 4 hours, preferably overnight in the refrigerator. Bring to room temperature before grilling.

2. To make the sauce, boil over high heat until reduced by half. In a blender or processor, pulse basil leaves 6 or 8 times. Add butter and pulse several times to blend. Return stock to boil, add lemon juice and whisk in basil butter a spoonful at a time until sauce glistens. Season with salt if necessary.

3. Grill chops over hot coals about 5 minutes per side; do not overcook. Insert a sharp knife point to test for doneness; chops should be pink inside.

4. To serve, place several tablespoons of sauce on warmed plates and lay 2 chops on top. Garnish with 1 large basil leaf or a trio of small ones.

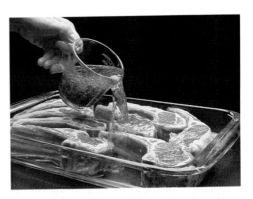

# GENNARO'S GRILLED LAMB CHOPS

Serves 6

When I visited Italy recently, my cousin Gennaro in Accettura grilled the most delicious lamb chops. He used a hibachi, but they can be cooked on almost any grill. Our meal began with slices of homemade salami and capocolla with home-baked bread. The grilled lamb followed, paired with a salad of fresh greens lightly dressed with oil and vinegar. Fresh fruit and local cheese rounded it out, and there was homemade red wine throughout.

### INGREDIENTS

12 lamb rib chops (1½ inches thick), fat trimmed
2 garlic cloves, finely chopped
2 tablespoons finely chopped fresh rosemary or 2 teaspoons dried, finely crushed
¼ cup olive oil
salt and freshly ground pepper

1. Make criss-cross cuts into the fat edges of the chops. Place them in one layer in a large glass dish or platter.

2. In a small bowl, combine all remaining ingredients and mix well. Brush both sides of the chops with the oil mixture and sprinkle with black pepper. Grill one side, then the other to desired doneness, about 10 minutes.

# LAMB CUBES IN A GARLIC AND ONION MARINADE

Serves 6

### INGREDIENTS

3 garlic cloves, peeled
1 medium onion
2 tablespoons fresh oregano or 1 teaspoon dried
1 tablespoon fresh rosemary or ½ teaspoon dried
¼ cup olive oil
juice of 1 lemon
salt and freshly ground pepper
2 pounds boneless lamb shoulder, cut into 1¼-inch cubes

1. Combine garlic, onion, oregano and rosemary in processor and blend almost to a paste. Add oil, lemon juice, salt and pepper and mix well.

2. Place meat cubes in a shallow glass or ceramic dish and pour marinade over, turning to coat. Marinate at room temperature for at least 2 hours.

3. Drain meat, reserving marinade. Thread the meat on 4 long or 8 short skewers, pressing pieces closely together. Season with salt and pepper.

# HERBED LAMB CHOPS WITH PARMESAN CHEESE

Serves 6

Oregano, mint and Parmesan flavor these chops, which take just a short time to grill. They are delicious with grilled potato and grilled onion salad, page 279.

### INGREDIENTS

6 center-cut loin lamb chops, each 1½ to 2
    inches thick, with apron
2 tablespoons olive oil
3 garlic cloves, minced
1 tablespoon finely chopped fresh oregano or 1
    teaspoon dried
1 tablespoon finely chopped fresh mint or 1
    teaspoon dried
1 teaspoon coarse salt
freshly ground pepper
⅓ cup freshly grated Parmesan cheese

**1.** Ask butcher to trim chops of excess fat. Wipe them clean and pat dry. Wrap fatty "apron" around chop (it is not necessary to secure it); the apron will keep the chop moist. With your hands or a brush, rub some of the olive oil well into both sides of chops. Smear remaining oil on the center of 2 sheets of heavy-duty foil, about 18 inches square; 3 chops will be wrapped in each.

**2.** In a small bowl, mix garlic, oregano, mint, salt, a liberal amount of pepper and the cheese. Divide into 6 portions. Press each portion onto both sides of each chop. Place 3 chops, side by side, in center of each piece of foil. Secure package using drugstore wrap.

**3.** When fire is ready, place packets on grid about 5 inches above heat source and grill for 15 minutes, turning packets once after 8 to 10 minutes.

Note: The coating of herbs and cheese may adhere to the foil. If this is the case, scrape it off and add to chop as it is being served.

# LAMB AND VEGETABLES, GREEK STYLE, IN A FOIL PACKET

Serves 4

One distinct advantage to foil cooking is the ease of preparing the entire main course at one time. This is a good example, as no precooking is required. Be sure the lamb is not overly fatty.

### INGREDIENTS

1½ pounds lean boneless shoulder of lamb, cut into 4 pieces
2 large garlic cloves, halved
4 small new potatoes, scrubbed and halved
4 whole mushrooms, stems trimmed, wiped clean
4 Italian frying peppers, stems, ribs and seeds removed, halved
2 medium onions, halved
4 eggplant slices (1 inch thick), skin on, each slice cut into 3 pieces
12 canned plum tomatoes, drained, seeded and coarsely chopped
2 tablespoons finely chopped fresh oregano or 2 teaspoons dried
salt and freshly ground pepper
8 tablespoons chicken stock
4 tablespoons olive oil

1. Cut 4 pieces of heavy-duty foil about 18 inches square, or large enough to envelop meat and vegetables.

2. Place one piece of lamb on each sheet and top with a garlic half. Add 1 potato, 1 mushroom, 1 pepper, ½ onion, 1 eggplant slice and 3 plum tomatoes.

3. Sprinkle oregano, salt, pepper, 2 tablespoons chicken stock and 1 tablespoon oil over each arrangement. Secure packets with a drugstore fold (see page 18).

4. When fire is ready, place packets on grid 5 inches over heat source. Cover and grill for 45 minutes, or cook on an open grill for 55 to 60 minutes, carefully turning after 25 minutes of cooking. Open a packet to test for doneness.

### Grilling with Foil

Corn has its own natural wrapper, the husk, and may be cooked in it directly on the grill. The moisture in the corn, when heated, turns to steam and this is how the corn cooks. This principle can be applied to other vegetables, meats and fish by enclosing any of them in a packet of heavy-duty aluminum foil.

Foil is always on hand and making packets is simple. Adding flavors is easy and a matter of taste. A piece of butter is a common enrichment, as are lemons, limes and oranges—their juices or zest. More stock, herbs, spices and any of the marinade ingredients could be added for flavor or additional moisture.

# SKEWERS OF LAMB, PINEAPPLE, PEPPERS AND OTHER THINGS

Serves 4

## INGREDIENTS

2 pounds boneless lamb shoulder, cut into 1¼-inch cubes

16 small onions, parboiled for 5 minutes

1 fresh pineapple, peeled, quartered, cored and cut into 1¼-inch cubes

3 Italian frying peppers, cored, seeded and cut into 1½-inch squares

10 small cherry tomatoes

½ cup soy sauce

2 tablespoons olive oil

2 garlic cloves, each cut crosswise into 4 pieces

1 teaspoon chopped fresh basil or ½ teaspoon dried

1 tablespoon grated fresh ginger or ½ teaspoon ground

freshly ground pepper

1. Combine all ingredients in a large glass or ceramic dish. Marinate in the refrigerator for 12 to 24 hours. Bring to room temperature before grilling; this will take about 2 hours.

2. On eight 10-inch skewers, alternate the lamb cubes, onions, pineapple, peppers and tomatoes. Grill the skewers about 4 inches from the heat, brushing frequently with the reserved marinade and turning often, for about 15 minutes or until done to your taste.

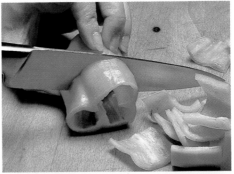

# LAMB KEBABS WITH ZEST OF CITRUS AND YOGURT SAUCE

Serves 4

This tender, flavorful skewered lamb created by Christopher Idone, is cooked briefly and served with lemon wedges, quartered tomato and onion salad. The simple yogurt sauce is the perfect accompaniment for the grilled lamb.

### MARINADE

¾ cup olive oil
1½ cups dry white or red wine
1 medium onion, chopped
2 bay leaves
2 tablespoons chopped fresh oregano, thyme, mint or rosemary, alone or in combination
2 strips of lemon zest, (2 × ½ inch each), chopped
2 strips of orange zest, (2 × ½ inch each), chopped

### INGREDIENTS

2 pounds boneless leg or shoulder of lamb, trimmed and cut into 1½-inch cubes
salt and freshly ground pepper
1 lemon, quartered and seeded
2 tomatoes, cored and quartered
1 small onion, thinly sliced
⅓ to ½ cup vinaigrette dressing
yogurt sauce (see below), well chilled

1. Combine the marinade ingredients in a glass or ceramic bowl.

2. Add the meat cubes. Refrigerate for at least 3 hours, tossing the mixture from time to time. Bring to room temperature before grilling.

3. Drain meat, reserving marinade. Thread the meat on 4 long or 8 short skewers, pressing pieces closely together. Season with salt and pepper.

4. Grill the skewers until the meat is pink and juicy, about 7 to 10 minutes, turning and brushing with the remaining marinade. For well-done meat, grill for 12 to 15 minutes.

5. Arrange skewer(s) of lamb on individual plates and place a lemon wedge alongside.

6. Combine tomatoes, onion and salad dressing. Toss and divide among the plates.

7. Pass the yogurt sauce in a small bowl.

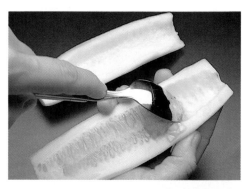

YOGURT SAUCE

Makes about 1¼ cups

INGREDIENTS

1 cup plain yogurt
1 garlic clove, minced
1 tablespoon chopped fresh mint
salt and freshly ground pepper
1 small cucumber, peeled, seeded and grated,
    optional

Combine all ingredients. Refrigerate for at least 1 hour before serving.

# BONED LEG OF LAMB
# WITH ROSEMARY
# AND WHOLE ONIONS

Serves 6

The foil-wrapped lamb is close enough to the coals that the meat will brown. Turn it over once to brown the other side. The sauce in the package will be mostly absorbed, but what little is left should be poured over the sliced meat.

### INGREDIENTS

1 whole leg of lamb (about 5 pounds), boned
¼ cup Worcestershire sauce
½ cup soy sauce
2 tablespoons chopped fresh rosemary (or 2
    teaspoons dried)
several sprigs of fresh rosemary, optional
4 garlic cloves, halved
freshly ground pepper
12 medium onions, peeled
salt
3 tablespoons olive oil

**1.** Trim all fat from the lamb. Be sure to check the weight of the boned leg and make a note of it. Place the lamb on a double sheet of foil large enough to envelop the meat and to seal with three folds on all edges (see drugstore fold, on page 18).

**2.** Rub or brush the Worcestershire and soy sauces over entire surface of the meat, using the entire amount. Sprinkle fresh or dried rosemary inside and out; add rosemary sprigs. Place 4 garlic halves inside the meat and the remainder over the top and sides. Season with pepper. Fold foil over the meat and secure the edges with triple folds.

**3.** Cut 6 double sheets of foil, each large enough to enclose 2 whole onions. Place onions in center; season with salt and pepper. Drizzle with olive oil and toss onions to coat. Secure packages with drugstore folds (see page 18).

**4.** Place lamb on the grill 5 to 6 inches above the coals and cook approximately 20 minutes per pound, turning once during cooking.

---

*Foil on the Table?*
*There is always the question of whether to serve the food in or out of the foil. Quite frankly, foil looks beautiful on the grill but not on the table. I carry the packet to the table, for it is always a joy to open it and see, hear, almost taste the steam escape. Then the food is transferred to a platter or individual plates, always pouring the juices over the food from the packet. If the food was packed in parchment paper and then in foil, remove the foil and serve the packet of parchment, which always makes an attractive presentation.*

# LAMB CUBES IN A SPICY YOGURT MARINADE

Serves 6

Lamb is a popular meat for skewering, and this marinade is deliciously tangy. The lamb sirloin costs a few cents more, but worth it.

### INGREDIENTS

2 cups plain yogurt
4 tablespoons butter, melted
juice of 1 lemon
2 garlic cloves, pressed
1 teaspoon ground cumin
1 teaspoon ground coriander
1 teaspoon mustard seeds
½ teaspoon cayenne pepper
salt
2 pounds lamb sirloin, cut into 1¼-inch
    cubes

1. Combine all ingredients except the meat in a medium bowl. Place the meat in a shallow glass or ceramic dish in one layer. Pour marinade over and turn meat to coat well. Marinate at room temperature for at least 2 hours.

2. Drain meat. Thread on 6 skewers and grill 10 to 12 minutes, turning to cook all sides.

# LAMB BURGERS

Serves 4

### INGREDIENTS

1 pound ground lean lamb
½ pound ground lean beef
1 small onion, minced
½ teaspoon ground ginger
juice of ½ lemon
salt and freshly ground pepper
2 slices bacon, cut in half lengthwise

1. Spread meat on counter or in bowl with splayed fingers. Add onion, ginger, lemon juice, salt and pepper and gently form into 4 burgers. Wrap one-half bacon slice around each burger and fasten with toothpicks.

2. When fire is ready, grill until browned and bacon is done. Remove toothpicks and serve on grilled rolls or bread with cole slaw.

# GRILLED MARINATED LAMB STEAK

Serves 4

Marcie Smith, of New York's Union Square Cafe, told me that this dish is Italian-inspired. Simple combinations of flavors bring out the best in a lesser cut of meat. While leg steaks tend to be a bit tough, the marinade gives them incredible flavor. One leg of lamb usually yields 4 to 6 steaks, with meat left over for brochettes.

### INGREDIENTS

3 cups dry red wine
1 cup olive oil
juice of 1 lemon
1 whole garlic bulb, halved and peeled
6 sprigs fresh rosemary
1 bay leaf
a small handful of black peppercorns, cracked
1 leg of lamb, cut into steaks
peanut oil
4 sprigs fresh rosemary for garnish

1. Combine wine, olive oil, lemon juice, garlic, 6 sprigs rosemary, bay leaf and peppercorns in a glass or ceramic dish. Add lamb and marinate for at least 6 hours, or preferably overnight in the refrigerator.

2. Drain the meat and pat dry. Coat with peanut oil. Grill over a hot fire to medium rare. Garnish with fresh rosemary.

# GRILLED LEG OF LAMB
# WITH YOGURT

Serves 6

According to Fereydoun Kia, of the chic restaurant Au Bon Air in Buenos Aires, the best meat in Argentina is lamb, not beef. "A lamb must walk a long distance to get its food," he explains, "and by walking it avoids getting fat." He claims the best lamb comes from the Middle Eastern countries, the second best from Patagonia (in Argentina) and the third best from Australia.

### INGREDIENTS

1 small leg of lamb with bone in (3 to 4 pounds)
4 garlic cloves, halved
2 cups plain yogurt
1 teaspoon saffron threads
salt and coarsely ground pepper

1. Cut small pockets into the fat or skin of the lamb with a small sharp knife and insert the garlic pieces.

2. Combine yogurt, saffron, salt and pepper. Cover the garlic-studded leg of lamb with yogurt mixture. Marinate in the refrigerator for 24 hours; the yogurt will turn a lovely golden-yellow color.

3. When the fire is ready, sear the lamb on all sides, about 5 minutes per side. If the fire flares up, move lamb to avoid charring. Raise grid and continue to cook lamb slowly until pink and moist on the inside, up to 1½ hours. To test for doneness, insert a metal skewer or sharp knife into the meat; if the end shows blood, the meat needs more cooking.

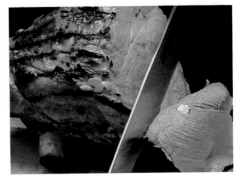

# BARBECUED SPRING LAMB WITH RHUBARB AND DANDELION

Serves 6 to 8

### MARINADE

½ cup chicken stock
¼ cup soy sauce
2 tablespoons fresh lemon juice
¼ cup spicy brown mustard
2 dashes hot pepper sauce
2 tablespoons chopped fresh thyme
4 finely chopped green onions, including light
  green parts (about ½ cup)
1 teaspoon finely chopped garlic

### INGREDIENTS

1 baby lamb shoulder (4½ pounds), trimmed,
  boned and slightly flattened ( 2½ to 3
  pounds trimmed weight)
8 ounces rhubarb stalks
2 cups water
¼ cup sugar
salt and freshly ground pepper
vegetable oil
2 tablespoons red wine vinegar
¼ cup olive oil
2 bunches tender dandelion greens, washed
2 tablespoons toasted almonds

1. Combine all the marinade ingredients in a glass or ceramic bowl.

2. Place the lamb in a glass or ceramic dish and pour the marinade over. Cover and refrigerate overnight.

3. Trim and wash the rhubarb and cut each stalk into 2-inch lengths. Cut each length into strips.

4. Combine water and sugar in a nonaluminum saucepan and bring to boil. Add the rhubarb, lower heat and cook gently for 2 minutes. Remove from heat and let the rhubarb cool in the liquid.

5. Remove lamb from the marinade; reserve marinade. Season meat with salt and pepper and rub it with a little vegetable oil. Grill over charcoal or on gas grill at medium to low setting until pink and moist inside, about 15 minutes or a bit more per side.

6. Meanwhile, bring the reserved marinade to boil and simmer for 4 minutes or until reduced by half, skimming off any foam that rises to the surface. Whisk the vinegar and olive oil into the hot marinade. Remove from heat and keep warm.

7. Toss the dandelion greens with a few tablespoons of the warm marinade and arrange on a serving platter. Drain the rhubarb and place it on the platter with the greens. Slice the lamb, place the slices on the greens and top with freshly ground pepper. Whisk the remaining dressing again and drizzle over the lamb, rhubarb and greens. Sprinkle with toasted almonds. Pass the rest of the dressing separately.

From Larry Forgione's An American Place, New York.

# GRILLED VEAL, VENISON, VARIETALS AND SAUSAGES

The rib and loin chop cuts of veal (the porterhouse) are delicious cooked on the grill. So are slices of the veal fillet, which when pounded become *paillards*. Boned shoulders, legs and whole loin of veal may be grilled, and are also well suited to spit-roasting and smoking. Veal is low in fat, so chops should be thick and cooked quickly to stay moist. Rolled veal is usually covered with some kind of fat to avoid drying out; the technique is exemplified in the Veal Roll with Hazelnut Butter on page 220.

Marinades give veal lots of flavor. The marinade for the veal chop recipe in this section is brushed on, but veal chops can also be marinated for several hours. Many types of marinades are suitable, including those with white wine, Marsala and lemon. When grilling veal chops, throw sprigs of oregano, rosemary or thyme on the fire for an aromatic sensation.

Liver is enhanced by grilling, as are other variety meats. Calves' liver is the most tender; it is excellent sliced and grilled or briefly marinated, as in the recipe in this section.

Sausages absorb the smoky flavors of grilling and are perfect when crisp on the outside and juicy inside. There are many kinds of sausages, in individual links or spiral form, in the markets or to be made at home. This section includes four of the best.

Use a needle or the sharp point of a small knife to lightly prick sausages before putting them on the grill. Fat will escape during cooking and will probably cause flareups, so don't grill over a very hot fire. Sausages need constant turning to brown all sides. They should not be eaten rare. The easiest way to test for doneness is to cut into a sausage to take a look. If grilling more than a few, consider using a hinged wire basket; rearrange the sausages several times to brown them on all sides.

# GRILLED VEAL CHOPS WITH BALSAMIC BUTTER SAUCE AND BELGIAN ENDIVE

Serves 4

This is sure to please any lover of grilled food. Simple, elegant and delicious.

### INGREDIENTS

4 Belgian endive
6 green onions
4 tablespoons butter
½ cup plus 2 tablespoons balsamic vinegar
¾ cup dry white wine
¾ cup beef stock
salt and freshly ground pepper
1 tablespoon olive oil
4 veal chops (8 to 10 ounces each)

1. Trim off root ends from endive and separate leaves. Cut leaves into 2 × ¼-inch julienne. Slice 4 green onions, including green parts, in the same fashion. Set aside.

2. Melt 1 tablespoon butter in a nonaluminum saucepan. Thinly slice remaining 2 green onions, including green parts, and sauté briefly in the butter. Add ½ cup vinegar and boil until reduced by half. Add wine and again reduce by half.

3. Boil beef stock in another saucepan until reduced by half. Add to vinegar mixture and simmer until sauce is thickened just enough to coat a spoon.

4. Whisk in remaining butter 1 tablespoon at a time, whisking each addition until incorporated before adding the next. Adjust seasoning with salt and/or pepper.

5. Combine remaining vinegar with olive oil and brush onto both sides of chops. Season with salt and pepper, and be sure chops are at room temperature before grilling. Grill until inside is slightly pink, about 10 to 15 minutes.

6. Fan out the julienned endive and green onion on each plate. Place a chop on top and spoon sauce overall.

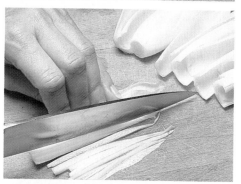

# GRILLED VEAL PAILLARD WITH SORREL SAUCE AND BABY VEGETABLES

Serves 6

Jean Michael Bergougnoux, a sous-chef at Lutèce in New York, grills the veal very briefly. It is delicious.

### INGREDIENTS

36 baby carrots
36 baby turnips
12 baby leeks
36 snow peas
2 tablespoons butter
1 large onion, sliced
3 garlic cloves, unpeeled
1 tablespoon all purpose flour
3 cups chicken stock
2 cups heavy cream
3 ounces fresh sorrel, stemmed and chopped
12 slices veal fillet (3 ounces each)
chopped fresh sorrel for garnish

1. Steam all the vegetables separately until crisp-tender. Keep warm.

2. Melt butter in a skillet over low heat. Add onion and garlic, cover and cook over low heat until tender, about 6 to 8 minutes; do not allow onion to color.

3. Add flour to onion mixture and blend well. Add chicken stock and cook slowly for 20 minutes. Strain, return mixture to saucepan

and add cream. Simmer briskly until sauce is thick enough to coat a spoon. Stir in chopped raw sorrel.

4. Flatten the pieces of veal with a meat pounder. Grill them quickly on both sides; this takes only a couple of minutes altogether.

5. To serve, spread sauce on warmed plates and arrange a piece of veal and some vegetables on it. Garnish with additional sorrel.

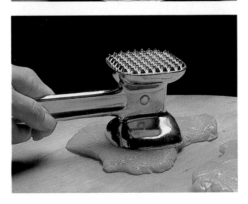

**4.** When fire is ready, place packets on grid about 4 inches above heat source. Grill for 30 minutes, turning carefully once.

Note: Most of the marinade in the packet will be absorbed during cooking and the shanks will be browned. They do not need another sauce, but if you want one, double the marinade ingredients and reserve one half. At serving time, heat the reserved marinade and spoon 2 tablespoons over each shank.

# VEAL SHANKS
# IN ORANGE ZEST MARINADE

Serves 6

Veal shanks, not used as much as they should be, make a flavorful packet when prepared this way. Lemon zest may be combined with or substituted for the orange. Serve the shanks with thin spaghetti with a tomato and butter sauce (see page 311) and a refreshing green salad.

### INGREDIENTS

6 veal shanks, about 2 inches thick
½ cup olive oil
½ cup white wine vinegar
2 tablespoons finely chopped orange zest
2 garlic cloves, minced
2 teaspoons coarse salt
1 teaspoon freshly ground pepper
1 tablespoon finely chopped fresh thyme or 1
    teaspoon dried

**1.** Wipe shanks clean and place them in a glass or ceramic dish in one layer.

**2.** Combine all remaining ingredients and mix well. Pour over shanks, coating all sides. Cover and let marinate overnight in the refrigerator; bring to room temperature before grilling.

**3.** Cut 2 pieces of heavy-duty foil, each about 18 inches square. Place 3 shanks in the center of each. Spoon half of the marinade over shanks in each packet and secure foil with drugstore wrap (see page 18).

# GRILLED VENISON CUBES IN BLACK PEPPER SAUCE

Serves 4

Venison fillets are very tender and use them if you can. If using frozen venison, be sure meat is thoroughly thawed before marinating. This black pepper sauce is great with venison.

### INGREDIENTS

1½ pounds venison fillets or steaks
1 cup dry white wine
3 tablespoons olive oil
1 small onion, coarsely chopped
1 small carrot, thinly sliced
2 parsley sprigs
2 sprigs fresh thyme or ½ teaspoon dried
salt and freshly ground pepper
black pepper sauce (see below)

1. Cut venison into 1-inch cubes. Place in a glass or ceramic dish.

2. Combine all remaining ingredients except sauce and pour over venison. Marinate at least overnight, or preferably for 2 nights.

3. Remove cubes from marinade and thread on skewer. Grill over hot coals to desired doneness, about 10 to 15 minutes, turning frequently.

### BLACK PEPPER SAUCE

Makes ¾ cup

### INGREDIENTS

½ cup white wine vinegar
10 peppercorns, crushed
1 cup veal or beef stock
2 tablespoons red currant jelly

1. Boil vinegar with peppercorns in a non-aluminum saucepan until reduced by half. Add stock, return to boil, lower heat and simmer until slightly syrupy and again reduced by half, about 30 minutes.

2. Add currant jelly and heat, stirring until dissolved. Strain sauce and distribute among warmed plates. Place venison atop sauce and serve immediately.

Note: Most of the marinade in the packet will be absorbed during cooking and the shanks will be browned. They do not need another sauce, but if you want one, double the marinade ingredients and reserve one half. At serving time, heat the reserved marinade and spoon 2 tablespoons over each shank.

# GRILLED SWEETBREADS
# WITH BUTTER

Serves 6

Because this often-overlooked part of the calf is such a delicacy, it is sometimes referred to as the "dish of kings," by Ann Lee Harris, owner of Harris' a popular steak house in San Francisco. They are served on toast points with a slice of grilled zucchini or fried eggplant. Bearnaise sauce, served on the side, is optional.

### INGREDIENTS

3 pounds sweetbreads
¼ cup vinegar
8 tablespoons butter, melted
salt and freshly ground pepper

1. Cover sweetbreads with water in a nonaluminum saucepan. Add vinegar. Bring to boil, lower heat and simmer for 15 minutes.

2. Plunge sweetbreads into cold water; allow to cool. Remove membrane and place sweetbreads on a platter. Cover with a plate or cutting board and top with a weight, such as several heavy cans. Refrigerate for several hours.

3. Slice the sweetbreads lengthwise about ⅓ inch thick. Dip in melted butter. Grill until lightly browned but still moist, about 2 minutes per side over medium heat. Season with salt and pepper.

> *Sweetbreads*
> *Sweetbreads are the two lobes of the thymus gland. They're a tender and subtly flavored delicacy, especially when grilled. The thymus disappears as the animal matures, so sweetbreads come from calves. They require soaking and peeling and also need to be weighted; do not skip this step of the procedure. The juice of one lemon may be used in place of the vinegar.*

# GRILLED *BOUDIN BLANC* WITH BRAISED RED CABBAGE AND BEARNAISE SAUCE

Serves 4

Boudin blanc is a tasty sausage of veal, chicken and pork. Its presentation is spectacular at the New York restaurant Quatorze: It is first poached in cream and water with herbs and vegetables, then grilled and served on warm braised red cabbage with bearnaise sauce and cornichons. Sam Hazen, the chef, says, "We always serve it with a mountain of *pommes frites.* One sausage makes an appetizer and two make an entree." He adds, "When you poach the boudin blanc, be careful not to break the casing."

### INGREDIENTS

2 cups light cream or half and half
1 cup water
½ onion, diced
1 carrot, diced
2 celery stalks, diced
1 tablespoon chopped fresh thyme
2 bay leaves
4 *boudin blanc* sausages, 4 ounces each
    (bratwurst or weisswurst can be substituted)
    substituted)
braised red cabbage (see below)
bearnaise sauce (see below)
8 cornichons, sliced

1. Combine cream, water, vegetables and herbs in a saucepan and bring to boil. Lower heat and simmer for a couple of minutes to enhance flavor. Add the sausages and simmer for 5 minutes. Remove sausages from liquid and transfer to hot grill. Cook for about 4 minutes, turning to grill all sides.

2. To serve, divide cabbage among warmed plates. Top cabbage with a *boudin blanc.* Add about ¼ cup bearnaise on the side and garnish with 2 sliced cornichons.

### BRAISED RED CABBAGE

Serves 4 to 6

### INGREDIENTS

12 tablespoons (1½ sticks) butter
1 head red cabbage, finely shredded
1 cup red wine vinegar
1 teaspoon chopped fresh thyme
4 bay leaves
2 tablespoons sugar
1 teaspoon salt
½ teaspoon freshly ground white pepper

1. Preheat oven to 350°F. Melt 8 tablespoons butter in an ovenproof saucepan with lid. Add the cabbage and toss to coat with butter.

2. Add the vinegar, thyme, bay leaves, sugar, salt and pepper and bring to boil, then remove from heat. Cover and braise in oven until tender, about 25 minutes.

3. Remove from the oven and discard bay leaves. Add remaining butter, toss and serve.

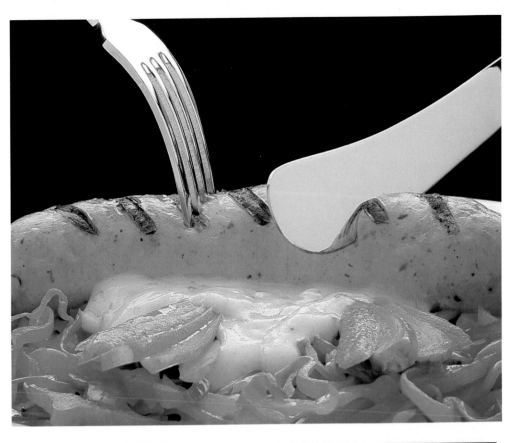

BEARNAISE SAUCE

Makes about 1½ cups

INGREDIENTS

4 egg yolks
1 teaspoon chopped shallot
¼ cup tarragon vinegar
2 tablespoons chopped fresh tarragon or 1½
    teaspoons dried
½ teaspoon chopped parsley
1 cup (2 sticks) melted butter, not warmer than
    115°F
1 teaspoon salt
½ teaspoon freshly ground white pepper

1. In a heatproof bowl combine yolks, shallot, vinegar, tarragon and parsley. Over a pan of hot water, beat yolks with whisk or hand mixer until they quadruple in volume.

2. Slowly whisk in butter a tablespoon at a time; sauce will resemble mayonnaise. Season with salt and pepper and serve hot. (Sauce can be held for several hours over warm water or in a vacuum bottle.)

## GRILLED HOMEMADE ITALIAN SAUSAGE

Makes about 3 pounds

Grilled sausage is a natural with grilled potatoes and a fresh green salad dressed with vinaigrette. Also delicious with it are grilled red bell peppers sprinkled with garlic and olive oil. Soaking the casing in orange juice beforehand freshens it up. Just-squeezed juice is best, but frozen or bottled will also work well.

### INGREDIENTS

3 pounds lean pork butt
1½ tablespoons salt
1 teaspoon fennel seed
1½ tablespoons paprika
½ teaspoon freshly ground pepper
2 yards sausage casing, soaked in ½ cup
  orange juice for 3 hours or overnight

1. Cut the meat into ¼-inch strips, then into ¼-inch dice. Combine in a large bowl with salt, fennel, paprika and pepper and mix well.

2. Thoroughly wash the casing in lukewarm water. Fit 1 yard of it over a sausage funnel. Tie the open end of the casing closed with strong string. Feed the meat through the funnel with your thumb, puncturing the casing with a needle to release air. The casing should be firmly packed. If it is too loose, squeeze the filling with your hand to compact it.

3. Tie the casing with string every 5 inches or so to form links; alternatively, arrange sausage in a spiral form without tying. If the casing breaks, stop funneling, remove sausage meat from that broken point, tie the casing off at the break and start funneling again to form a new link. At this point the sausage may be refrigerated, covered lightly, for 10 days or so. Bring to room temperature before grilling.

4. Grill sausage in a hinged wire basket over a charcoal or wood fire or a gas grill, turning so all sides are cooked. Be sure sausage is thoroughly cooked; the best way to test is to cut it open.

*Angela's Homemade Sausage*
*My family made sausage. Once a year, 200 to 250 pounds were put up. Some of it was eaten fresh, some was kept in the refrigerator for a couple of weeks and the rest was dried, then canned in rendered pork fat — to last all year long.*

*It seems I always had to explain this family sausage-making ritual to friends who, when they visited, would see sausage links hanging from poles all over the house. We often grilled sausage for them, and most of the time they carried some home.*

*I've heard my colleague Christopher Idone remark, "No one really wants to make sausage any more." I think he may have a point, and I don't make it that often. But there is something special about homemade sausage, especially when it is grilled.*

# GRILLED CALVES' LIVER WITH BALSAMIC VINEGAR

Serves 4

My friend and fellow cookbook writer, Hedy Giusti-Lanham Allen, makes beautiful *Fegato alla Veneziana*, which is calves' liver cut into thin slices and sautéed with parsley, salt, pepper, stock and vinegar. Hedy inspired the following preparation. Serve it with a Valpolicella from Lake Garda or a Merlot from Friuli (which is near Venice) or California.

### INGREDIENTS

6 slices calves' liver, about ⅓ inch thick
   (approximately 2 pounds)
5 tablespoons butter
4 tablespoons olive oil
3 tablespoons balsamic vinegar
salt and freshly ground pepper
3 white onions, cut into ½-inch slices
1 purple onion, cut into ½-inch slices
6 red potatoes, boiled and halved

1. Trim away any veins or membranes from the liver slices. Let liver stand at room temperature in a glass dish while you prepare the rest of the recipe.

2. In a small saucepan, melt 3 tablespoons butter. Remove from heat and add 3 tablespoons olive oil, 2 tablespoons vinegar, salt and pepper. Pour mixture over the liver, being sure that each slice is coated on both sides. Marinate for about 30 minutes.

3. Make a foil package of double thickness for the onion slices, both white and purple. Dot remaining 2 tablespoons butter over the onions; sprinkle with remaining 1 tablespoon olive oil. Add salt and pepper and secure the package. Place foil package on grill and cook for 20 to 30 minutes (if you use a covered grill they will cook faster).

4. Salt and pepper the potato halves and add them to the grill cut side down. Cook until they show grill marks, then turn and grill the uncut sides. Move them to the side of the grill to clear space for the liver slices.

5. Drain liver, reserving marinade. Place liver on the grill and cook each side for only 1 to 2 minutes, depending on the heat and thickness of the meat. Baste with reserved marinade. The liver should acquire grill marks, but be careful not to overcook.

6. Overlap liver slices on warmed large white oval platter. Brush with remaining 1 tablespoon vinegar. Place grilled potatoes at one end of platter.

7. Quickly open the onion package and, with a wide spatula, transfer onions to the grill for a minute or two; do not turn. Lift onions with the spatula and invert them onto the platter, showing the crisped edges. Serve immediately.

# GRILLED WINE-SOAKED SAUSAGE ON WINE-SOAKED TOAST

Serves 4

This is a unique hors d'oeuvre or appetizer. The key is to choose a flavorful sausage that stands up to the wine. Marcie Smith is responsible for this and her sausage comes from Salumeria Biellese at 376 Eighth Avenue, New York.

### INGREDIENTS

1 piece fresh garlic sausage, about 6 inches long and 2½ inches thick
3 cups full-bodied red wine, such as Cabernet Sauvignon
4½-inch-thick slices of dense-textured white bread, such as sourdough
3 tablespoons butter

1. Place the sausage in a nonaluminum pot just large enough to hold it and add 2 cups wine. If the wine does not completely cover the sausage, it will have to be turned during cooking. Bring the wine to a simmer and gently poach the sausage for 25 to 30 minutes. Transfer sausage to another container and allow to cool in the poaching liquid. It will keep, covered and refrigerated, for up to 4 weeks.

2. Soak the slices of bread in the remaining 1 cup wine. Heat a sauté pan over high heat; add the butter. As it turns brown, lower the heat and sauté the soaked bread as you would French toast, until it is brown and crisp on each side.

3. Meanwhile, slice the sausage into ¼-inch rounds. Grill them on a lightly oiled charcoal or wood grill (2 to 4 pieces per serving) until they have grill marks. Layer the grilled sausage on top of the toasts and cut in half to serve.

# DUCK SAUSAGE WITH PORT AND GREEN PEPPERCORNS

*Makes 14 sausages; serves 7*

Tim McGrath is in charge of the kitchen at the Columbia Bar & Grill in Hollywood. He enjoys this preparation because the sausages, pears and port wine sauce can all be made ahead. Tim grills over oak charcoal.

### INGREDIENTS

3 ducks, skinned and boned
2 tablespoons green peppercorns
½ teaspoon freshly ground white pepper
1 tablespoon finely chopped shallot
1 tablespoon finely chopped garlic
1 cup dry white wine
½ cup port
1 teaspoon ground mace
1 teaspoon dried thyme
1 teaspoon herbes de Provence
1 tablespoon coarse salt
6 to 7 feet washed hog casings
poached pears (see below)
port wine sauce (see below)
fresh thyme sprigs for garnish

1. Grind together first 11 ingredients. Cook a small amount in a skillet; taste and adjust seasonings. Stuff into casings, tying every 3 inches. Refrigerate sausages overnight; bring to room temperature before grilling.

2. With a fork, prick sausages all over. When fire is ready, grill them about 4 minutes per side.

3. Slice pears and fan one out on each plate. Put sausages on plates and spoon sauce over. Garnish with thyme sprigs.

### POACHED PEARS

Serves 7

### INGREDIENTS

1 cinnamon stick
1 tablespoon sugar
3 whole cloves
1½ quarts water
7 firm pears, peeled and cored

In a 2-quart saucepan, combine all ingredients except pears and bring to boil. Lower heat, add pears and poach for about 10 minutes, or until tender. Serve warm or at room temperature.

### PORT WINE SAUCE

Makes about 2 cups

### INGREDIENTS

1 quart chicken stock
1 cup port
2 tablespoons unsalted butter
salt and freshly ground white pepper

In a heavy saucepan, boil chicken stock until reduced by half. Add port and continue to reduce until sauce coats a spoon, about 20 minutes. Gradually whisk in butter.

# GRILLED POULTRY AND GAME

A chicken in every pot has surely become a chicken on every grill. Chicken is a mainstay all over the world. Although some cooks consider it bland, its versatility presents challenge upon challenge; sometimes it seems there are as many ways to prepare chicken as there are all other foods combined. There is a movement afoot in this country to improve the bird's natural flavor, so the advent of the free-range chicken is upon us — a trend that may well provide a permanent source of better-tasting chicken.

The grill cook looks at chicken the way a painter looks at a blank canvas. The cook's art is to give the bird a new identity by mopping it, rubbing it, cutting it in many ways and creating infinite recipes for grilling, spit-roasting and smoking it. Poultry is a good source of protein, and it is produced in a shorter time at lower cost than either fish or meat. Why shouldn't it be on every grill?

Birds of all kinds are suited to the grill — rock Cornish game hens, pigeons, squabs, ducks, turkeys, quail and pheasant. Flatten and grill whole tender quail; smoke turkeys and rock Cornish hens; grill poultry parts in and out of wire baskets; insert herbs and spices under their skins and in their cavities; and spit-roast all of them. The recipes in this section give the details.

## POULTRY SELECTION AND PORTION SIZE

CHICKEN: Buy broilers — whole or halved, ready-to-cook, fresh, ice-chilled or quick-frozen. Provide one half-broiler or about 12 ounces per person; a 3-pound broiler serves four. Or have a half or whole chicken breast, two drumsticks or two thighs per person.

OTHER BIRDS: One squab or Cornish hen or a half-duckling per person. Turkeys come in many sizes, and all can be grilled:

broiler-fryers . . . . . . . . . . . . . 3 to 4 pounds
small roasters . . . . . . . . . . . . 5 to 8 pounds
larger young hens . . . . . . . . 12 to 16 pounds
tom turkeys . . . . . . . . . . . 18 to 30 pounds

# GRILL RULES AND SOME ADVICE

1. If possible, buy poultry at special meat counters where a butcher is on duty rather than opting for packaged chicken. If only the second option is available, check the "sell by" date on the package.

2. Consider spending a little more and ask your butcher about the availability of free-range chicken.

3. Of all grilled foods, chicken (because of its fat and skin) causes the most flareups. Remove the fat and cut off up to half of the skin, especially when grilling pieces.

4. Don't hesitate to use zesty barbecue, lemon, soy and other marinades to gain flavor. The same is true with herbs.

5. Learn to cook chicken without drying it out, especially when grilling halves; usually the breast is overdone and the thigh or leg underdone unless the half chicken is positioned to give the leg and thigh more heat. Poultry should not be cooked "well done." Think in terms of "medium," as for grilling steaks.

6. Test for proper doneness — a thermometer should register 170°F to 175°F. Or puncture the thigh with a small skewer; the juices should run clear with barely the faintest trace of pink. Be sure to let a whole bird rest for 8 to 10 minutes — its internal temperature will rise by 5 or 10 degrees, thereby cooking it further and firming the meat for carving.

7. While grilling, baste as often as is practical. Apply sweet mops toward the end of grilling time. If spit-roasting, baste with juices in the drip pan. Start grilling skin side down; the other, bone side should stay longer towards the fire than the skin side.

---

### Poultry Sizes

*Poultry is usually classified by weight, as shown below. For grill cooking, only fryers or broilers are used — quartered, halved or whole. Capons can be spit-roasted or smoked.*

| Approximate Weight | Known As |
|---|---|
| 1½ to 2½ lbs | fryer |
| 2½ to 3½ lbs | broiler |
| 3½ to 5 lbs | roaster |
| 5 lbs and over | fowl |

Capons and turkeys are over 5 pounds and are the only available poultry this size. These plum birds are excellent for spit-roasting or smoking, and can be grilled if cut into serving parts or butterflied.

---

### Poultry Types

*The three main chicken breeds today are Cornish Rock, Plymouth Rock and White Rock. Leghorns are scrawny and are used mainly for egg production. For clarification:*

*SQUAB is a domestically raised pigeon*

*SQUAB CHICKEN is a young chicken, also known as spring chicken*

*POUSSIN is the French name for squab chicken or spring chicken*

*ROCK CORNISH GAME HEN is a special breed of small chicken, 1 to 1½ pounds, a cross between the Cornish and White Rock breeds. Not to confuse, but this is the "poussin" (or squab chicken, or spring chicken) of that particular breed.*

*DUCK, in the U.S., is commercially dressed; Long Island duckling, for instance, weighs in consistently at 4 pounds. It has a very thick layer of fat between the flesh and skin but this helps keep the meat moist in grilling. Most producers call for puncturing the skin to release fat as the duck cooks. There are less well known but excellent ducks from other parts of the U.S., including Maryland and Michigan.*

# GRILLED CHICKEN BREAST WITH TARRAGON AND GARLIC BUTTER SAUCE

Serves 4

Elka Gilmore, a well-known chef working in California, grills chicken breasts this way.

### INGREDIENTS

#### MARINADE

¼ cup dry white wine
¼ cup olive oil
2 garlic cloves, sliced
salt and freshly ground white pepper
4 chicken breast halves, boned and skinned

#### SAUCE

3 cups Chablis or Chardonnay
2 shallots, minced
2 cups tarragon vinegar
2 white peppercorns, cracked
salt
juice of 1 lemon
¼ cup heavy cream
1 cup (2 sticks) unsalted butter
1 teaspoon finely chopped fresh tarragon
1 garlic clove, minced

1. Combine the marinade ingredients and mix well.

2. Place chicken breasts in a glass or ceramic container. Pour marinade over and allow to marinate for at least 2 hours, or overnight in the refrigerator. Bring to room temperature before grilling.

3. To prepare sauce, combine wine, shallots, tarragon vinegar, peppercorns and lemon juice in a heavy nonaluminum saucepan and boil until about 1 tablespoon is left and liquid is syrupy. Add heavy cream and reduce for another moment. Over low heat, whisk in butter piece by piece until it is all incorporated. Add tarragon and minced garlic.

4. When the fire is ready, grill breasts for 4 minutes on each side, basting frequently and turning only once. Do not overcook. Transfer to warm plates and nap with sauce.

---

*Garlic*

*There are many varieties of garlic, including white-, pink- and mauve-skinned. Bulb and clove sizes vary, too. The best garlic comes from warm climates. It may be native to Asia but we know the plant has been cultivated around the Mediterranean since early Egyptian times. Look for a hard bulb whose cloves are not shrunken away from their papery sheaths. If you find any discoloration in a clove cut it away and discard it; faded cloves leave a bad taste and will spoil a dish.*

*When I was growing up I was told that the lives of some close relatives had been spared during the World War I Spanish flu epidemic owing to their heavy consumption of garlic. And, in fact, garlic is very healthy. It has been reported that it reduces blood pressure, clears bronchitis and tones up the digestive system because of its inherent antiseptic properties. Years ago, I read that Caesar's soldiers ate garlic for extra energy before going into battle, and that it was fed to cocks before a fight.*

*Many great dishes include lots of garlic — and I've eaten plenty of dishes that would have benefited by it. Italian, French and Chinese, the world's three great cuisines, all use garlic generously, and the current food revolution uses lots of the lovely clove.*

# GRILLED CHICKEN BURGS WITH HERBS

Serves 6

This recipe is from Craig Claiborne, truly a household name; as food editor of *The New York Times* he has probably influenced every table in America. More than anyone I know, he has helped to create an atmosphere in this country that allows its young chefs and culinary students to propel the food revolution forward.

### INGREDIENTS

2 pounds skinless, boneless chicken breasts
¼ cup heavy cream
salt and freshly ground pepper
2 tablespoons finely chopped fresh tarragon
1 cup fine fresh breadcrumbs
4 tablespoons butter
2 teaspoons fresh lemon juice
2 tablespoons finely chopped parsley
¼ teaspoon hot pepper sauce, optional

1. Trim the breasts to remove all nerve fibers, cartilage and so on. Cut the chicken into small cubes.

2. Place the chicken in a food processor and grind coarsely. Gradually add the cream, blending briefly; do not overblend. The mixture should not be pasty.

3. Scrape the chicken into a mixing bowl. Add salt, pepper, tarragon and breadcrumbs, beating rapidly with a wooden spoon.

4. Divide the mixture evenly into 12 portions. Using dampened hands, shape the portions into flat, round patties. Chill thoroughly until ready to cook.

5. Preheat a gas or charcoal grill to high. Brush the surface evenly with a little oil. Grill the patties for about 4 minutes. Carefully turn with a spatula and cook about 4 minutes longer.

6. Heat the butter almost but not quite to the simmering point. Stir in the lemon juice, parsley and hot pepper sauce and pour over the patties. Serve immediately.

# GRILLED BONED CHICKEN BREAST WITH SWEET GARLIC ON A BED OF CURLY ENDIVE WITH PINE NUTS

Serves 4

### INGREDIENTS

#### SWEET GARLIC
1 large garlic bulb
1 teaspoon extra virgin olive oil
1 bay leaf, cracked
1 sprig fresh thyme

#### CHICKEN
2 tablespoons softened butter
1 tablespoon finely chopped fresh tarragon or 1
    teaspoon dried
1 tablespoon coarse-grained mustard
salt and freshly ground pepper
4 chicken breast halves, boned, with skin on
olive or peanut oil

#### SALAD
¼ cup tarragon vinegar
⅓ cup olive oil
⅓ cup peanut oil
1 to 2 heads curly endive, trimmed, washed
    and dried
¼ cup toasted pine nuts

1. To make the sweet garlic, preheat oven to 325°F. Trim away the top quarter of the tapered end of the garlic head. Place garlic on a sheet of aluminum foil. Drizzle oil over cut end and place bay leaf and thyme on top. Seal with foil. Bake for 1½ hours. Allow to cool,

lay bulb on its side and press gently with your hand to release the pulp. Combine the puree with the butter, tarragon, mustard, salt and pepper; set aside.

2. Wash and thoroughly dry the chicken breasts and lay them on a work surface skin side up. Divide garlic butter into 4 parts and spread with your fingers, as evenly as you can, under skin of each breast half. Brush chicken lightly with oil.

3. Grill the breasts on both sides, skin side down first, for a total of about 15 minutes or until cooked through.

4. For salad, combine the vinegar, ⅓ cup each of olive and peanut oil, salt and pepper and shake or whisk to blend. Dress the curly endive with the mixture, add the pine nuts and toss well. Divide salad among 4 plates. Add a piece of chicken to each and serve.

*The Breast of a Chicken*
A chicken has one breast. Some people think it has two because the breast thins as it crosses the breastbone and thickens again into what seems like a second breast.

Supermarkets have created this dilemma because when they pack breasts in plastic, they cut the meat through the breastbone, creating two breast halves. It actually is this chicken breast half that is usually served. It's not the chicken breast; it is the chicken breast half.

Some people may think the chicken half breast is to be cut in two to create a chicken breast half. 'Taint so. That would be a quarter of a chicken breast.

When cutting up a chicken at home, cut through the ribs to detach the breast from the chicken. Then, along the breastbone, cut the breast in half. Remove the breastbone halves.

# GRILLED CHICKEN BREAST PIECES IN SPICY ANISE SAUCE

Serves 4

Here the whole chicken breasts are chopped into smaller pieces — about three per half breast. After marinating in an unusual sauce including red chilies and dried star anise, the chicken is skewered and grilled. Dried anise stars, available in most Chinese and other food specialty shops, are inexpensive but flavorful. Throw six or eight of them on the fire and lower the grill cover for added flavor.

### INGREDIENTS

4 large chicken breasts (about 1½ to 2 pounds)
¼ cup dry sherry
¼ cup peanut oil
⅓ cup soy sauce
1 tablespoon sesame oil
4 green onions, trimmed and cut into 1-inch pieces
12 dried Chinese black mushrooms
2 tablespoons grated fresh ginger
4 small whole dried red chilies
4 dried star anise
1 tablespoon sugar
salt, optional

1. Remove about half of the skin from each chicken piece. Chop breasts into 2-inch pieces with breastbone in. Wash and dry well. Place in one layer in a glass, ceramic or stainless steel dish.

2. Mix all other ingredients and pour over chicken pieces. Marinate overnight in refrigerator, turning meat several times, or marinate at room temperature for 3 hours.

3. When the fire is ready, remove chicken pieces from marinade and skewer them; reserve marinade. If you have extra star anise, add some to the fire. Grill, basting frequently with leftover marinade.

4. Bring leftover marinade to boil. Distribute by spoonfuls onto 4 warmed plates. Add 1 star anise and 1 small red chili for garnish to each plate. Place grilled chicken pieces over sauce and serve.

---

*Star Anise*
*Star anise is always available in Chinese and Latin markets. It is refreshing in this recipe and is often used with duck and pork. The aromatic Chinese mixture known as "five spices" always includes it.*

---

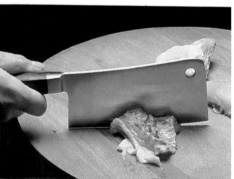

# GRILLED CHICKEN BREASTS WITH GULF SHRIMP AND ARTICHOKES ON SAFFRON FETTUCCINE

Serves 8

T his dish is the creation of Marcel Desaulniers, who grew up in a French Canadian family in Woonsocket, Rhode Island, and graduated from The Culinary Institute of America. He has been nominated by both *Cook's Magazine* and *Food And Wine* as an outstanding American chef, and is a co-owner of The Trellis, a well-known cafe, restaurant and grill in Williamsburg, Virginia.

### INGREDIENTS

8 chicken breast halves (4 ounces each) skinned and boned
8 tablespoons fresh lemon juice
6 tablespoons dry white wine
salt and freshly ground pepper
4 medium artichokes (about 8 ounces each)
3 cups chicken stock
10 tablespoons (1¼ sticks) softened unsalted butter
2 tablespoons minced shallots
1¼ pounds medium shrimp, peeled, deveined and cut in half lengthwise
8 portions saffron fettuccine (see below)
1 tablespoon chopped parsley

1. Sprinkle chicken with 2 tablespoons each lemon juice and white wine. Add salt and pepper to taste. Individually wrap each piece in plastic and refrigerate until needed.

2. Acidulate 1½ quarts water with 2 tablespoons lemon juice. Prepare the artichokes by removing all leaves. Slice straight across the flower about ¾ inch above the choke. Use a sharp-edged spoon to remove the purple and white thistle, or choke, from the center of the artichoke heart. Cut away all but ¼ inch of the stem. As soon as you cut and trim each one, place artichoke hearts directly into acidulated water.

3. Meanwhile, bring 2 quarts lightly salted water to a boil with 4 tablespoons lemon juice. Drain and rinse the prepared artichokes and drop into boiling water. Cook them for 10 to 12 minutes, until a knife inserted in center of artichoke encounters firmness but no resistance. Drain cooked artichoke hearts, then plunge them into ice water. When cool, remove from water and cut into julienne strips. Refrigerate until needed.

4. Preheat oven to 225°F. Season chicken breasts with salt and pepper. Grill over a medium-hot charcoal or wood fire for 3 to 4 minutes on each side, turning only once. Transfer to a baking sheet and hold in oven while completing recipe.

5. Bring chicken stock to boil.

6. Heat 2 tablespoons butter in a large non-stick sauté pan over high heat. When butter is hot add shallot, season with salt and pepper and sauté 1 minute. Add remaining 4 tablespoons wine and allow to simmer for 10 to 15 seconds. Add shrimp, season with salt and pepper and sauté for 2 minutes. Add artichokes and hot chicken stock. Bring to a boil, then remove from heat.

7. Cook pasta in 3 quarts boiling salted water for 30 seconds to 1 minute, until

tender but still firm to the bite. Drain cooked pasta in a colander and toss with remaining 8 tablespoons butter.

8. Divide pasta among 8 warm 9- to 10-inch soup/pasta plates. Place the shrimp mixture on top of the pasta and divide the cooking liquid among the plates. Place a chicken breast on top of each portion. Garnish with chopped parsley and serve immediately.

## SAFFRON FETTUCCINE

Serves 8

### INGREDIENTS

2 tablespoons warm water
1 teaspoon saffron
4½ cups all-purpose flour
4 large eggs
1 tablespoon olive oil
1 teaspoon salt
cornmeal

To prepare pasta by hand:

1. Combine warm water and saffron. Allow to steep at room temperature for 30 minutes.

2. Place 4 cups flour on a clean, dry cutting board or similar work surface. Make a well in the center and add the eggs, saffron water, olive oil and salt. Using a fork, combine the ingredients in the well. When thoroughly mixed, begin to work the flour into the center a small amount at a time. When enough flour has been added that you can handle the dough, begin kneading by hand; knead until all the flour has been incorporated, about 10 minutes. Cover the dough with plastic wrap and allow to relax at room temperature for 1 hour.

3. Cut the pasta dough into 8 equal portions. Roll and knead each portion of dough through the pasta machine, using the extra ½ cup flour as necessary to prevent dough from becoming tacky. Cut sheets of dough into fettuccine. To prevent sticking, toss cut pasta with cornmeal. Place on a baking sheet lined with parchment paper. Cover tightly with plastic wrap and refrigerate until needed.

To prepare pasta in processor:

1. Break the eggs directly into processor work bowl and blend lightly by pulsing twice.

2. Add olive oil, warm water, saffron and salt and pulse two more times.

3. Add 1 cup flour and process for 5 seconds. Repeat with 3 more cups flour, processing for 5 seconds after each addition.

4. The dough will become a ball and climb up the center of the chopping blade. Turn dough out onto work surface and knead lightly. Divide in half and form 2 balls. Cover each half with a bowl or cloth towel and let rest for 1 hour.

5. Proceed with cutting as in Step 3 above.

---

*Saffron Pasta*
*If the pasta dough is too moist, the strands will stick together and it may not cut properly on the pasta machine. If this occurs, air-dry the sheets of pasta for 10 to 15 minutes, then cut.*

*Fresh-cut pasta may be wrapped loosely and refrigerated for 24 to 48 hours. Before cooking, be certain to shake off the excess cornmeal. Remember, fresh pasta cooks very quickly, so taste frequently to determine the degree of doneness.*

---

## CHICKEN BREASTS WITH A STUFFING OF ALMONDS, MUSHROOMS AND GREEN ONIONS

**Serves 4**

The chicken cooks quickly, especially in a covered grill. The stuffing will brown somewhat and pick up that grilled flavor.

### INGREDIENTS

4 boneless chicken breasts (about 5 ounces each)
2 slices bacon
⅔ cup water
6 tablespoons butter
2 cups herbed breadcrumbs*
4 green onions, thinly sliced
4 mushrooms, sliced
½ cup slivered almonds
6 tablespoons softened butter
salt and freshly ground pepper
12 baby carrots, washed, with 2 inches of stem
1 tablespoon chopped fresh thyme or 1 teaspoon dried

1. Wash and dry breasts; set aside.

2. Sauté bacon until almost crisp. Remove from pan and set aside. Discard bacon fat or save for another use.

3. Heat water and 6 tablespoons butter in a large saucepan. When butter is melted, remove from heat. Add breadcrumbs, green onions, mushrooms and almonds. Crumble or chop bacon and add to crumb mixture. Toss well.

4. Cut 4 sheets of heavy-duty foil, 18 inches square. Smear each chicken breast with softened butter and season with salt and pepper. Place in center of each sheet of foil. Evenly divide stuffing into 4 parts. Lightly shape each portion into an oval patty and place on top of chicken. Mold stuffing to cover breast. Add 3 baby carrots to one side of breast and sprinkle stuffing with thyme. Enclose chicken with a drugstore wrap (see page 18).

5. When fire is ready, place packets 5 to 6 inches above heat source. Close cover and grill for 25 to 30 minutes, carefully turning packet once after 15 to 20 minutes.

*Note: Use herbed packaged breadcrumbs or make your own in the food processor, adding 2 tablespoons fresh herbs of your choice or 1 teaspoon dried.

# GRILLED HERBED CHICKEN

Serves 4

Mark DiGiulio and Peter Meltzer, two charming restaurateurs, are responsible for creating a charming "real French Bistro" in New York — Quatorze, on West 14th Street. They feature several excellent grilled dishes on their menu. Two outstanding ones are Grilled Chicken and Grilled Boudin Blanc, both excellently prepared by their chef, Sam Hazen, a native New Yorker who graduated from The Culinary Institute in Hyde Park, New York.

Sam prefers Pulia brand olive oil. He always uses fresh herbs in the marinade for the grilled chicken; that, he insists, is the way to get flavor. He also prefers duck fat to clarified butter for sautéing the chicken before grilling it. "Be sure to cut the chicken in pieces," he says, "so you have more control over the cooking times." At Quatorze they use a gas grill with lava stones.

All herbs should be fresh. Remove the stems as necessary and chop the leaves coarsely; a food processor may be used for this. If this is not possible, substitute dried but reduce amounts by half. *Pommes frites* and a vegetable make excellent accompaniments.

## INGREDIENTS

2 whole chickens, 2½ pounds each
½ cup duck fat or clarified butter

## MARINADE

2 bunches chives, chopped
2 tablespoons chopped fresh thyme
2 tablespoons chopped fresh tarragon
2 tablespoons chopped fresh oregano
2 tablespoons chopped fresh marjoram
4 bay leaves
2 cups fresh lemon juice
2¼ cups olive oil
¼ cup chopped garlic
1 teaspoon salt
1 tablespoon white pepper

1. Cut chicken into parts in order to have 1 breast, 1 leg and 1 thigh per person, or ask your butcher to cut it in this fashion for you. Place chicken in a glass or ceramic dish.

2. For marinade, add the chopped herbs and bay leaves to the lemon juice and slowly whisk in the olive oil until emulsified. This is important; emulsification will ensure even marination. Add garlic, salt and pepper and pour over chicken. Toss to be sure all pieces are coated. Marinate for 2 to 3 days in refrigerator.

3. Preheat oven to 250°F. Heat duck fat or clarified butter in an iron skillet and sauté chicken, skin side down first, until both sides are browned. Chicken will cook further on grill, so do not attempt to cook it through in the skillet. Transfer pieces to oven to keep warm as they are cooked, then place on grill for 8 to 10 minutes until lightly golden. Chicken pieces are done when juices run clear.

# GRILLED CHICKEN WITH MISANTLE BUTTER

Serves 4

The combination of sesame and pumpkin seeds, poblano and chipotle peppers, and a little lime juice originated in the Yucatan region of Mexico. The creator of this recipe, chef Jimmy Schmidt, has transformed it into a compound butter.

### INGREDIENTS

8 tablespoons toasted pumpkin seeds
4 tablespoons toasted sesame seeds
½ chipotle pepper, rehydrated (if dried) or canned
½ poblano pepper, roasted, peeled and seeded
4 tablespoons unsalted butter
1 tablespoons red wine vinegar
2 tablespoons fresh lime juice
salt
4 chicken halves, boned except for wing and drumstick
olive oil
4 red and poblano pepper tamales (see below)
4 herb sprigs for garnish

1. In a mortar, combine ¼ cup pumpkin seeds, 2 tablespoons sesame seeds and chipotle pepper. Grind with pestle until a smooth paste is obtained. Transfer to food processor. Add poblano pepper and butter and puree until combined. Add vinegar and lime juice. Season with salt. Transfer to small bowl. Fold in remaining pumpkin and sesame and refrigerate. (Misantle butter can be made several days ahead.)

2. Preheat grill or broiler to 450°F. Rub chicken surfaces very lightly with olive oil. Place skin side to heat until seared and golden, about 7 minutes. Turn and cook to desired doneness, about 13 minutes. Transfer to plate. Spread some of misantle butter across skin.

3. Meanwhile, remove tamales from steamer and position on upper half of serving plates. Arrange chicken on lower half of plate. Spread with remaining butter on chicken and garnish with herbs and serve.

### RED AND POBLANO PEPPER TAMALES

Makes 4

### INGREDIENTS

Poblano Pepper Masa:
½ cup milk
1 tablespoon unsalted butter
salt
¼ cup rice flour
2 tablespoons masa harina
2 tablespoons yellow cornmeal
½ cup roasted, peeled, seeded and pureed poblano pepper

Red Pepper Masa:
½ cup milk
1 tablespoon unsalted butter
salt
¼ cup rice flour
2 tablespoons masa harina
3 tablespoons yellow cornmeal
½ cup roasted, peeled, seeded, and pureed red pepper
8 large cornhusks, soaked in water
½ cup diced husked tomatillos

1. For poblano pepper tamales, combine milk, butter and salt in a small saucepan and bring to simmer over medium-high heat. Add rice flour, masa harina and cornmeal and cook, stirring constantly, until very thick, about 4 minutes. Add pepper puree and mix until combined.

2. Repeat procedure with ingredients for red pepper masa.

3. Place 2 cornhusks overlapping on a flat surface. Spoon 2 tablespoons of each masa randomly over center of husks. Spoon 2 tablespoons of tomatillos over masa. Cover tomatillos with a bit of additional masa. Fold husks around masa to form a tight tamale, tucking in ends.

4. Place tamale in steamer and steam over high heat for about 5 minutes. Serve by opening husks to reveal filling.

# CHICKEN AND GREEN MANGO KEBABS

Serves 2

Chicken teams well with many other foods, and this is one particularly special combination from Christopher Idone, the author of *Glorious Food* and *Glorious American Food.*

### INGREDIENTS

2 whole chicken breasts, boned and skinned
1½ cups coconut milk
juice of 1 lime
1 small fresh chili pepper, seeded, deveined and finely diced
1 teaspoon coriander seeds, crushed
½ cup olive oil
1 firm mango
½ cup toasted sesame seeds

1. Wash and dry chicken and cut into 2-inch cubes.

2. Combine the coconut milk, lime juice, chili, coriander and oil in a large bowl and add the chicken. Refrigerate for at least 3 hours. Bring chicken to room temperature.

3. Peel the mango and slice into cubes about the size of the chicken pieces. Thread the chicken and fruit alternately on skewers. Set the skewers on a hot grill and cook until the chicken is lightly charred, about 8 minutes.

4. Sprinkle the grilled kebabs with the sesame seeds and serve.

# GRILLED HERBED CHICKEN *AL MATTONE* WITH SWEET POTATO SHOESTRINGS

Serves 6

This recipe, from Mary Etta Moose, chef at the Washington Square Bar & Grill in San Francisco, illustrates the method of grilling on a flattop. It works equally well over medium coals.

### INGREDIENTS

3 chickens (3½ pounds each), halved

#### MARINADE

3 tablespoons chopped fresh thyme
3 tablespoons chopped fresh rosemary
3 tablespoons chopped fresh basil
1½ tablespoons chopped fresh mint
6 tablespoons chopped flat parsley leaves
1½ tablespoons finely chopped garlic
½ teaspoon freshly ground pepper
1 tablespoon coarse salt
1 cup (or less) extra virgin olive oil

#### BASTING MIXTURE

½ cup fresh lime juice
½ cup extra virgin olive oil
¼ teaspoon coarse salt
¼ teaspoon freshly ground pepper
sweet potato shoestrings (see below)

1. Taking care not to tear the skin, partially bone the chicken halves as follows: cut off wing tips; remove drumstick bones and breastbones. Leave the wing bones, thigh bones and ribs in place to retain shape. Wipe chicken clean with a damp cloth.

2. Combine marinade ingredients, using just enough olive oil to make a spreadable paste (you may need less than the cup specified). Coat the chicken halves with the paste inside and out. Marinate, covered, overnight in the refrigerator.

3. Bring chicken to room temperature. Preheat a clean flattop grill to medium temperature, 325°F to 350°F. Lightly oil the preheated grilltop. Taking care not to disturb the marinade coating, arrange the chicken halves on the grill without touching. Top each piece with a heavy flat weight, or with a brick, to flatten it during cooking.

4. Combine basting mixture ingredients. After 5 minutes, drizzle 1 teaspoon of the basting mixture over each piece, using a spoon, not a brush, to avoid breaking the crust. Baste again in the same way after another 5 minutes, and carefully turn the pieces over. Gently replace the weights. Baste again after 5 and after 10 minutes, just before chicken comes off the grill.

## Serves 6

If you can find Japanese sweets, with their taste between chestnuts and sweet potatoes, use them. Garnish the plates with a bouquet of herbs used in the marinade.

### INGREDIENTS

2 pounds sweet potatoes
3 cups corn oil
coarse salt
herb sprigs for garnish

1. Peel potatoes. Cut into shoestring strips about ⅛ inch thick. Wrap tightly in towels to prevent discoloration before frying. Just before cooking, place half of potato strips in deep frying basket.

2. Bring oil to 370°F. Lower potatoes into the oil and immediately raise the heat until the oil returns to 370°F. Fry strips for about 3 minutes, until outsides are crisp.

3. Drain the fries on paper towels and sprinkle them with coarse salt. Have a helper distribute them on 3 serving plates while you fry a second batch. Garnish with herbs and serve.

# HONEY-GLAZED GRILLED CHICKEN

## Serves 6

### INGREDIENTS

12 chicken thighs (about 4 pounds)
juice of 1 lemon
½ cup peanut oil
½ cup honey
½ cup cream sherry
¼ cup soy sauce
1 medium onion, finely chopped
2 garlic cloves, finely chopped
1 tablespoon chopped fresh ginger or ½ teaspoon ground
½ cup flaked coconut
salt and a generous sprinkle of freshly ground pepper

1. Remove about half the skin and all the fat from the chicken. Rinse chicken and pat dry. Place in a bowl with the lemon juice and let stand for 15 to 30 minutes. Drain, dry and place in a clean bowl.

2. Combine all remaining ingredients. Pour over chicken and marinate for 3 hours at room temperature or overnight in the refrigerator. Bring the chicken to room temperature before grilling.

3. Grill for 15 minutes, skin side up. Turn and grill skin side down for another 15 minutes, basting frequently with marinade. Turn and grill a final 15 minutes, basting every 3 or 4 minutes. Total grilling time should be about 45 minutes over grayed hot coals.

# GRILLED THAI GARLIC CHICKEN WITH CHILI HONEY SAUCE (*Kai Yang*)

Serves 8

Regal, romantic, relaxed and refined are words often used to describe The Siamese Princess restaurant in Los Angeles. One might wonder if the food measures up to the decor and ambiance — but taste the satay, grilled chicken or steamed goose salad and wonder no more. Some food experts claim that the restaurant's chef/owner, Victor Sodsook, is responsible for influencing local farmers to grow authentic Thai produce.

### INGREDIENTS

1 cup grated fresh or packaged coconut
1 cup water
2 tablespoons minced garlic
1 tablespoon curry powder
1 bunch fresh coriander, with root, washed and dried
2 tablespoons Thai fish sauce
½ teaspoon salt
1 teaspoon freshly ground pepper
1½ tablespoons Thai yellow curry paste

3 chickens (about 3 pounds each), cut into serving pieces
honey sauce (see below)

1. For coconut milk, combine coconut and water in a saucepan and bring to boil. Remove from heat and let stand 30 minutes. Drain coconut in strainer, pressing on solids to extract all liquid; you should have about 1½ cups. Discard coconut.

2. Combine coconut milk with remaining ingredients in a blender or food processor and blend until very smooth.

3. Transfer marinade to a very large bowl. Place chicken pieces in the marinade and refrigerate for at least 12 hours, turning occasionally. Bring chicken to room temperature before grilling. Drain, reserving marinade.

4. Grill chicken over charcoal, brushing with marinade toward end of cooking time.

5. Before serving, dip grilled chicken pieces in the honey sauce.

### HONEY SAUCE

Makes 1 cup

1 cup honey
2 teaspoons brown sugar
1 small red chili pepper, stemmed, seeded and ground in blender or spice grinder
½ teaspoon salt

Combine all ingredients in a small saucepan and bring to boil. Lower heat immediately and simmer for 2 minutes; be careful not to scorch. Serve hot or at room temperature.

# GRILLED CHICKEN THIGHS AND LEGS WITH SAFFRON AND LIME

Serves 8 to 12

Derek H. N. Foster, the wine and food critic for the *Buenos Aires Herald* in Argentina, says this is one of the best grilled chicken dishes he has ever eaten. I enjoyed it at the home of its creator, Fereydoun Kia, a leading restaurateur in Argentina.

### INGREDIENTS

24 chicken legs and thighs (12 of each), from small (about 2-pounds) chickens
½ cup olive oil
3 large onions, grated
1 teaspoon saffron threads
salt and freshly ground pepper
¾ cup fresh lime juice

1. Wash and dry the chicken pieces. Place in one or more glass or ceramic dishes in one layer. Combine all remaining ingredients except ½ cup lime juice. Pour the marinade over the chicken and toss to coat all the pieces. Cover and marinate at least 15 hours in the refrigerator; bring to room temperature before grilling.

2. Just before grilling, pour the remaining ½ cup lime juice over the chicken. Brush the grill with oil and place the chicken on it. Grill for 20 to 30 minutes, turning the chicken pieces 3 or 4 times.

> *An Outdoor Grill in Argentina*
> "The harder the wood, the better," said Fereydoun Kia as he explained quebracho wood. "Quebracho means 'ax breaker.' It's grown in Argentina and Brazil, and the wood is so hard that it sinks fast in water." Fereydoun never mixes quebracho with charcoal; he uses one or the other to make a fire.

# GRILLED BABY CHICKEN WITH LENTIL SALAD AND SAUTÉED SPINACH

Serves 6

Contributed by Pitita Lago, who was born and raised in Puerto Rico and attended art school in Florence and Madrid. Her cooking career began by accident in Washington, D.C.: she was an unemployed art student, and nearly broke, when she decided to take a job as a dishwasher at one of Washington's top restaurants.

### INGREDIENTS

6 baby chickens (poussins), about 1 pound
    each, at room temperature
⅔ cup extra virgin olive oil
2 tablespoons finely chopped fresh rosemary
15 garlic cloves, thinly sliced
salt and freshly ground pepper
lentil salad (see below)
sautéed spinach (see below)

1. Cut chickens in half and remove necks, backbones and wing tips. Marinate chickens in oil, rosemary and garlic for 8 to 10 hours.

2. Remove from marinade and season with salt and pepper on both sides. Grill over a medium flame for about 8 to 10 minutes per side or until the meat feels springy to the touch. Serve with lentil salad and spinach.

## LENTIL SALAD

Serves 6

### INGREDIENTS

1 pound lentils
6 ounces bacon, cut into 1-inch pieces
1 onion, halved
1 bay leaf
2 teaspoons salt
1 red and 1 yellow bell pepper, stems, ribs and
    seeds removed, cut into ¼-inch dice
2 serrano chilies, seeded and finely chopped
1 red onion, chopped
2 tablespoons chopped fresh coriander
juice of 1 lime
¾ cup extra virgin olive oil
¼ cup red wine vinegar
salt and freshly ground pepper

1. Rinse the lentils in cold water. Pick through them and remove any foreign matter. Cook with bacon, onion, bay leaf and salt in water to cover until tender, skimming often. Rinse under warm water and discard the bacon, onion and bay leaf. Drain lentils well.

2. Add all remaining ingredients and toss well. Adjust the seasonings. Serve at room temperature.

## SAUTÉED SPINACH

Serves 6

### INGREDIENTS

2 pounds fresh spinach
4 tablespoons butter
salt and freshly ground pepper
pinch of freshly grated nutmeg
fresh coriander sprigs for garnish

1. Wash and stem the spinach. Dry well. In a large skillet, sauté spinach in butter over high heat, in batches if necessary, until barely cooked. Season with salt, pepper and nutmeg.

2. Arrange the spinach on the center of each serving plate. Place chicken on top and surround with lentil salad. Garnish with sprigs of coriander.

---

*Lentils*
*Included in the dried beans category, along with black-eyed peas, chickpeas, and cranberry, great northern, kidney, lima, navy, pink and pinto beans, lentils are among the least expensive but most nutritious foods. When served with rice, they provide almost complete protein and are cholesterol-free.*

*Native to Central Asia, lentils are known as dahl in India, where they are served daily. In addition to protein, they are rich in Vitamin B, iron and phosphorus. If for some reason you don't want to use lentils in this salad, substitute black-eyed peas, chickpeas or one of the beans.*

---

# GRILLED BARBECUED CHICKEN PIECES

Serves 4 to 6

The tenderest chicken pieces come from birds no heavier than about 3 pounds. The pieces may be marinated overnight or not. This barbecue sauce is special enough to make a good barbecued chicken without marination, but if you have the time, marinate them.

### INGREDIENTS

2 broiler-fryers (about 3 pounds each)
barbecue sauce with horseradish (see page 34)

1. Cut chicken into serving pieces as you wish: halves, quarters, breasts, legs and so on. If you use smaller pieces, you may want to use a hinged wire grill to facilitate turning.

2. When fire is ready, grill skin side first, about 6 inches over heat, for about 10 minutes or until lightly browned. Turn and brown on other side. Lightly brush on barbecue sauce.

3. Additional cooking time will be about 20 to 30 minutes. Turn every 5 minutes, basting lightly each time. Do not burn chicken.

4. Serve any remaining sauce hot on the side.

# GRILLED SONOMA SQUAB MARINATED IN BOURBON, HONEY AND SOY

Serves 6

This special squab presentation was created by Joyce Goldstein, chef/owner of Square One in San Francisco. Serve the squab with rice sprinkled with chopped green onions, and with stir-fried snow peas, grilled Japanese eggplant or sautéed spinach.

### INGREDIENTS

6 squab (about 16 ounces each)
2 cups soy sauce
1 cup bourbon
1 cup honey
8 garlic cloves, minced
2 tablespoons grated fresh ginger
freshly ground pepper

1. Prepare each squab for grilling by removing the head, feet and wing tips. Insert a sharp knife through the neck cavity and carefully split the bird down the back, keeping the breast intact. Remove the backbone, then carefully remove the breastbone, central cartilage and ribs. The bird will look like a butterfly with only wing and leg bones attached.

2. Place the squab in a shallow glass or ceramic dish and add the remaining ingredients. Cover and refrigerate overnight. Do not marinate more than a day, or the ginger will cause the meat to break down and become mushy.

3. Prepare the grill and bring the squab to room temperature. Sprinkle squab with pepper. When the fire is ready, grill the squab skin side up for 4 minutes, then turn and grill for 3 minutes on the skin side. Do not worry if the bird turns quite dark; the honey causes it to caramelize on the outside, but it will not taste burned (unless, of course, you overcook it or place it too close to the flame and really scorch it). Squab are best served rare; the longer you cook them, the tougher they become. A home broiler will take a bit longer than a mesquite flame or charcoal. Test squab for doneness rather than trusting to suggested written times; the cooking times suggested here are for high heat.

# SPATCHCOCK GRILLED PIGEON WITH STUFFED MUSHROOMS

Serves 4

For about 10 years, Nicola Cox has done the cookery demonstrations at the Game Fair, a remarkable exhibition set up annually in the park of one of Britain's stately homes to display everything having to do with country sports and pursuits. Nicola's Spatchcock Grilled Pigeon with Stuffed Mushrooms is based on an older recipe for grouse that she inherited from her Scottish great-great-grandmother. The pigeon recipe can also be adapted for squab or quail. To "spatchcock" means to slit a bird down the back and open it up flat. Young pigeons, at their best from June to November, are chosen for their rosy to blue-tinged skin and soft down. Older birds have darker skin, skinny feet and thin necks. The pigeons are best eaten within 12 to 48 hours (depending on the weather) because they lose their flavor if kept too long.

## INGREDIENTS

4 tender young pigeons or squab
salt and freshly ground pepper
4 large mushroom caps (chop and reserve
   stems)
½ shallot or 2 very small onions, minced
a handful of chopped fresh parsley
small sprig of fresh lemon thyme
¼ cup whole-grain breadcrumbs
4 tablespoons butter, melted

2 large tomatoes, halved, optional
1 bunch watercress
vinaigrette dressing

1. Spatchcock each pigeon by cutting down the back, snipping out the backbone and through the wishbone with a pair of kitchen shears. Press bird flat, tuck wings under carcass and keep in place with cocktail picks. Cut slits in the skin on each side of the lower back and tuck in drumstick ends. Season with salt and pepper.

2. To make the mushroom stuffing, combine mushroom stems, shallot, parsley, lemon thyme, breadcrumbs, and salt and pepper to taste. Add 1 tablespoon melted butter to bind.

3. When the fire is very hot, grill breast side of pigeons for 6 to 8 minutes. Meanwhile, brush mushroom caps with remaining butter and grill for 1 to 2 minutes, flat side down. Fill mushrooms with stuffing. Turn pigeons, at the same time adding stuffed mushrooms and tomato halves to grill; cook for 5 to 6 minutes longer, or until pigeon meat is just pink.

4. Dip watercress sprigs in vinaigrette and shake off excess. Serve pigeons surrounded by the stuffed mushrooms, grilled tomato halves and watercress.

# MUSTARD-MARINATED PIGEON WITH LARDONS AND PEARL ONIONS

Serves 4

From Brian Whitmer, the young Kansas City-born chef at Montrachet, one of New York's truly stellar new restaurants.

### INGREDIENTS

4 pigeons (about 1 pound each), boned except for thighs
2 tablespoons Dijon mustard
1 cup olive oil
4 shallots, thinly sliced
4 garlic cloves, thinly sliced
4 sprigs fresh marjoram, lightly crushed
4 sprigs fresh thyme, lightly crushed
2 strips slab bacon (8 × ¼ inch each), rind removed
24 pearl onions
2 cups Savoy cabbage cut into 1-inch cubes (about ¼ of a large head)
1½ cups *jus* (see below)
salt and freshly ground pepper
2 tablespoons butter
1 teaspoon chopped parsley
4 sprigs fresh marjoram for garnish

1. Rub the pigeon all over with mustard and set aside.

2. Combine marinade ingredients and stir well. Pour some of marinade into a glass or ceramic dish large enough to hold the pigeons in one layer. Add the pigeons and pour the remaining marinade over. Cover and marinate for 2 nights in the refrigerator. Bring birds to room temperature before grilling.

3. Cut bacon strips into ¼-inch-thick matchsticks. Cook in a skillet over low heat until fat is rendered and bacon is slightly underdone. Remove lardons from fat; reserve fat in skillet.

4. Blanch onions in boiling water for 3 minutes. Remove skins and cut off root ends. Add onions to bacon fat in skillet and cook very slowly, stirring frequently, until browned on all sides. Remove onions with a slotted spoon; reserve fat in skillet.

5. Blanch cabbage in boiling salted water for 1 minute. Drain and dry.

6. Return lardons to skillet and reheat until crisped. Add cabbage to skillet, toss and cook over medium-high heat until lightly browned. Add onions and *jus* and bring to boil. Taste for seasoning, adding salt and pepper as needed. Stir in butter and parsley, remove from heat and keep warm.

7. Grill pigeons skin side down over a medium-hot charcoal fire. Turn over and cook only until breasts are rare. Move birds to lower heat on the grill and arrange so thighs receive the most heat; the thigh should be cooked while the breast remains pink.

8. Distribute sauce among 4 warmed plates. Place a pigeon on top and set a small sprig of marjoram on each bird.

Makes 1½ cups

2 tablespoons olive oil
1 small carrot, thinly sliced
1 large celery stalk, thinly sliced
1 small leek, thinly sliced
1 shallot, thinly sliced
2 garlic cloves, minced
1 teaspoon cracked white pepper
4 cups chicken stock
2 sprigs fresh thyme
2 sprigs fresh marjoram

**1.** In a large skillet or saucepan, brown bones in olive oil over high heat. Add carrot, celery, leek, shallot, garlic and white pepper. Toss until vegetables are browned.

**2.** Add chicken stock, thyme and marjoram and simmer over medium-low heat for about 1 hour or until reduced to 1½ cups.

# GRILLED TURKEY BREAST IN SHERRY WITH ROSEMARY

Serves 6 to 8

INGREDIENTS

1 turkey breast (3 to 4 pounds), skinned
2 cups dry sherry
2 tablespoons dried rosemary, crushed
8 tablespoons (1 stick) butter, melted
salt and freshly ground pepper

**1.** Cut the breast into 1-inch-thick slices. Cut the slices into 1-inch strips and the strips into 1-inch cubes. Place in a large shallow glass or ceramic dish, in one layer if possible. Pour the sherry and crushed rosemary over.

**2.** Marinate at room temperature for 2 to 3 hours; the turkey may absorb the sherry completely.

**3.** Skewer the turkey pieces and brush liberally with melted butter. Grill until pieces are browned at edges, about 15 minutes, turning and basting frequently with butter and any remaining sherry; basting is important to keep the turkey pieces moist. Test for doneness by removing a piece of turkey from the skewer and tasting it.

# GRILLED
# WHOLE TURKEY LOCO
# WITH LIME, OREGANO AND
# CRANBERRY SALSA

Serves 6

This unusual dish, and so easy grill is from Gene and Jerry Ann Woodfin. The cranberry salsa is a delightful accompaniment.

### INGREDIENTS

1 turkey (12 pounds)
8 tablespoons (1 stick) butter
juice of 6 limes
2 tablespoons tequila
2 tablespoons finely chopped fresh oregano or 1
    teaspoon dried
salt and freshly ground pepper
cranberry salsa (see below)

1. Ask your butcher to butterfly the turkey, cutting off excess skin and lumps of fat. Wash and dry the bird and insert a meat thermometer in the thickest part, not touching the bone.

2. Melt butter and add the lime juice, tequila, oregano, salt and pepper.

3. Place bird skin side down on oiled grill, about 6 inches above heat. Mop bird with lime mixture. Grill for about 15 minutes, turn and mop some more. Grill another 15 minutes.

4. Turn and mop with lime sauce every 20 minutes or so until the thermometer registers 170°F, about 1½ to 2 hours.

### CRANBERRY SALSA

Makes about 2 cups

#### INGREDIENTS

2 cups fresh or frozen cranberries
4 teaspoon grated orange zest
2 large oranges, peeled, membranes removed
¼ cup finely chopped onion
1 tablespoon minced fresh coriander
1 tablespoon minced fresh ginger
1 tablespoon minced jalapeño, pepper, seeded
salt

Chop cranberries coarsely in food processor. Transfer to bowl and add orange zest. Coarsely chop oranges in processor and add to cranberries with all remaining ingredients. Mix well and allow flavors to blend for at least 30 minutes. Serve at room temperature.

# ROCK CORNISH HENS AND VEGETABLES IN WHITE WINE AND TARRAGON

Serves 6

This is a complete and flavorful meal, all grilled at once in individual foil packets. When cooked, transfer the birds to serving plates and put vegetables on individual side plates.

### INGREDIENTS

6 rock Cornish hens (about 1¼ pounds each), split in half*
salt and freshly ground pepper
12 long carrots, peeled and halved lengthwise
6 small potatoes, peeled and halved
3 zucchini (about 1 × 6 inches), ends trimmed, halved crosswise
1½ red bell peppers, stems, ribs and seeds removed, cut into 12 strips lengthwise
3 onions, halved
3 celery heart stalks with leaves
1 cup dry white wine
12 tablespoons butter, cut into 12 pats
3 tablespoons finely chopped fresh tarragon or 1 teaspoon dried
½ cup light corn syrup
6 sprigs fresh tarragon, parsley or watercress for garnish

1. Rinse and dry the poultry pieces. Arrange 2 halves, skin side down, on heavy-duty foil sheets at least 18 inches square. Salt and liberally pepper each half on both sides. (These packets will not be turned; skin will brown in packet.)

2. Distribute vegetables equally among packets.

3. Sprinkle some wine over each arrangement and add 2 pats of butter to each. Season with salt to taste, a liberal amount of pepper and the tarragon. Secure each packet with a drugstore wrap (see page 18), leaving some air inside.

4. When fire is ready, place packets on the grid, close cover and grill for about 30 minutes. Do not turn packets.

5. Open each packet and drizzle 1 tablespoon corn syrup over contents. Loosely close packet and let rest for 5 to 10 minutes. To serve, transfer hens to individual plates, turning skin side up. Arrange vegetables on side plates. Pour juices over both. Garnish with a sprig of tarragon, parsley or watercress.

*Note: Three 2½-pound chickens may be split in half and used in place of rock Cornish hens.

# FIREPLACE QUAIL
# WITH WINTER GRATIN

Serves 4 to 6

Chef Larry Forgione suggests that to cook the quail in a fireplace, rig supports at each side of the fire to support the skewers. Use bricks or, if the fireplace is large enough, logs. You may cook the birds on an outdoor grill but use wood, not charcoal for intense heat. You may also oven-broil them 5 to 6 inches from the heat, 5 to 7 minutes to a side.

### INGREDIENTS

#### MARINATED QUAIL

8 to 12 quail (5 ounces each), trussed
salt and freshly ground pepper
¼ cup coarse-grained mustard
2 tablespoons cider vinegar
2 tablespoons honey
¼ cup dry white wine
1 teaspoon chopped fresh thyme or ½
   teaspoon dried

#### WINTER GRATIN

1½ pounds boiling potatoes
1½ pounds sweet potatoes
2½ cups heavy cream
2 garlic cloves, crushed
2 teaspoons salt
½ teaspoon freshly ground white pepper
pinch of nutmeg
1 large tart baking apple (about 8 ounces),
   peeled, cored and grated
½ cup fresh breadcrumbs

1. Season the quail with salt and pepper. Combine mustard, vinegar, honey, wine and thyme. Rub each quail with this until well coated. Place birds in a shallow dish and pour any remaining marinade over. Refrigerate for 6 to 8 hours, turning occasionally.

2. Preheat oven to 375°F. Bake white and sweet potatoes until barely tender and a sharp knife inserted into them meets some resistance, about 40 to 45 minutes depending on size. Allow to cool. Peel carefully. Using the large holes of a cheese grater, grate the white and sweet potatoes into two separate bowls.

3. In a heavy saucepan, slowly heat cream, garlic, salt, pepper and nutmeg until scalded. Reduce heat and simmer 5 to 7 minutes. Strain half of hot cream mixture over each bowl of potatoes and toss well.

4. In a lightly buttered 2-quart casserole, layer ⅓ of the sweet potatoes, ⅓ of the grated apple and ⅓ of the grated white potatoes. Repeat twice more, ending with a layer of white potato and spooning liquid into dish as you add potatoes. Top with breadcrumbs.

5. Preheat oven to 375°F. Place casserole in a shallow baking pan and add boiling water to come halfway up sides of casserole. Bake until breadcrumbs are golden, about 25 minutes. Reduce oven temperature to 250°F to keep casserole warm until quail are cooked.

6. Remove quail from refrigerator and turn in marinade. Skewer quail through the cavities; more than one will fit on each skewer. Cook 9 inches above glowing red logs, turning every 3 to 5 minutes and basting with marinade, for about 12 to 15 minutes or until legs move easily in sockets and juices run clear. Remove skewers. Serve with potato gratin.

# CHARCOAL-GRILLED QUAIL WITH WARM CURLY ENDIVE SALAD

Serves 4

### INGREDIENTS

8 quail (about 4 ounces each)
5 tablespoons oil (vegetable, corn, peanut or
    safflower)
juice of ½ lemon
1 tablespoon white wine vinegar
2 tablepoons Dijon mustard
1 large garlic clove, finely chopped
1 tablespoon finely chopped fresh tarragon or 1
    teaspoon dried
salt and freshly ground pepper
curly endive salad (see below)

1. Ask your butcher to remove backbones and breastbones of quail so the birds lie flat.

2. Combine all other ingredients and mix well. Coat quail with the marinade and place in a glass or ceramic dish. Cover and marinate in refrigerator overnight or at room temperature for 3 hours. If refrigerated, let stand at room temperature for about 1 hour before grilling.

3. Grill quail skin side down over high heat approximately 5 minutes; turn and grill other side an additional 5 minutes.

4. Arrange salad on plates, place 2 quail on each plate and serve.

### INGREDIENTS

2 heads curly endive
½ cup oil (vegetable, corn, peanut or
    safflower)
3 tablespoons balsamic vinegar
½ cup finely chopped green onions
salt and freshly ground pepper

1. Remove tough outer leaves from endive and use hearts only. Wash, drain, and dry.

2. In a skillet or small nonaluminum saucepan, bring all remaining ingredients to boiling point. Pour over salad greens and toss well. Serve immediately.

---

*Quail*
*The terms quail and partridge are used interchangeably in the United States. Some call the bird "bobwhite" from the sound of its call. As a rule, names of the quail species include a location, such as mountain quail or California quail.*

*Quails are trussed like squab and are becoming more popular on American restaurant menus. Talented chefs across the country are creating marvelous-tasting preparations. A good example is the marinated quail with winter gratin on page 215. The recipe on this page is also to be recommended.*

# GRILLED BONELESS DUCK BREAST WITH WILD RICE GRIDDLE CAKES AND MANGO

Serves 6

Tim McGrath is chef at the Columbia Bar & Grill, one of Hollywood's most beautiful places to dine *alfresco*. This intriguing combination of grilled duck breast, wild rice griddle cakes and mango is just one example of Tim's lively and satisfying cuisine.

### INGREDIENTS

12 boneless fresh duck breasts, trimmed
½ cup olive oil
1 small orange, sliced
3 garlic cloves, crushed
1 tablespoon each coarsely chopped fresh
    thyme, sage, tarragon and rosemary
wild rice griddle cakes (see below)
mango sauce (see below)
6 watercress sprigs for garnish

1. Place duck breasts in a glass or ceramic dish. Combine olive oil, orange, garlic and herbs and mix well. Pour over breasts, being sure that all are thoroughly coated. Cover and marinate in refrigerator overnight, turning the breasts several times. Bring to room temperature before grilling.

2. With hands, wipe off excess herbs and marinade. Place breasts on grill, meat side down, and cook 5 minutes. Transfer breasts to cast iron skillet skin side down and sauté on grill for about 5 minutes to render fat from skin. When fat is rendered, place breasts on grill skin side down for about 1 minute to crisp skin.

3. Arrange 3 griddle cakes along outer rim of each plate. Ladle some sauce onto center of plates. Slice duck breasts on the bias and fan out opposite the griddle cakes. Add 3 mango slices to each plate and garnish with a sprig of watercress. Serve immediately.

## WILD RICE GRIDDLE CAKES

Makes about 18

### INGREDIENTS

2 tablespoons butter
½ onion, finely chopped
¼ cup wild rice, rinsed in cold water and
 drained
2 bay leaves
¾ cup water
1 cup all purpose flour
½ teaspoon salt
1 teaspoon sugar
1 large egg, beaten
1½ cups milk
1 teaspoon vanilla
2 tablespoons butter, melted
½ cup clarified butter

**1.** Melt 2 tablespoons butter in saucepan and sauté onion over medium heat until translucent. Stir in rice, bay leaves and water. Bring to boil, reduce heat to low, cover and cook until rice is tender, about 35 minutes. Drain and spread on a baking sheet or platter. Cool in refrigerator.

**2.** In a bowl, combine flour, salt and sugar. In another bowl, combine eggs, milk and vanilla. Whisk together dry and liquid mixtures, adding 2 tablespoons melted butter. If necessary, strain to get a smooth batter.

**3.** When rice is cooled, stir into batter.

**4.** Place skillet over medium heat and coat bottom with a small amount of clarified butter. Ladle in small amounts of batter to make cakes about 2 to 3 inches in diameter. Brown on both sides. Keep warm until needed.

## MANGO SAUCE

Makes about 2½ cups

### INGREDIENTS

3 medium-size ripe mangoes
1 tablespoon sugar
¼ cup red wine vinegar
2 cups demiglace or brown sauce
salt and ground white pepper

**1.** Peel the mango vertically, slicing around the pit. Reserve slices in refrigerator. With paring knife, trim excess fruit from pit. Reserve.

**2.** Place the sugar in a 1-quart nonaluminum saucepan and caramelize over medium heat. Quickly add mango trimmings. Add vinegar and cook 2 minutes. Add demiglace or brown sauce, bring to boil, lower heat and simmer for 10 minutes. Puree in blender or processor in 2 or 3 batches. Add salt and pepper to taste.

# SPIT-ROASTING

The beauty of spit-roasting is indirect heat. The meat, poultry or fish to be spit-roasted is not seared at a high temperature; instead, it is constantly revolved over lower heat that roasts evenly and allows the food to self-baste.

To many people's surprise, this is one of the best ways to barbecue ribs. Because a rack of ribs is thin, it will only be moist and tender if cooked slowly over low heat. When a sparerib rack is grilled over direct heat, it can scorch if constant attention is not given. Often trimming of fat and parboiling are essential to avoid flareups and blackened ribs. In spit-roasting, these concerns disappear. It is easy to thread the rack on the spit and to cook the ribs slowly and evenly.

Quail, duck, goose, lamb, rabbit and beef prime rib are a few candidates for spit-roasting, but there are many others. The fully flavored, fat-wrapped veal loin is a stellar spit roast, as are rock Cornish hens with herb bouquets and the spicy cinnamon pork loin.

When spit-roasting it is important to secure the prongs of the spit forks into the meat. First slide one spit fork onto the spit shaft and tighten the thumbscrew, using pliers if necessary. Then insert the pointed end of the shaft through the center of the meat or the cavity of the fowl. Slide the other fork onto the shaft and secure it also. Test for proper balance by turning the shaft in the palms of your hands; this will prevent unnecessary strain on the motor. Drumsticks, wings and odd-shaped meats need to be tied, trussed and balanced to provide for proper roasting.

A drip pan (and they can be homemade) must be placed under the meat.

To make a foil drip pan:

1. Tear off two sheets of 18-inch-wide heavy-duty foil. Each sheet should be about 6 inches longer than the food to be spit-roasted.

2. Place one sheet on top of the other and fold in half along the length of foil. This will give you four thicknesses of foil 9 inches wide and 6 inches longer than the food.

3. Fold the ends and sides up about 2 inches high. Pull out the four corners and fold each one back against the sides.

4. Place foil pan under food and in front of fuel when grilling on spit.

Remove the cooking grid and place the spit over the drip pan and indirectly over the coals. If you are using a gas grill, put the drip pan on the lava rocks or rearrange the rocks around the pan. Most spits are adjustable in height and are either electric or battery-operated. A closed hood will produce smoky flavors, less so if the hood is half opened. For maximum smoke flavor, use the lowest spit setting with a closed hood. Basting will be necessary in either case.

Spit-roasting is one of the best ways to grill, and one of the most relaxing. Once the spit is set up and the motor begins, the grill cook can rely on the spit to do most of the work. Most basting is done toward the end of cooking, but do check the spit from time to time throughout to be sure all is well.

# SPIT-ROASTED VEAL ROLL WITH HAZELNUT BUTTER

Serves 6

Serve this with garlicky potatoes and a crisp hearts of escarole salad with light mustard dressing. Warm goat cheese, sprinkled with an herb of your choice (such as basil, thyme, tarragon, or oregano), completes the meal.

### INGREDIENTS

1 boned veal shoulder (4 pounds), trimmed of fat

#### FILLING

4 tablespoons softened unsalted butter
¼ cup finely chopped hazelnuts
1 tablespoon finely chopped lemon zest
juice of 1 lemon
¼ cup finely diced red bell pepper
1 garlic clove, minced
2 tablespoons finely chopped parsley
salt and freshly ground pepper

#### MARINADE

3 tablespoons olive oil
1 large garlic clove, minced
juice of ½ lemon
2 tablespoons sherry vinegar
8 ounces thinly sliced fresh pork fatback
hazelnut butter (see below)

1. Have the butcher tie the veal in a roll. At home, untie the veal roll and spread it open. If it needs to be cut open further, do so.

2. For filling, combine butter, hazelnuts, lemon zest, juice of 1 lemon, red pepper,

1 garlic clove, parsley, salt and pepper and mix well. Spread mixture over veal. Reroll and tie to keep together while marinating.

3. For marinade, combine olive oil, 1 garlic clove, juice of ½ lemon and vinegar and pour into a glass or ceramic container. Roll the veal in marinade to coat and let stand at room temperature for about 3 hours or refrigerate overnight (if refrigerated, bring to room tem-

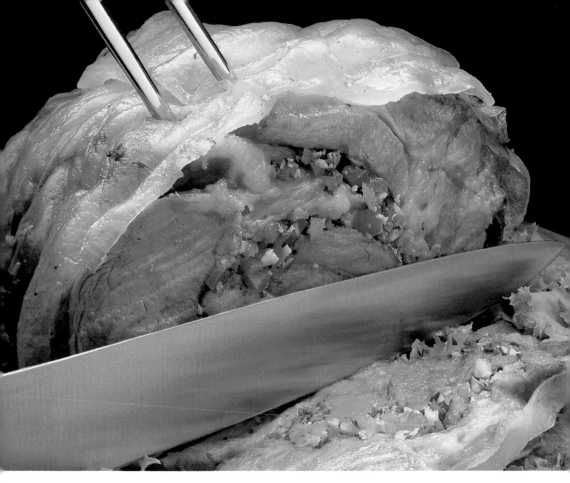

perature before roasting). Remove string from roll, bard with strips of pork fat and tie neatly and securely.

4. Arrange the spit by first sliding one of the forks onto the spit rod. Run the spit through the length of the veal roll, keeping an eye on balance and forcing spit through the other end of the meat. Add the second fork and secure both. Test by rolling in the palm of your hands. Adjust spit if necessary.

5. Prepare the fire, setting a drip pan under the spit to catch the drippings.

6. Arrange spit over fire, using lowest rung if adjustable heights are available. The veal roll can be set fairly close to the fire.

7. Close cover of grill partially or fully, depending on how much smoke flavor is desired. Roast veal slowly and steadily for 20 to 30 minutes a pound, or a total of 1½ to 2 hours. Serve with hazelnut butter.

HAZELNUT BUTTER
Makes about ½ cup

INGREDIENTS

4 tablespoons butter
¼ cup chopped hazelnuts
juice of 1 lemon
2 tablespoons finely chopped parsley
salt and freshly ground pepper

Melt butter in a small skillet. Add hazelnuts, lemon juice, parsley, salt and pepper. Mix well and serve hot.

# SPIT-ROASTED SWEET BOURBON RIBS

Serves 4 to 6

This is so good with a side of pork ribs, and roasting the whole side at one time keeps the ribs moist. When the cover is closed, grill another 20 minutes, basting with marinade 10 minutes before done.

### INGREDIENTS

½ cup firmly packed brown sugar
½ cup bourbon
¼ cup soy sauce
juice of 1 lemon
½ cup beer
1 whole side of spareribs (4 to 5 pounds),
    trimmed of fat and membrane
salt and freshly ground pepper

1. In a small saucepan, combine all ingredients except ribs and heat, stirring constantly, until sugar is dissolved. Remove from heat. Lay ribs flat in a glass or ceramic dish and coat with marinade.

2. Marinate ribs for several hours at room temperature or overnight in refrigerator, turning several times.

3. Thread ribs onto spit and secure with prongs. Cook uncovered for about 20 minutes, then close cover partially or completely to gain desired amount of smoke flavor. Reheat marinade and serve with ribs.

### Lemon

The colored part of the lemon peel, or "zest," contains the fruit's essential oil. Cut a thin piece of lemon peel and, under good light, bend the ends together; you'll see the oil burst forth. The juice, though not aromatic, is used in marinades in place of or in conjunction with vinegar. When a recipe calls for lemon juice, always use fresh.

### Bourbon

"Discovered" in the late 18th century, bourbon is made of corn with a little rye and barley malt, all combined with limestone-filtered water. The liquor is named for Bourbon County (first in Virginia, today also in Kentucky), which in turn was named for the French royal family. Labels on many bourbon bottles carry the phrase "sour mash." This simply means that some of the undistilled liquid from yesterday's fermented grain mash goes into today's supply. This is a "blood transfusion," if you will — a way of assuring continuity in the brew's character and flavor. Bourbon is peculiar to the United States, just as Scotch whiskey is made only in Scotland and Cognac only in France. Many years ago, James Beard wrote that bourbon isn't used half enough in cooking. Agreed: bourbon leaves an exciting and haunting flavor.

## SPIT-ROASTED CHILI-BARBECUED RIBS

Serves 4

The tangy tomato-chili barbecue sauce will glaze the ribs; the dry heat of the coals will crisp and brown them. Just hope you've grilled enough: the tantalizing aroma will whet your appetite. You'll have more sauce than you need, so save the remainder for future use (it's also great with hamburgers).

### INGREDIENTS

4 tablespoons butter
1 onion, finely chopped
2 garlic cloves, finely chopped
4 cups canned plum tomatoes, put through a
    food mill
2 teaspoons chili powder
1 cup dry red wine
½ cup soy sauce
2 tablespoons cornstarch
1 tablespoon sugar
salt
½ cup chicken stock
1 whole rack of spareribs (4 to 5 pounds),
    trimmed of fat and membrane

1. Melt butter in saucepan or skillet over medium-high heat and sauté onion until soft. Add garlic and cook a minute longer. Add all remaining ingredients except meat and bring to boil. Reduce heat and simmer for several minutes. Remove from heat and set aside.

2. Thread ribs onto spit and secure with prongs. Close cover about two-thirds of the way. Spit-roast ribs for about 30 minutes, then baste with sauce every 10 minutes or so for another 40 minutes, or until juices run clear. Place several tablespoons of sauce on each plate and serve with ribs.

> *Barbecued Ribs*
> *Barbecued ribs are one of life's treats, but a common complaint in grilling them is the difficulty of holding down flareups.*
> *Spareribs are fatty; excess fat should be removed before grilling. Cooking on a spit takes a little longer but the ribs require less attention. Though the ribs will need frequent basting, it doesn't begin, as a rule, until they are at least half cooked.*

## SPIT-ROASTED CINNAMON PORK

Serves 6

Try serving this with cole slaw and mustard sauce.

### INGREDIENTS

1 center-cut pork loin, boned
   (3½ to 4 pounds)
2 tablespoons cinnamon
2 teaspoons salt
1 teaspoon freshly ground white pepper
2 teaspoons sugar
1 onion, finely grated (about ½ cup)
4 garlic cloves, minced (about 2 tablespoons)
1 to 3 tablespoons soy sauce

1. Prepare the pork for the rub by scoring the surface in 1-inch diamonds with a sharp knife; cuts should be ⅛ to ¼ inch deep.

2. Combine all other ingredients except soy sauce. When well mixed, blend in 1 tablespoon soy sauce. If mixture is not spreadable, add another 1 to 2 tablespoons soy sauce.

3. Rub mixture into loin as completely as possible, using your hands and penetrating the scored lines. Let pork stand at room temperature for 3 hours or refrigerate overnight. Bring to room temperature before grilling.

4. Secure pork on the spit. Arrange coals at far end of grill. Set drip pan under spit and insert spit when fire is ready. Roast for 1½ to 2 hours or until pork is slightly pink inside, basting with juices from drip pan; do not overcook. Allow to rest for 5 to 10 minutes before cutting into thin slices.

# SPIT-ROASTED PORK LOIN WITH MADEIRA AND ORANGE ZEST

Serves 6

**2.** Secure pork on the spit and set it over the grill when the fire is ready. Roast about 1 to 1¼ hours, or until pork is slightly pink inside (do not overcook). Transfer to a warm platter and cover with foil. Allow to rest for 5 to 10 minutes before slicing.

If you are using a covered grill, add soaked wood chips for more flavor. I usually cover the grill halfway through the cooking time for that extra smoky taste. Serve hot or cold.

### INGREDIENTS

½ cup Madeira
¼ cup honey
½ cup fresh orange juice
¼ cup soy sauce
2 tablespoons finely chopped orange zest
2 garlic cloves, minced
1 tablespoon chopped fresh sage or 1 teaspoon dried
1 pork loin (3 to 4 pounds), trimmed of fat and tied

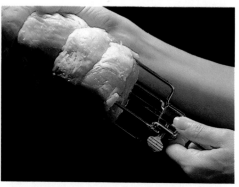

**1.** Combine all ingredients except the pork and stir well to dissolve honey. Add pork marinade, cover and let marinate for at least 4 hours at room temperature or, better still, overnight in the refrigerator. Bring to room temperature before cooking.

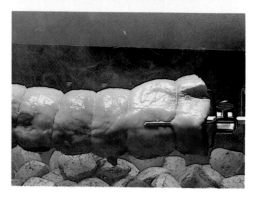

# SPIT-ROASTED TENDERLOIN OF BEEF

Serves 6 to 8

You can spit-roast a smaller tenderloin than called for here; for example, a 2-pound tenderloin, which will serve 3 or 4 people, will take 30 to 40 minutes to cook. Whatever the size, allow the meat to rest for 10 minutes or so after removing it from the fire and spit. Close the cover partially during cooking. If you like, try different aromatic woods or chips, such as mesquite or hickory, though they are not really necessary to achieve a beautifully spit-roasted tenderloin. This is one of the simplest recipes in the book. Little or no checking is needed; just keep an eye on the clock. Add butter, salt and pepper after the meat is removed from the fire. The tenderloin is a little thicker at one end than the other, but this is a convenience — it provides slices of varying doneness to suit every taste.

### INGREDIENTS

1 beef tenderloin (4 to 5 pounds), trimmed
2 tablespoons butter
salt and freshly ground pepper

**1.** Meat must be at room temperature. Secure it on the spit, insert the prongs at each end and test for balance by rotating the spit on the palms of both hands.

**2.** Build a fire with briquettes at the rear of the grill and allow it to reach the gray ash stage. Gently tap the briquettes to shake off ash. Place drip pan in front of fire and under the spit. Attach the spit and start the motor.

**3.** The slow, steady turn of the spit allows the meat to baste itself, so no basting is required except for an occasional brush with drippings. Roast for about 45 minutes or to desired doneness. When done, remove the spit. Butter, salt and pepper the tenderloin. Allow it to rest for about 10 minutes before cutting into thin slices.

---

*Spit-Roasting a Beef Rib Roast:*

1. *Ask your butcher to free rib bones from meat and to remove the last couple of inches of rib bones, without cutting off the meat attached to those bone ends.*

2. *Lay a thin piece of suet between the rib meat and the rib bones.*

3. *Fold the meat flap (where the tips of the bones were removed) over bone ends.*

4. *Secure roast by tying with cord every 1½ inches or so to keep end flap of meat and suet in place.*

5. *Set one spit fork on rod, insert rod through center of meat and add second fork. Be sure forks are secure, tightening with pliers if necessary.*

6. *Test for balance by rotating rod in the palms of your hands.*

---

# LEG OF LAMB ON A SPIT WITH A COFFEE BASTE

Serves 6 to 8

Howard Erskine is a topnotch theatrical producer (he won a Tony award for his production of *Desperate Hours*, starring Paul Newman), as well as a great chef. He was given this recipe by the famous actor Alfred Lunt.

### INGREDIENTS

1 leg of lamb (5 to 6 pounds), bone in,
    trimmed
salt and freshly ground pepper
4 whole garlic cloves, unpeeled
2 cups brewed coffee with cream and sugar

1. Secure leg of lamb on the spit and check for balance by rotating spit on the palms of your hands. Season liberally with salt and pepper.

2. Start the lamb turning on the spit, then immediately smash a clove of garlic and throw it directly on the fire. Repeat every 4 to 6 minutes with the remaining garlic cloves, closing the cover to allow the aroma of the smoking garlic to be absorbed by the still-uncooked lamb.

3. Roast for about 2 hours or to desired doneness, basting with coffee every 15 to 20 minutes. A delightful crust will result. Let meat rest for about 10 minutes before slicing.

# SPIT-ROASTED ROAST BEEF

Serves 6

The perfume of beef-on-the-spit is one sure stimulant to one's appetite.

### INGREDIENTS

1 3½-pound rib roast
8 tablespoons (1 stick) butter, melted
⅓ cup red wine
Salt and freshly ground pepper

1. Ask your butcher to bone and roll a rib roast, to be spit roasted. Insert rod and forks and check for balance. Add drip pan to fire box and spit roast for 45 to 60 minutes.

2. Combine butter, wine, salt and pepper and baste as frequently as you can during the roast.

3. Serve with garlicky potatoes (see page 278) and a fresh green salad.

---

*Spit-Roasting Leg of Lamb*
1. Ask the butcher to remove 2 or 3 inches of bone from shank end of leg, leaving meat in place as a flap.

2. Fold up flap of meat and insert rod through it, proceeding all the way through center of leg.

3. Secure spit forks.

4. Test for balance by rotating rod in the palms of your hands.

# CHICKEN(S) ON A SPIT WITH CELERY AND GREEN ONION

Serves 2 to 3

The quantities below are for a small chicken; double or triple them for a larger bird. A 3½- to 4-pounder will take 1 to 1¼ hours to cook, and a 4- to 5½-pound chicken or capon will need 1¼ to 1½ hours.

### INGREDIENTS

1 whole chicken (2½ to 3 pounds)
1 recipe marinade (see page 34 )
1 celery stalk, cut into 3 pieces
2 green onions, halved
1 sprig each fresh tarragon, thyme and
   rosemary

1. Wash and dry the chicken and place in a glass or ceramic dish. Pour marinade over chicken, rubbing some inside the cavity.

2. Tie the celery, green onions and herbs together. Dip into the marinade and place inside the chicken. Let marinate at room temperature for 2 to 3 hours or overnight in the refrigerator. Bring to room temperature before grilling.

3. Secure the chicken on the spit. Tie legs together, then tie wings. Roast over glowing coals for 45 to 60 minutes, basting frequently with marinade for additional flavor.

*More than One Chicken or Game Bird:*

1. Dovetail chickens or game birds on the rod. Skewer or use cord to secure wings as above. Use cord to tie legs as above.

2. Use spit forks at each end to further secure birds to rod. Be sure fork screws are tightened.

3. An alternative method is to thread birds on the spit sideways, centering each, rather than lengthwise. Secure with spit forks and tie wings and legs as above.

---

*Spit-Roasting Turkey*

1. *Secure the neck skin to the back skin with a small skewer by laying bird on its breast and bringing neck skin up over neck opening. Secure by looping cord around skewer, making a figure eight. Skewer or tie wings to body.*

2. *Turn turkey breast side up and run rod through the body cavity, starting at center of neck and coming out slightly above tail. Secure one fork in breast end and one in tail end. Use cord to tie legs and tail to rod.*

3. *Test for balance by rotating rod in the palms of your hands.*

---

*Spit-Roasting Poultry*
*One Chicken or Game Bird:*

1. *Run the spit through the breast, parallel to the backbone, and out through the body opening. Make sure the rod is centered.*

2. *Attach spit forks in breast and tail areas to secure bird.*

3. *Tie wings by starting a piece of cord at the back, looping it around each wing and tying it closed. Or secure each wing with a small skewer.*

4. *To secure legs, loop a piece of cord around the tail and rod and tie it tightly around the crossed legs.*

5. *Test for balance by rotating rod in the palms of your hands.*

# ROCK CORNISH GAME HENS WITH HERB BOUQUETS

Serves 2 to 4

These are tasty, bouquet-fragrant birds. Serve them with brandied or pickled fruit — pears, peaches, figs or watermelon rind.

### INGREDIENTS

2 rock Cornish game hens (about 1½ pounds each)
2 tablespoons olive oil
salt and freshly ground pepper
1 celery stalk, cut into 4 pieces
6 sprigs each fresh rosemary, parsley and tarragon
2 garlic cloves, halved
2 teaspoons fresh lemon juice
zest of 1 lemon, coarsely chopped

1. Wash and dry the hens inside and out. Rub oil, salt and pepper over entire surface and inside cavity.

2. Using 4 of each of the herb sprigs, make 2 herb bouquets by cradling herbs and garlic pieces between 2 pieces of celery and tying them. Place one in cavity of each bird, trimming celery to fit if necessary. Pour a teaspoon of lemon juice into each cavity. Truss both birds.

3. Secure birds onto spit with neck ends at center. Adjust spit to one of the lowest positions. For a smoky flavor, close the cover and open vents about halfway; for a less smoked flavor, close hood only partially. Make a fire to the rear of a covered grill and set a drip pan under spit. Pour 1 cup warm water into the drip pan and add the lemon zest and remaining herb sprigs.

4. Roast for about 1 hour, basting with mixture in the drip pan every 10 minutes or so. Omit basting for the last 15 minutes to crisp the skin.

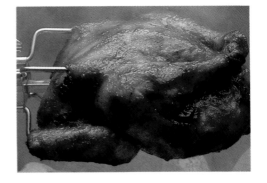

## BUTTERY BARBECUED ROCK CORNISH HENS

Serves 2 to 4

Baked or grilled potatoes and sautéed spinach go well with these birds.

### INGREDIENTS

2 rock Cornish game hens (about 1½ pounds each)
2 tablespoons olive oil
salt and freshly ground pepper
2 green Italian frying peppers, stemmed and seeded
1 onion
6 sprigs parsley, stemmed
2 garlic cloves
1 cup barbecue sauce (see page 24)
½ teaspoon freshly grated nutmeg

1. Wash and dry the hens inside and out. Rub the oil, salt and pepper over entire surface and inside cavity.

2. Chop peppers into 5 or 6 pieces. Coarsely chop onion, parsley and garlic and place in food processor with the green pepper. Add ¼ cup barbecue sauce and pulse 8 to 10 times. Transfer to a bowl, add nutmeg and mix well. Place half of mixture into each cavity and sew opening closed.

3. Secure birds onto spit with neck ends at center. Adjust spit to one of the lowest positions. For a smoky flavor, close the cover and open vents about halfway. Make a fire to the rear of a covered grill and set a drip pan under the spit.

4. Roast hens for about 1 hour, basting with remaining barbecue sauce every 10 minutes or so. Omit basting for the last 15 minutes to crisp the skin.

5. Clip threads at opening of cavity and scoop out stuffing. Serve with hens. If you wish, accompany with additional barbecue sauce.

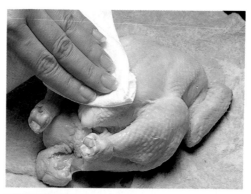

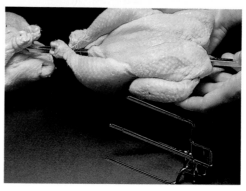

*Spit-Roasting Hens*

*The rock Cornish hens are secured to the spit and suspended above a drip pan that is surrounded by glowing coals. The hen is basted with a tangy barbecue sauce as it spit roasts. Peppers, onion, parsley, garlic and nutmeg form a "stuffing" to add flavor to the bird.*

*Mount each bird, one at a time, on the spit, making sure it is centered and balanced. Secure with spit forks. Tie wings and legs. To tie wings, start cord at the back, go around each wing, and tie across breast. To secure legs, loop cord around the tail, then bring it tightly over both legs (crossed) and tie tightly.*

*Don't forget to place drip pan in grill.*

# SPIT-ROASTED GRILLED CHICKEN WITH ROASTED CHILI SAUCE

Serves 2 to 4

Serve with *pico de gallo* and hot flour and corn tortillas advises Clive DuVal, a master with grilled foods.

### INGREDIENTS

½ fresh pineapple, peeled, cored and chopped
4 heaping tablespoons Koon Chun brand lemon or lime sauce*
2 cups fresh orange juice
¼ cup safflower oil
2 tablespoons cracked black pepper
2 tablespoons coarse salt
3 medium jalapeño peppers, stemmed, seeded and chopped
¼ cup chopped fresh basil
¼ cup chopped fresh coriander
1 free-range chicken fryer (3½ pounds)
roasted chili sauce (see below)

1. Puree all ingredients except basil, coriander, chicken and chili sauce in a food processor or blender. Whisk in the herbs and pour marinade over the chicken, making sure the cavity is filled with the marinade. Refrigerate, covered, for 3 hours. Bring to room temperature before roasting.

*You may substitute 2 tablespoons fig or peach preserves, ¼ cup fresh lemon or lime juice and ¼ cup fresh orange juice.

2. Drain chicken, reserving the marinade. Spit-roast the chicken over mesquite charcoal for 20 minutes. Remove from heat and marinate again for 30 minutes. Meanwhile, place a handful of pecan shells or hickory chips in water to soak for 30 minutes. Split chicken in half and place directly on medium-hot grill, skin side up, for 10 minutes.

3. Drain the pecan shells or hickory chips and add to the fire. Grill chicken for 10 minutes more. Remove and dip chicken in marinade again.

4. Cut leg joint slightly so chicken lies flat. Grill breast side down for 5 minutes more or until done (total grilling time is about 45 minutes). Accompany with chili sauce.

### PICO DE GALLO

Serves 6

### INGREDIENTS

4 medium tomatoes, chopped
1 medium-size white onion, chopped
2 garlic cloves, minced
3 fresh jalapeño or serrano peppers, finely chopped
⅓ cup finely chopped fresh coriander
3 tablespoons fresh lime juice
2 tablespoons safflower oil
1 teaspoon chopped fresh basil
1 teaspoon chopped fresh marjoram
1 teaspoon chopped fresh tarragon
2 firm avocados, peeled, pitted and chopped
salt and freshly ground white pepper

Combine all ingredients in a bowl. Serve immediately, or cover and refrigerate. Bring to room temperature before serving.

## ROASTED CHILI SAUCE

Makes about 3 cups (6 servings)

The dried chilies, pumpkin seeds and *mole* are available at Latin markets. Koon Chun barbecue sauce is a mixture of plum and hoisin sauces, which can be substituted.

### INGREDIENTS

1 teaspoon each dried chervil, tarragon and oregano
1 teaspoon whole cumin seeds
1 tablespoon ground ancho chili
1 tablespoon ground cascabel chili
1 tomato, roasted, peeled and seeded*
1 red bell pepper, roasted, peeled and seeded
2 poblano chilies, roasted, peeled and seeded
2½ cups chicken stock
4 tablespoons unsalted butter
1 jalapeño pepper, stemmed, seeded and minced
2 garlic cloves, minced
2 green onions, minced
1 teaspoon minced fresh ginger
¼ cup Marsala
¼ bottle (6 tablespoons) beer
¼ cup hulled and ground unsalted pumpkin seeds
1 teaspoon brown sugar
1 tablespoon Koon Chun brand barbecue sauce, optional
1 tablespoon prepared *mole* sauce
fresh lime juice
coarse salt
cayenne pepper

1. Combine dried herbs, cumin, ground chilies, roasted vegetables and 1½ cups chicken stock in a blender and puree.

2. Melt butter in a skillet over low heat. Add jalapeño, garlic, green onions and ginger and sauté for 3 to 4 minutes, taking care not to burn garlic. Deglaze with Marsala and then beer, and simmer 2 to 3 minutes.

3. Add remaining stock, then the pureed mixture and simmer 2 to 3 minutes. Whisk in pumpkin seeds, brown sugar, barbecue sauce and *mole*.

4. Simmer until sauce thickly coats the back of a spoon. Season to taste with lime juice, coarse salt and cayenne. Serve hot.

> *To roast the tomato, place in a dry heavy skillet over high heat. The tomato will start to char quickly. Keep turning it until all surfaces are black and the skin begins to peel.

# SPIT-ROASTED DUCK
# WITH HONEY

Serves 6

Honey and orange flavors penetrate these ducks and the same procedure may be used for a goose up to 10 pounds.

### INGREDIENTS

2 4-pound ducks
juice of 1 lemon
2 tablespoons vegetable oil
salt and freshly ground pepper
4 oranges, halved
½ cup honey
¼ cup soy sauce
2 sticks butter
2 tablespoons orange zest
¾ cup orange juice, fresh
3 spring onions, including green part, finely
   sliced

1. Prepare ducks for spit-roasting by thawing, if frozen, and removing fat. Wash and dry the birds. With a needle, puncture large fat accumulations above the thighs and under the wings where the skin looks pale and different from the rest of the bird.

2. Rub the inside and outside of the ducks with lemon juice, oil, salt and pepper. Put 4 orange  halves into each cavity. Cut off the tip and first joint of each wing. Secure the flap of the neck skin over neck opening with a skewer and then tie wings with a string. Put one fork on spit and slide on one duck by splitting through tail cavity, coming through neck flap. Insert second duck, add another fork to secure both ducks. Check for balance.

3. Put a drip pan in the center of the grill, with plenty of coals all around. Add 1 cup water and any leftover lemon juice into drip pan.

4. Combine honey and soy sauce. When fire is ready, spit-roast ducks until skin is tanned. Prick once again above thighs and under wings to allow fat to escape. Brush with honey/soy sauce frequently. Allow to spit roast for about 2 hours or until ducks are done. Do not baste for last 15 minutes to crisp skin. Duck is done when juices run clear. Let rest for 10 or 15 minutes.

5. Before ducks are done, heat butter, orange zest and juice and spring onions for about 20 minutes over low heat. This is the sauce for the ducks. Keep warm.

6. To serve, discard orange halves. Slice duck and serve with sauce.

# SMOKE COOKERY

The mystery and excitement of smoke cookery create challenge and fun in addition to delicious food. Experimentation with different marinades and aromatics can be never-ending because there are so many variables in ingredients, fuel and timing.

There are several types of equipment for smoking. It may be done in a covered kettle, a square or rectangular grill or an electric smoker (these are known as dry smokers), or in the charcoal water smoker (known as a wet smoker). All operate on a kindred principle: the heating element, whether electric, gas or charcoal, is at the bottom of the unit with a grid over it on which to place the food. Some grills can be converted into wet smokers by adding specific equipment — or simply a bowl of water or other liquid below the food.

Covered grills can smoke foods if they have high domes or tight-fitting covers. Not much charcoal is required, about 20 briquettes, and the indirect heat method is used (briquettes are arranged on one or two sides of the firebox with a drip pan directly below the food). Be sure the charcoal is dry. The smoky flavor comes not from the briquettes but from the addition of the presoaked aromatic wood chips or vines; the amount added will determine the degree of smokiness. It's difficult to discuss amounts of wood or chips as tastes differ, but an average would be about 2 to 4 cups of chips.

Do not add raw charcoal to the smoker. If more is needed, start it in a chimney-type cone and let it burn down to gray ash stage before adding it to the fire in the smoker. And never use starter fluid, which will spoil the flavor you're seeking.

When a covered grill is used for smoking, the vents should be open and the lid closed. Avoid peeking at the food inside, because every time the cover is lifted at least 10 to 15 minutes will have to be added to the total cooking time. It is best to keep a thermometer inside the grill to check temperature if there is not a built-in heat gauge. Internal temperatures should be kept at about 150°F; this can usually be maintained by adding or removing one or two pieces of charcoal.

The charcoal water smoker is an updated version of an ancient cooking method that combines heat from charcoal, smoke from aromatic woods, chips or vine cuttings, and moisture from liquid vapors to baste meat, poultry or seafood. The food cooks slowly, with little or no attention needed, until it is done to a tender and succulent state.

Two important advantages of water smoking are that basting is rarely necessary except to glaze the food, and that the smoked food may be kept in the refrigerator for up to two weeks.

Salting or curing meats before smoking them is an old-time procedure that is still popular today. However, marinades flavor and tenderize foods more quickly and easily than dry cures or brine, and their variety is almost infinite. Suggestions on brine and dry cures are given on page 19).

Smoking food is an outdoor activity. Keep safety in mind: place the smoker on a level, heatproof surface, away from windows, house, barn or any flammable materials. Bear in mind that extra cooking time — up to an hour — is needed if the weather is cool, the wind is strong or the altitude is high.

Foods cooked in a smoker will look different from those cooked in other ways. For example, turkey will be pink inside and pinkish-red on the outside. If this color doesn't please, glaze the bird by combining equal parts of jelly and wine in a small saucepan, heating and stirring until the jelly is melted. Use this as a baste during the last hour of smoking, but add more time to the total cooking time to compensate for opening the cover. Glazing helps appearances for those who can't quite make the shift from oven-baked to smoked foods.

One final note: I write down almost everything I do when I cook. There's hardly anything more aggravating than not remembering what made the beef chuck so good the last time it was smoked. Keep notes with your recipes and keep adding and referring to them.

## THE CHARCOAL WATER SMOKER

Here is the detailed procedure for using this equipment. Although most water smokers employ basically the same operating principle, it is always best to consult the manual provided by the manufacturer.

1. Line both the coal and water pans with foil to ease cleanup later, but be careful not to block any vents.

2. Use only top-quality charcoal briquettes. Start some briquettes in chimney-type starter to get the fire going. Place these in the smoker bowl, then add the remainder needed. Do not add the meat until all briquettes are ready — that is, uniformly covered with gray ash.

3. Be sure to fill the water pan. Use hot tap water if the weather is cool. Check the recipe to see if something other than water is required; some recipes call for other liquids.

4. Place food in one layer on the grill over the water pan. If there are separate pieces of food, leave a little space in between. If a second grill is needed, put it in place and spread food on it also.

5. When the fire is ready, place any aromatic wood or chips you wish on the coals. Carefully place the smoker body containing the water and the food on top. Lock it in place.

6. If cooking time is more than 5 or 6 hours, check to be sure the water has not evaporated. If it has, more will need to be added. There is usually an opening to allow access to the pan. Do not open and close the cover to check whether or not the food is smoking; each time the cover is lifted, more cooking time will have to be added.

7. Good-quality briquettes burn a long time. When the main food has been smoked, use the remaining coals to flavor nuts, cheeses and other foods, but first remove the water pan and the cooking grill. Add more aromatics to the coals, replace water pan and grill and then add whatever extra food you may wish to smoke.

There is no reason for any mishap with a charcoal water smoker if several rules are observed. They add up to common sense, but are emphasized here especially if children are to be around equipment.

1. Place the smoker away from buildings, trees and windows (very little smoke emerges from the smoker, but there will be some). Be sure the ground is level so the smoker won't tip over.

2. Without exception, charcoal *must not* be used for indoor cooking or heating. Toxic carbon monoxide fumes may build up to lethal levels. Do *not* use kerosene, gasoline, or alcohol to light the fire. Instead, use the simple Easy Ember-type cone to start a fire with newspaper and a match.

3. Do not leave ashes in the bowl between uses. Each time you use the smoker, dump the ashes after making sure the coals are dead. Also clean the equipment after each use. Simply wash the water pan and grills with warm water and soap, and use paper towels or old rags to remove the grease from inside the smoker.

4. Refrigerate smoked foods as soon as you can. It is permissible to keep the food warm in the smoker — for example, a roast that has been served and is waiting for seconds. But once the meal is completed, move all food into the refrigerator.

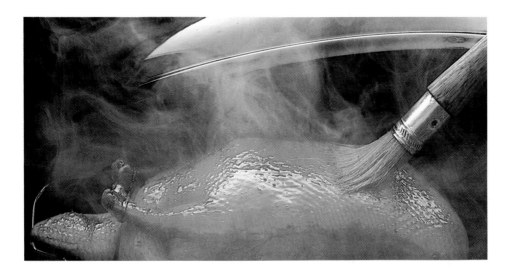

# SMOKED FETTUCCINE WITH FONTINA CHEESE

Serves 6

A covered grill or a smoker is required for this pasta and cheese dish, which goes well with many grilled preparations. For the best smoke flavor, soak a handful of hickory, apple or other hardwood chips in water for half an hour, then add them to the fire.

### INGREDIENTS

1 pound fettuccine
6 tablespoons butter
¼ cup freshly grated Parmesan cheese
12 ounces Fontina cheese, cut into ½-inch
    cubes or grated
1½ cups chicken stock
1 teaspoon whole cumin seed
2 tablespoons kirsch
freshly ground pepper
½ cup finely chopped parsley

1. Build a fire in the grill or smoker. While coals heat up, soak a handful of hardwood chips and bring a large pot of salted water to boil for pasta.

2. Cook the fettuccine until al dente. Drain and return to the pan. Add 4 tablespoons butter, cheeses, stock, cumin, kirsch, pepper and parsley and toss well.

3. Double-fold foil to make an open container approximately $6 \times 14 \times 1\frac{1}{2}$ inches. Coat the foil with the remaining 2 tablespoons butter. Place the fettuccine mixture in the container and spread it evenly.

4. Add wood chips to the fire. Place the container of pasta on the grill, close the cover and smoke until bubbly, about 20 minutes.

### Grating Parmesan

Hard cheeses such as Parmesan and Romano can be grated easily in a food processor. The cheese is easier to grate if it's at room temperature. Cut it into slices about 1 inch thick, then into 1-inch cubes. Fill the processor bowl about ¼ full of cheese cubes and pulse with the steel blade until the cheese resembles fine breadcrumbs. Store in a tightly covered jar in the refrigerator.

### Cumin

Essential in Mexican and Indian cooking and becoming more common in other cuisines, cumin is sold in seed or ground form and has a pungently aromatic flavor. Americans use it in chili and other Tex-Mex foods, which are popular these days. Ground cumin loses its flavor more quickly than the seed form. Mexican cooks believe that the seeds should be rubbed between the palms of the hands as they are added to foods to get the fullest flavor.

# SMOKED CORNISH HENS
# WITH TAWNY PORT
# AND RED CURRANT SAUCE

Serves 6

Add moistened wood chunks or chips to the fire; apple lends itself especially well but other aromatics will work too.

### INGREDIENTS

6 Cornish Game hens (1 pound each)
2 onions, thinly sliced
2 carrots, cut into 2 × ¼-inch julienne
1 celery stalk, cut into 2 × ¼-inch julienne
salt and freshly ground pepper
6 slices bacon, halved crosswise
tawny port and red currant sauce (see below)

1. Wash and dry hens inside and out. Evenly divide onions, carrots and celery and place inside hens; season with salt and pepper. Secure wings behind the birds' backs and tie legs together with string; cut strings off at knots to make them tidy. Cross 2 bacon strips over each hen's breast. Sprinkle with salt and pepper.

2. Ready the fire for the water smoker, with water pan ¾ full. Set hens on top of the grill. Cover and smoke for 3 hours, basting with the sauce during the last 15 minutes or so. To test for doneness, move a leg; if it rotates easily in socket, birds are cooked. Serve with remaining sauce.

## TAWNY PORT AND RED CURRANT SAUCE

Makes about 1 cup

½ cup tawny port
1 cup red currant jelly
½ teaspoon grated lemon zest
2 tablespoons red wine vinegar
salt and freshly ground pepper

Combine all ingredients in a small nonaluminum saucepan and stir over low heat until jelly melts.

---

*Red Currant Sauce*
*A well-chosen sauce can transform these birds into something special. Sophisticated or simple, original or traditional, a sauce adds individuality to food. In this case, the red currant sauce gives character to the smoked rock Cornish hens, perfumed on the inside by the sweetness of carrots and onions, perfumed again on the outside with red currant jelly and tawny port. This uncomplicated sauce, which also serves as a baste, is delicately sweet and sour and colors the birds as they smoke; it is a perfect match for young tender hens that retain their moisture during the smoking process. The sauce may be used with other poultry and is delicious with game birds, grilled venison and pork. Fresh red currants, almost translucent, are bright red and small (slightly smaller than blueberries). Dried currants, actually Corinth grapes, are a different fruit, and are used like raisins.*

---

# SMOKED BARBECUED PORK RIBS WITH MOLASSES

Serves 4 to 6

Best of all are pork baby back ribs; they are truly succulent.

### INGREDIENTS

1 rack of spareribs or baby back ribs (5 pounds)
⅓ cup red wine vinegar
¼ cup soy sauce
¼ cup dark molasses
⅓ cup Dijon mustard
1 tablespoon Worcestershire sauce
dash of hot pepper sauce or a pinch of red pepper flakes

1. Wipe rack of ribs and place in a large glass or ceramic dish.

2. Combine all remaining ingredients and mix well. Molasses, like honey, has a tendency to settle, so stir a few times while marinating. Pour mixture over ribs, coating both sides well. Marinate 4 to 5 hours at room temperature, or better, overnight in the refrigerator. Bring to room temperature before smoking.

3. Prepare the charcoal water smoker using about 7 pounds of charcoal for the fire and adding 4 quarts water to the water pan. Add hickory chunks or presoaked chips to the fire. Place ribs on grill above the water pan and pour marinade over ribs, allowing it to fall into the water. Close cover and smoke for about 3½ hours, adding more hickory chunks or chips as you wish. To test for doneness, cut off a rib and taste to see if it is done to your liking. The meat should be cooked through but still moist.

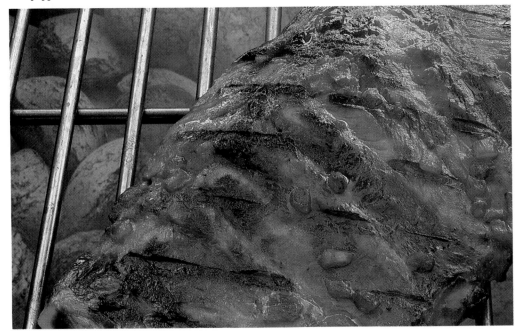

# SMOKED SCALLOPS
# AND SHRIMP
# IN PINK SAUCE
# OVER BRAZILIAN RICE

Serves 6

Clive DuVal, the chef/owner of Tila's Cantina & Taqueria in Houston, makes his own version of a smoker by boring holes in the bottom of a large wok. He places the wok on the grill over hot coals to smoke delicate seafood such as scallops, shrimp, lobster and fish fillets.

### INGREDIENTS

24 sea scallops
24 fresh shrimp (20 to 25 count)
5 tablespoons cracked black pepper
½ cup fresh lime juice
½ cup olive oil
pink sauce (see below)
Brazilian red rice (see below)
freshly grated Parmesan cheese
chopped parsley

1. Combine sea scallops, shrimp, pepper, lime and oil. Mix well and let stand at room temperature for 15 minutes. Remove seafood and reserve marinade.

2. Prepare smoker with medium-hot mesquite charcoal and 2 handfuls of cherrywood chips, soaked for 30 minutes. Add shrimp and smoke until shells turn pink, about 5 minutes. Remove and peel.

3. Place scallops in smoker and smoke until outside has a sweet, smoky flavor but inside is still moist and fresh, about 3 to 4 minutes.

4. Pour reserved marinade into large non-aluminum sauté pan and bring to boil. Add smoked scallops and shrimp and cook until almost done. Add pink sauce, bring to boil and remove from heat.

5. Place Brazilian rice on a large warm platter and cover with the shrimp and scallops. Sprinkle with Parmesan and parsley and serve immediately.

Makes about 4 cups

⅓ cup canned mango juice
2 large tomatoes, roasted, peeled and seeded
2 cups light cream or half and half
1 cup heavy cream
1 tablespoon minced fresh ginger
1 teaspoon oyster sauce
3 tablespoons unsalted butter
½ zucchini, sliced
4 mushrooms, sliced
2 poblano chilies, seeded and sliced
2 green onions, minced
2 garlic cloves, minced
1 jalapeño pepper, chopped
kernels from 1 ear of corn
1 pound fresh spinach, stemmed and chopped
¼ cup dry white wine
¼ cup orange liqueur
1 cup chicken stock
seasoning to taste: coarse salt, white pepper,
    chopped fresh basil, cayenne pepper and
    fresh lime juice

1. Puree first 6 ingredients in food processor and reserve.

2. In a large skillet, melt butter over medium-high heat and sauté zucchini, mushrooms, poblanos, garlic, jalapeño, corn and spinach until slightly soft. Deglaze with white wine. Add liqueur and simmer 1 minute. Add chicken stock and reserved puree and combine well.

3. Season to taste. Simmer until sauce thickly coats the back of a spoon.

Serves 6

2 tablespoons *achiote* (annatto) seeds*
1 tablespoon grated orange zest
1 tablespoon grated lime zest
¾ cup olive oil
1 small white onion, thinly sliced
2 garlic cloves, minced
2 teaspoons freshly ground white pepper
3 cups long-grain rice
3¼ cups chicken stock
juice of ½ orange
1 tablespoon paprika
1 small red and 1 small green bell pepper,
    stems, ribs and seeds removed, sliced
3 mushrooms, sliced
1 medium carrot, julienned

1. In a large ovenproof skillet, cook annatto seeds and grated zests in oil for 20 minutes over medium heat; oil will turn pink. Discard seeds. Sauté onion, garlic and white pepper in the oil until the vegetables are soft and translucent; take care not to burn garlic.

2. Add rice and stir to coat thoroughly with oil. Sauté until rice turns opaque. Add stock, orange juice, paprika and remaining vegetables.

3. Preheat oven to 450°F. Bring to a boil and stir carefully. Lower heat to medium and cook 5 minutes. Stir again carefully and cook until liquid has evaporated completely. Cover and bake for 10 minutes. Remove from oven and let stand, covered, for 10 more minutes before serving.

*found in food specialty stores

## SMOKED SALMON

Makes 16 to 24 appetizer servings

### INGREDIENTS

1 half salmon (about 5 to 6 pounds), cut lengthwise
2 tablespoons coarse salt
2 tablespoons cracked white peppercorns
fresh dill to cover surface of salmon (10 to 15 sprigs)

1. Place salmon skin side down on a flat work surface. Carefully run fingers over fish, barely touching it, to locate bones (once located, they usually run in a line down the length of the salmon). Extract each bone with long-nosed pliers by pulling straight out, gently pressing down on salmon around bone to help expose end of bone for easy removal. (You'll be amazed at how well this works; all bones can be removed in a couple of minutes.) When all bones are removed, wash and dry salmon.

2. Lay salmon skin side down and rub in salt and pepper. Press dill sprigs lightly onto salmon.

3. If using a kettle, square or rectangular grill with cover, smoke salmon over indirect heat. Center salmon over a drip pan skin side down, close cover and smoke for 1½ hours or until internal temperature reaches 140°F to 150°F. If using a charcoal water smoker, fill drip pan with water. Cooking time will be between 1 and 2 hours or until salmon flakes. Use a fork to test for doneness.

# SMOKED PORK CHOPS WITH HONEY AND SOY

Serves 4 to 6

All pork chops are not created equal. They will cost a few cents more, but buy center loin chops, called either loin or rib chops. These are the best quality and most tender.

### INGREDIENTS

8 rib pork chops, 1½ inches thick
¼ cup honey
½ cup soy sauce
1 tablespoon sesame-chili oil (available at Oriental markets), or substitute sesame oil and additional pepper
2 tablespoons grated fresh ginger
2 garlic cloves, minced
salt and freshly ground pepper

1. Remove excess fat from chops and check for stray pieces of bone or cartilage. Wipe chops dry. Arrange in one layer in a glass or ceramic dish.

2. Combine all remaining ingredients and mix until oil is combined. Pour over chops, turning all sides. Marinate for 2 hours at room temperature or overnight in refrigerator. Bring to room temperature before smoking.

3. If using kettle, square or rectangular grill with dome cover, smoke over indirect heat but first sear the chops directly over the coals for 2 to 3 minutes on each side. Then center them over a drip pan half filled with water and the remaining marinade. Close cover and smoke for about 1 hour; chops should be slightly pink inside and still moist.

---

*Pork Chops*
*The richest known food source of Vitamin $B_1$ (thiamine) is fresh pork. As for fat content, lean pork and lean beef are about on a par. Pork, of course, is considerably cheaper than beef, yet Americans eat about twice as much beef than pork. Look for lean, young chops when buying pork. If young, the fat is pure white, the meat a gray/pink. Older pork is usually not as firm as young pork and has a deeper coloration—rose to red. Also look for the small chop, another sign of the younger animal, and aim for the center-cut loin chops.*

## SMOKED RABBIT WITH WATERCRESS, FENNEL, TOASTED PINE NUTS AND BALSAMIC DRESSING

Serves 8

Rabbit, smoked in this way by Marcel Desaulnier, an outstanding chef in Williamsburg, Virginia, is simply delicious.

### INGREDIENTS

2 small dressed rabbits (about 2 pounds each)
½ cup coarse salt
2 tablespoons sugar
1 cup warm water
1 cup cool water
4 ounces pine nuts
¾ cup olive oil
¼ cup balsamic vinegar
salt and freshly ground pepper
3 large bunches (1 to 1¼ pounds) watercress,
    stemmed, washed and dried
1 large fennel bulb (1 pound), cored and cut
    into 1¼ × ⅛-inch strips
1 tablespoon fennel leaves

1. Remove all bones from rabbit except for leg bones. Trim away all tendons and sliver membrane from loins, tenderloins, hind leg and thigh section.

2. Dissolve salt and sugar in 1 cup warm water, then stir in 1 cup cool water.

3. Dip rabbit meat momentarily in the brine. Remove and drain on paper towels.

4. Line the center shelf of a smoker with parchment paper. Place rabbit meat on the parchment. Place shelf in the smoker and smoke rabbit for 3 hours. Remove from smoker, transfer to a baking sheet and bake for 5 minutes in a preheated 300°F oven. Cool rabbit at room temperature for a few minutes, then refrigerate for 30 to 40 minutes until thoroughly chilled. Cut into 1¼ × ¼-inch julienne strips. Refrigerate until needed.

5. Toast pine nuts on a baking sheet in a preheated 300°F oven for 15 minutes.

6. To prepare dressing, whisk together olive oil and balsamic vinegar. Adjust seasoning with salt and pepper.

7. Cover 8 chilled 9- to 10-inch plates with watercress. Sprinkle smoked rabbit and fennel julienne over watercress on each plate.

8. Drizzle 2 tablespoons dressing over each plate. Sprinkle with pine nuts and fennel leaves and serve.

## SMOKED CHICKEN WITH SASSAFRAS

Serves 4 to 6

Instead of using a smoker, you can also bake this in a 400°F oven for 1 hour; just layer the sassafras leaves above and below the chicken, advises the chef, Felipe Rojas-Lombardi.

### INGREDIENTS

1 chicken (3½ pounds), butterflied
2 garlic cloves
2 tablespoons coarse salt
¼ teaspoon freshly ground white pepper
⅛ teaspoon cayenne pepper
1 teaspoon ground cardamom
2 tablespoons fresh lemon juice
¼ cup olive oil
large bunch sassafras leaves*

1. Wash and dry chicken. Set aside.

2. In a mortar, grind garlic, salt, white pepper, cayenne pepper and cardamom to a paste. Stir in lemon juice, then olive oil.

3. Rub the chicken thoroughly, inside and out, with the spice mixture. Let stand at room temperature for 1 to 2 hours before smoking.

4. Prepare a fire in a covered grill. When fire is ready, place generous amount of sassafras, sticks and leaves, on the grid. Place chicken skin side up on top of the sassafras. Cover the entire chicken with more sassafras. Close the cover of the grill and smoke for about 1 hour. To check for doneness, pierce a joint; the juices should run clear.

5. Remove the chicken and sassafras from the fire and transfer to a large pan. Let stand for 10 minutes undisturbed. Then remove the sassafras and cut and serve the chicken.

*Sassafras leaves may be obtained in some specialty food shops, such as Dean & DeLuca in New York.

---

*Seeds of Paradise*
*A pretty name in the Orient for cardamom, a popular spice carried from Asia to Europe over the old overland spice routes. A member of the ginger family, it was used by the Greeks and Romans to make perfume. Today we use dried pods, which come in different colors and sizes. Tiny seeds are inside the pods; they are often bleached to present a more palatable color. You probably know their flavor in liqueurs, pastries, teas, coffees and curries. Here is an unusual use of the spice.*

# SMOKED ROCK CORNISH HENS WITH ORANGE-SHERRY GLAZE

Serves 6

The taste of smoked poultry is changed considerably by the addition of aromatic wood chunks or chips. When you're ready to start grilling, try adding 1½ cups chips, presoaked for 30 minutes, to the fire. Hickory chips are flavorful here; if you want a less pronounced hickory flavor, decrease the amount of chips. The marination is optional. Even without it, the hens will be moist, tender and richly colored.

### INGREDIENTS

6 rock Cornish game hens (a little over 1 pound each), cleaned and giblets removed
2 cups chicken stock
2 garlic cloves, sliced
1 onion, sliced
½ cup soy sauce
¼ cup vegetable oil, optional

### GLAZE

⅓ cup fresh orange juice
⅓ cup sweet sherry
¼ cup soy sauce
⅓ cup orange marmalade

1. Rinse hens and dry well. If you plan to marinate them, combine chicken stock, garlic, onion and soy sauce. Add enough water to make mixture fill the smoker's water pan. Place hens in mixture and marinate in refrigerator overnight. If you plan to smoke hens without marinating them, rub oil all over them and set aside at room temperature.

2. Prepare the fire in a covered grill. When fire is ready, pour marinade into water pan and set it in place in the smoker.

3. Arrange hens on grid in smoker. Close cover and smoke for about 2½ hours; hens are done when legs move easily in their sockets.

4. One hour before hens are cooked, combine glaze ingredients in a saucepan and boil briskly to reduce by ⅓. Brush birds liberally with glaze several times during last 30 minutes of smoking. Serve warm or cold.

---

*Smoke Rings*
*To preserve meat, it was once cured, smoked or aged. Rather than preservation, the primary concern today is taste. Smoking procedures are considered top secret by some people. Flavor depends on the type of wood used. Hickory is suggested here, but some grill experts prefer oak chips, some juniper, others beech. Try them all and then decide. Remember, the process smoking adds flavor, color and character.*

# SMOKED DUCK
# WITH SMOKED GARLIC SAUCE

Serves 12

This recipe is from Carolyn Buster, talented chef/owner of The Cottage restaurant in Calumet City, Illinois. The stuffing of fruits and vegetables and an apple cider marinade result in slightly sweet, fruity and very moist birds.

### INGREDIENTS

4 ducks (4 to 4½ pounds each)
spiced butter (see below)
2 cups each chopped celery, onions, carrots,
    tart apples and oranges
1 large bunch parsley, chopped
1 gallon apple cider
4 whole garlic bulbs
smoked garlic sauce (see below)

1. Wash ducks inside and out; dry thoroughly. Generously rub inside of ducks with some of the butter mixture. Combine celery, onions, carrots, apples, oranges and parsley and pack into cavities of ducks. Place an additional dollop of spiced butter on top and some into skin. Stand ducks tail end up in a stainless steel or plastic container and pour cider over. Top with a weight if necessary to keep ducks submerged in liquid. Marinate in refrigerator for 18 to 24 hours.

2. Prepare fire in smoker and arrange some soaked hickory, mesquite or osage chips over fuel. Place water pan in position and fill ⅔ full with some of the marinade. Position ducks on rack above water pan, breast side out and tail end up. Place whole heads of garlic in center.

3. Cover smoker and smoke for approximately 2½ hours, turning duck breasts to inside after 30 minutes. It may be necessary to rotate ducks if smoker has hot spots.

4. Remove ducks and cool to room temperature. Peel garlic cloves.

5. Set 2 ounces of smoked garlic aside. Skim fat from smoking juices and transfer to a skillet (reserve juices for sauce). Place over medium-high heat, add remaining garlic cloves and sauté until golden brown.

6. Bone the ducks. Gently warm the breasts in a small amount of sauce with a few sautéed garlic cloves. Thinly slice warmed meat and arrange on plates. Spoon sauce around meat and add a little on top. Garnish with remaining garlic cloves and serve.

## SPICED BUTTER

Makes 2 pounds

2 pounds softened butter
2 shallots, minced
6 garlic cloves, minced
1 tablespoon chopped parsley
1 tablespoon black peppercorns
2 teaspoons salt
1 teaspoon chili powder
½ teaspoon dried oregano
½ teaspoon ground cumin
¼ teaspoon ground coriander
1 teaspoon curry powder
1 teaspoon dried basil
4 dashes Worcestershire sauce
4 dashes hot pepper sauce

Combine all ingredients in processor or electric mixer bowl and blend well.

## SMOKED GARLIC SAUCE

Makes 4½ to 5 cups

4 cups strained duck smoking juices
1 cup red currant jelly
½ teaspoon salt
⅛ teaspoon ground ginger
¼ teaspoon cinnamon
2 bay leaves
pinch of ground cloves
¼ teaspoon white pepper
2 ounces peeled smoked garlic, pureed (3 tablespoons)
⅔ cup port
2 to 3 tablespoons cornstarch

Strain smoking juices through cheesecloth. Place strained juices in saucepan and add all remaining ingredients except wine and cornstarch. Simmer for 15 minutes. Combine cornstarch with enough wine to make a thin paste; gradually stir in remaining wine. Add mixture to sauce and stir over medium heat until thickened. Strain again if you wish.

## SMOKED DUCK
## WITH HONEY-ORANGE GLAZE

Serves 6

### INGREDIENTS

2 ducklings (4 to 5 pounds each)
3 oranges
8 green onions
8 parsley sprigs
2 garlic cloves, crushed
¼ cup honey
⅔ cup soy sauce

**1.** Wash ducklings under cool water inside and out; drain and dry well. If using frozen ducks, be sure they are fully thawed.

**2.** Peel 2 of the oranges; finely chop enough zest to make 2 teaspoons. Squeeze ¼ cup juice from the remaining orange.

**3.** Place a whole peeled orange inside cavity of each duck along with 4 green onions, 4 parsley sprigs and 2 garlic cloves. Puncture duck skin between breast and wing joints to allow fat to drain off. Tie legs and tail together and cut off excess string to tidy. Secure wings behind back, and flap excess neck skin over the back to tidy it also.

**4.** Prepare the fire in the smoker. Insert the water pan, filled with 6 quarts water, and set food grid in place. Arrange ducks on grid (use 2 levels if you wish), cover securely and smoke for about 5 hours, until legs move easily in sockets and the ducks' juices run clear.

**5.** In a saucepan, combine honey, reserved orange juice, orange zest and soy sauce and heat through to make the glaze. Glaze the ducks liberally several times during the last hour of smoking.

### Soy Sauce

A most common ingredient in marinades and barbecue sauces, soy sauce has been enthusiastically adopted in the U.S. The soybean, native to southeast Asia, was cultivated as early as 3000 B.C. in China. Now it is grown all over the world and many consider it the single most important crop. Rich in protein and oil, it has many uses in the culinary and industrial worlds. To make soy sauce, cooked soybeans and wheat or barley flour are salted and fermented. The resultant liquid, salty and dark brown with a taste of reduced bouillon, is soy sauce. Its influence in grilling is so strong that it is difficult to imagine cooking without it; soy sauce has become an American staple like olive oil and red wine vinegar.

# SMOKED SPICY BEEF

Serves 8

The meat will be moist, tender and full of flavor. If you wish, double the marinade recipe and keep half of it in a covered jar in the refrigerator. At serving time, heat it and serve with the beef as a barbecue sauce.

### INGREDIENTS

4 pounds beef chuck, boned and most fat
    removed
⅓ cup catsup
⅓ cup soy sauce
⅓ cup sherry vinegar
1 tablespoon dry mustard
¼ cup vegetable oil
1 large garlic clove, minced
salt and freshly ground pepper

**1.** Put meat in a glass or ceramic dish and set aside.

**2.** In a bowl, combine catsup, soy sauce, vinegar and mustard and whisk until well mixed. Add remaining ingredients and whisk again until oil is emulsified. Pour over meat, turning to coat all sides. Cover securely with plastic wrap and refrigerate overnight, turning meat several times. Bring meat to room temperature before smoking.

**3.** Prepare a charcoal fire in the water smoker. When it is ready, add 4 to 5 quarts water to the water pan. Set grill over water pan. Place meat on grill and pour remaining marinade over the meat into the water pan. (No aromatic chunks or chips are needed on the fire, as the marinade provides lots of flavor, but hickory can be added if you like.) Smoke for about 5 hours, checking water pan after 4 hours or so. (Beef will be cooked through and will appear well done.) Serve beef hot or cold.

---

*Dry Mustard*

"Mustard as we know it today is the innovation of an obscure old lady simply known as Mrs. Clements of Durham (England)."* It was her idea, in 1729, to grind mustard seeds in a mill exactly like wheat. She sold them as fine powder and is supposed to have made a small fortune from what people called "Durham mustard" all over England. Mrs. Clements was able to secure the patronage of King George I.

Dry mustard is usually prepared by adding water to the powder, making a smooth paste, similar to custard in consistency. These days, dry mustards are combined with wines or vinegars, cider or cream, herbs or spices, onions or garlic, or any combination of these. Dry mustard is used as an ingredient for "dry" rubs, in marinades, sauces and accompaniments when preparing meats or fish for the grill or serving them after grilling. With good effect it is combined here with other flavoring agents to smoke beef chuck.

*Simon and Howe: Dictionary of Gastronomy, McGraw-Hill, 1970.

## DAMSON PLUM-GLAZED SMOKED HAM

Serves 12 to 16

### INGREDIENTS

1 fully cooked ham (12 pounds)
whole cloves
1 bottle (750mL) port
8 ounces (1 cup) damson plum jelly
2 teaspoons dry mustard
1 tablespoon grated orange or lemon zest
horseradish cream sauce (see page 309)

1. Cut off the rind, if any, of the ham. With a sharp knife, score fat into 1-inch squares or diamonds. Insert a clove wherever the lines cross, covering the entire top side of ham. Place on a platter and pour several table-spoons port over ham, several times.

2. Prepare a fire in the water smoker. When ready, add 1 quart water to the water pan. Set rack on top and place ham on the rack. Pour any wine on the platter over the ham, allowing it to fall into the water pan. Add all but ¼ cup port to the water pan. Cover and smoke for 3½ hours.

3. Combine reserved ¼ cup port, jelly, mustard and citrus zest in a small saucepan over medium-low heat and stir until jelly is dissolved. Remove from heat. Brush glaze thickly over ham 2 or 3 times during the last 30 minutes of smoking.

4. Serve with horseradish cream sauce.

> *Zest of Orange or Lemon*
> *The zest is the colored part of the rind, with almost no pith (the white, bitter layer under the skin). Special zest peelers are available and work well but you can easily use an ordinary vegetable peeler without cutting deeply into the pith. Use the zest as fresh as can be—that is, as soon as it is peeled away and minced, as I use it in this recipe. But dried zest works well, too, as its flavor lasts a long time.*

## SMOKED GRAPEVINE-SCENTED TURKEY

Serves 12 to 16

Grapevine cuttings impart an unusually delicate and sweet flavor to turkey and other foods. Vine cuttings are becoming easier to buy for those who don't live near vineyards; many come from California and other wine-growing regions.

### INGREDIENTS

1 fresh or thawed frozen turkey (10 to 12 pounds)
salt and freshly ground pepper
2 cups grapevine cuttings
1 cup dry vermouth
2 tablespoons chopped fresh rosemary or 1 tablespoon dried

1. Wash the turkey inside and out. (The giblets are not needed for this recipe.) Dry the bird and season liberally with salt and pepper. Bring to room temperature while preparing the fire. Insert meat thermometer into thickest part of leg, avoiding the bone, if you prefer to gauge doneness this way.

2. Start some charcoal in chimney-type starter, and when red hot, place in the smoker firebowl. Add as much additional charcoal as the bowl will hold, about 10 to 12 pounds.

3. Place vine cuttings in another bowl and cover with water. Soak 30 minutes — about as long as it will take the coals to be ready for smoking.

4. Drain about ½ cup vine cuttings and place on top of the coals. When the fire is ready, place 5 quarts hot tap water, vermouth and rosemary into water pan of smoker. Set cooking grid in place and put turkey on it. Secure cover and smoke for 5 to 7 hours, or until the bird's legs move easily in their sockets and juices run clear; add ½ cup drained vine cuttings every hour or so (add through the window, if your smoker has one, and not by removing the cover).

*Carving the Smoked or Spit-Roasted Turkey*
*Think ahead and decide how the carved turkey will be served. On individual plates? On a large (warmed) platter? Arrange to have the plates or platter nearby. Transfer turkey to a carving board, countertop or any comfortable place. Do not try to carve on the small arm or shelf of a grill.*

*Place the turkey directly in front of you. Insert a large fork into the top of the breast and slice down through the joint where the legs join the body to remove the legs.*

*Slice down where the wings are attached to the body to remove the wings.*

*Cut down from the breast tip at an angle following the body curve to produce even slices. Repeat with other side when needed.*

# VEGETABLES

Vegetables are beautiful things to look at and to grill. What can compare to the shape, color or gleam of a glistening, deep purple eggplant? A smooth-as-silk bright red tomato? The soft patina of a white mushroom? The gentle orange of carrots, with soft green fern-like tops? A family of garlic cloves? The freshness of pale green chicory leaves? Forest-green clusters of broccoli? The heavenly layers of endive leaves? The beauty and mystery of the inner rings of an onion? The variety is infinite. There are so many vegetables and so many ways to grill them.

But there are also many things to consider — first at the vegetable stand, where your job begins. Don't select vegetables that are bruised, wilted or damaged in any way. Improper handling and bruises destroy vitamins. Not every grocery store or even green-grocer receives fresh vegetables every day. Learn about your store's shipments so you can shop on the days when the produce is freshest. It follows, of course, that you should eat the fresh vegetables as soon as you can to get the most vitamins; deterioration begins after about five days.

Vegetables should be stored in a cool, humid place until ready for use; it is not necessary to wash them before storage. Rinse the vegetables in cool water before eating. Do *not* soak them, as soaking draws out essential vitamins.

Try not to peel vegetables unless it is necessary; scrubbing is better to preserve nutrients. When the peel of a zucchini is scraped away, all the vitamins go down the drain. It is not necessary to peel eggplant. And why not boil potatoes with their skins on, or slice them unpeeled for grilling? There has been much in the literature about the need for dietary fiber, and one solution is to retain as much of the skin as possible. Grill vegetables instead of boiling them to retain more nutrients; even frozen vegetables lose fewer vitamins if they are cooked over fire, not in water.

Vegetable Grilling Guideline

- Select dark green, yellow and orange vegetables, fresh or frozen.

- Pass by damaged or wilted produce.

- Refrigerate fresh vegetables without washing.

- Prepare vegetables shortly before serving time. Avoid peeling or soaking.

- Rinse and scrub vegetables instead of peeling. Trim away as little as possible.

- Remember that grilling causes minimal loss of nutrients.

# GRILLED ARTICHOKES
# WITH WHOLE GARLIC BULBS

Serves 6

Garlic becomes sweet when it is grilled; the taste is quite different from that of its raw state. Release the cooked clove by squeezing it out of the skin, as in skinning almonds, or lay the whole bulb on its side and press down to release the pulp all at once. The butter, oil, salt and pepper add more flavor as the garlic cooks. It's a natural companion to the artichoke; spread the garlic on toast or on the artichoke leaves themselves.

### INGREDIENTS

6 whole garlic bulbs
6 fresh artichokes
juice of 1 lemon
½ tablespoon unsalted butter
⅓ cup olive oil
6 sprigs fresh thyme or 2 teaspoon dried
salt and freshly ground pepper

1. Remove papery skin from outside of garlic, leaving bulbs whole. With a sharp knife, slice off top quarter of each bulb to expose the top ends of the cloves.

2. Trim the artichokes with scissors by snipping off the points of the outside leaves. Cut off stem end and top quarter of artichokes. Quarter the artichokes and immediately immerse in cool water acidulated with the lemon juice. Keep the artichokes submerged by laying a plate on top of them in the bowl.

3. Cut 6 sheets of heavy-duty foil about 12 inches square. Place 1 garlic bulb and 4 artichoke quarters on each sheet, lifting artichoke pieces directly out of their bath to the foil without draining. Add 2 tablespoons butter, some on the garlic but most of it on the artichoke quarters, and sprinkle some oil overall. Place herb sprig across artichoke and garlic, season with salt and pepper, and secure package with drugstore wrap (see page 18).

4. When fire is ready, place packets on grid over hot coals and cook for about 40 minutes, turning carefully several times. Serve directly from foil.

**Artichokes**

Don't keep artichokes in acidulated water for more than 30 minutes or they'll taste sour. Drain and rinse the artichokes before placing them in the cooking liquid.

Use stainless steel knives when working with artichokes. And use vessels of stainless steel, glass or ceramic, otherwise the artichokes will darken unattractively. Cook artichokes all the way through; undercooked ones will be discolored and hard.

# SWEET AND SOUR
# COLE SLAW

Serves 8

### INGREDIENTS

2 pounds cabbage, shredded
1 medium onion, finely chopped
1 medium bell pepper, finely chopped
2 tablespoons sugar
½ cup white wine vinegar
½ cup vegetable oil
1 teaspoon salt
1 teaspoon dry mustard
1 teaspoon celery seed

1. Combine cabbage, onion, pepper and sugar and mix well.

2. In a nonaluminum saucepan, bring the remaining ingredients to a boil. Remove from heat and pour over slaw. Cover and refrigerate for 2 hours before serving.

---

*Cabbage*
*A cabbage is mature when it starts to split and when it develops an odor. Buy tender young cabbage; they don't smell as strong and their leaves are tightly packed. Remove outer leaves, and note that there is less waste on a younger head because fewer leaves have to be discarded.*

---

# GRILLED BUTTERED
# TURNIPS

Serves 4 to 6

Many people do not like turnips — and if they are just boiled, they may have a point. But the vegetable takes on a different flavor when grilled, and they couldn't be easier to prepare.

### INGREDIENTS

6 turnips (about 1 pound)
2 tablespoons butter
salt and freshly ground pepper

1. Clean and trim turnips and place in a saucepan. Add water just to cover. Bring to boil, lower heat and simmer until turnips are barely cooked. (Insert knife to test for doneness; it should meet just a little resistance.) Drain turnips and cut into ½-inch-thick slices. Lay the slices flat and dot with butter.

2. Grill the slices on both sides until they show grill marks. Add salt and pepper and serve immediately.

# GRILLED WHITE CHICORY
# WITH OLIVE OIL
# AND SMOKED MOZZARELLA

Serves 4

## INGREDIENTS

4 heads of green chicory
4 tablespoons olive oil
4 thin slices smoked mozzarella

1. Remove the green leaves from each head of chicory so only the hearts are left. Trim each head, wash and drain. It is not necessary to dry the chicory if it is well drained.

2. Heat a gas-fired flattop until very hot. Place the 4 heads of chicory on the grill and sprinkle each with 1 tablespoon oil. With a spatula, press down on each head and cook for about 30 seconds. Quickly turn and, pressing down with the spatula again, grill for about 15 seconds. The chicory will begin to brown in this time if the heat is high.

3. Just before removing the chicory from the flattop, add a slice of mozzarella to each head; in a few seconds, the cheese will begin to melt. Serve immediately.

---

*Chicory*
*What we in the U.S. know as chicory is called endive in England and elsewhere. A beautiful pink-and-red chicory called* Cicoria di Treviso, *grown in Italy, is also popular in France and Switzerland. The vegetable has a touch of bitterness and, although it is most popular as a salad green, be sure to try it grilled.*

---

*Grilled Chicory - Cantinori*
*Lavagna is the Italian word for slate. This black stone from Liguria is a key piece of equipment at Il Cantinori, a Tuscan restaurant on East 10th Street in New York City. Pino Luongo said the slate is first oiled, then heated in the broiler until almost literally red hot. At this point it is put on a heatproof countertop, and there vegetables of almost any description are grilled. The* lavagna *stays hot enough to grill for at least 30 minutes. Nothing other than a little oil and black pepper is added; the object is to allow the individual flavors to sing. A gas-fired flattop grill can be substituted for slate with excellent results.*
*Other vegetables can be grilled using the same technique as the one given here for white chicory. Consider using radicchio, Belgian endive, raw sliced fennel, sliced beets (but steam them first), raw turnip slices, small whole fresh leeks, sliced eggplants, fresh asparagus spears or sliced raw zucchini. Add a sprinkle of olive oil and, if you like it, black pepper. Salt is really not necessary, but if you insist, add it after the vegetable is removed from the grill.*

## BUTTERED FRESH CORN

Serves 4

The fresher the corn the better. To vary it, add to the packet a fresh herb of your choice; basil is delightful. Chop the herb and sprinkle over the buttered corn before closing the packet.

### INGREDIENTS

8 ears very fresh corn
softened butter
salt and freshly ground pepper

1. Husk the corn and put 2 ears on each of 4 heavy-duty foil sheets large enough to securely envelop the ears.

2. Spread 1 tablespoon butter on each ear of corn, covering all sides.

3. Salt and pepper the corn on all sides. Sprinkle a few drops of water over the corn in each package. Fold over the foil to make snug packages.

4. Place corn on the grill for about 10 minutes, turning the packets 3 times so that each faces the heat for about 2½ minutes. Serve with additional butter, salt and pepper.

## FRESH CRANBERRIES WITH ORANGE ZEST AND WHITE WINE

Serves 6

This complements smoked, spit-roasted or grilled poultry and pork.

### INGREDIENTS

2 cups fresh cranberries
2 tablespoons finely chopped orange zest
½ cup sugar
½ cup dry white wine
salt

1. Pick over cranberries, rinse and drain well. Put in a bowl.

2. Add zest, sugar, wine and salt to taste and mix well. Transfer to a foil tray. Cover tray with a piece of foil.

3. Cook at edge of grill over indirect heat until cranberries pop and sugar is dissolved, about 30 minutes. (Or cook over heat but cut time in half.) Serve as a relish.

# ORZO WITH RED BELL PEPPERS AND CURRANTS

Serves 4

### INGREDIENTS

½ cup currants
½ cup dry white wine
1 red bell pepper, stem, ribs and seeds removed,
    cut into ¼-inch dice
3 tablespoons olive oil
3 tablespoons butter
2 green onions, thinly sliced
salt and freshly ground pepper
1 cup orzo
½ cup freshly grated Parmesan cheese,
    optional

1. Combine currants and wine and let stand for about 30 minutes.

2. Sauté red pepper in the olive oil and 1 tablespoon butter for 4 to 5 minutes. Add currants and wine and bring to boil; simmer a few minutes longer to cook off some of the wine. Add green onions. Season with salt and pepper to taste.

3. Cook orzo in boiling salted water until al dente, about 10 minutes; drain. Add remaining 2 tablespoons butter to pan in which orzo cooked, return orzo to pan and toss to coat. Stir in currant mixture and top with Parmesan if desired.

Variation: Substitute 2 small (1 × 6-inch) zucchini for red pepper. Cut zucchini into ¼-inch dice and proceed as above.

# ASSORTED GRILLED VEGETABLES WITH ROUILLE SAUCE

Serves 6

### INGREDIENTS

2 yellow bell peppers
12 cherry tomatoes
3 zucchini, 1 x 6 inches each
12 artichoke hearts, quartered, fresh or bottled
juice of 1 lime
½ cup olive oil
1 teaspoon finely chopped fresh thyme or ½
    teaspoon dried
salt and freshly ground pepper
Rouille sauce (see page 311)

1. Wash and dry the vegetables. Cut peppers in 1¼-inch lengths. Trim artichoke hearts and remove tomato stems, if necessary.

2. Combine lime juice, oil, salt and pepper in a large bowl. Add vegetables and toss.

3. Soak 6 wood skewers in water for ½ hour. Thread skewers with vegetables in a pattern suited to your taste.

4. When fire is ready, grill vegetables until done, turning carefully as needed. Use any leftover oil/lime juice to baste vegetables while grilling.

5. Serve grilled vegetables on skewers and pass sauce. Sauce should be put on individual plates by tablespoon(s) to the side of skewered vegetables.

# GRILLED EGGPLANT WITH CAPER AND ANCHOVY SAUCE

Serves 6

This can be made ahead of time — in fact, it is more flavorful that way. Allow grilled eggplant rolls to marinate in sauce before serving.

### INGREDIENTS

2 small eggplants (about 12 ounces each)
salt
⅓ cup olive oil

### SAUCE

½ cup olive oil
¼ cup red wine vinegar
1 anchovy
2 garlic cloves, minced
¼ cup chopped parsley
2 tablespoons chopped shallot
2 tablespoons drained capers
freshly ground pepper

1. Cut the ends off the eggplants but leave them unpeeled. Stand each on end and cut lengthwise into ¼-inch slices. Salt lightly, lay in colander and allow to drain for about 30 minutes. Dry each slice. Brush oil on both sides and grill slices over a medium-hot fire until tender, turning once; do not char. Remove slices as they are cooked and roll up each one. Set on a platter.

2. For the sauce, combine oil and vinegar, then mash in the anchovy. Add garlic, parsley, shallot, capers and pepper. Pour over eggplant rolls and let marinate at least 30 minutes. Serve at room temperature.

## GRILLED EGGPLANT WITH CHINESE BLACK VINEGAR

Serves 6

Arecipe from Selma Nemer, chef/owner of Eartha's Kitchen in Saratoga, N.Y., who says that these eggplant slices are also delicious served on a base of shredded lettuce or cellophane noodles lightly tossed with sesame oil.

Makes about 1 cup

INGREDIENTS

6 tablespoons Chinese black vinegar
4 teaspoons sugar or honey
2 tablespoons chopped fresh coriander
½ cup sesame oil
1 tablespoon chili paste with garlic

Combine vinegar, sugar or honey and coriander in a small bowl. Slowly whisk in the sesame oil; continue whisking until emulsified. Whisk in chili paste. (Alternatively, combine all ingredients in a processor and blend until emulsified.)

INGREDIENTS

6 small eggplants
½ cup (about) extra virgin olive oil
½ cup soy sauce
Chinese black vinegar sauce (see below)
green onion flowers and pickled ginger for
    garnish

1. If Chinese eggplants are used, cut them lengthwise into ¾-inch-thick slices; if regular eggplants, slice into ¾-inch rounds. Brush both sides with olive oil and let stand while preparing fire. When fire is ready, grill eggplant until tender, 3 to 4 minutes per side, basting constantly with soy sauce and oil. Grilling will take less than 10 minutes.

2. Place eggplant on a large platter and spoon some Chinese black vinegar sauce over. Garnish with green onion and pickled ginger and serve.

---

*Eggplant*

Mela insana, *which means "raging apple," was the Italian name for eggplant for many, many years. It was always soaked in water and salt to remove its "insanity." I salt and drain it not because its juice is poisonous, but because I want it less bitter. Most young, small eggplants do not require this treatment so look for small Italian, Japanese and Chinese types. Larger ones will almost always need salting and draining. Look for eggplants with the lovely green capelike bracts and stems firmly attached; if the bracts are loose, the eggplant has aged and started to spoil. Be sure the vegetable is firm. Eggplant is very popular for grilling and the treatment is usually simple — often just a smear of good olive oil, salt and pepper.*

# GRILLED BELGIAN ENDIVE WITH PINK AND GREEN PEPPERCORN MOUSSELINE

Serves 6

A wonderful way with endive as prepared by Selma Nemer.

### INGREDIENTS

½ cup extra virgin olive oil
2 tablespoons soy sauce
6 fresh Belgian endive, halved lengthwise
1 small bunch arugula, stemmed
peppercorn mousseline sauce (see below)
12 thin red bell pepper slices for garnish

1. Combine olive oil and soy sauce and brush over endive.

2. Prepare the fire, adding mesquite, cherry or applewood chips that have been soaked in water at least 30 minutes. Grill the endive cut side down for about 3 minutes, basting with oil and soy marinade. Turn and baste again for another 3 minutes.

3. Line individual plates with arugula leaves. Place grilled endive on arugula. Add a dollop of peppercorn mousseline and garnish with red pepper strips.

Makes about 1½ cups

This is a versatile sauce. Omit the peppercorns and add grated orange zest and some juice to create an orange mousseline, or do the same with grated fresh ginger for a ginger mousseline. All are particularly good accompaniments to grilled fish.

### INGREDIENTS

12 pink peppercorns
12 green peppercorns
⅓ cup dry white wine
2 tablespoons chopped fresh tarragon
¼ cup Dijon mustard
2 tablespoons tarragon mustard
salt and freshly ground pepper
2 egg yolks
2 tablespoons softened butter
½ cup heavy cream, whipped to soft peaks

1. Combine peppercorns and wine and let steep for 10 minutes.

2. In the top of a double boiler, combine the tarragon, mustards, salt, pepper and egg yolks. Whisk over gently simmering water until mixture is pale yellow and tripled in volume, and until it ribbons when dropped from the whisk.

3. Remove from heat, whisk in the butter and cool.

4. Fold in the whipped cream and drained peppercorns. Chill until ready to use.

# GRILLED BELGIAN ENDIVE, ITALIAN PORCINI MUSHROOMS AND JAPANESE EGGPLANT WITH GINGER SOY SAUCE

Serves 4

Each vegetable is worth grilling. Together, they create an international taste sensation, especially when napped with the ginger soy sauce.

### SAUCE

### INGREDIENTS

1 tablespoon peanut oil
1 tablespoon chili oil
4 green onions, thinly sliced
2 tablespoons grated fresh ginger
⅓ cup dry vermouth
⅓ cup soy sauce

### VEGETABLES

### INGREDIENTS

2 Belgian endive, trimmed and halved
   lengthwise
8 large fresh porcini (2 to 3 inches in
   diameter), stemmed
2 Japanese eggplants, stemmed and cut into
   ¼-inch lengthwise slices
½ cup (or more) olive oil
salt and freshly ground pepper

1. For sauce, heat oils in a skillet, add green onion and ginger and sauté over medium heat until onion softens. Add the vermouth and soy sauce and bring to boil. Reduce heat and simmer for a few minutes. Remove from heat and keep warm.

2. For vegetables, brush each piece with olive oil on both sides; sprinkle with salt and pepper to taste. Grill over a hot fire for 5 to 6 minutes or until tender, turning 2 or 3 times and removing vegetables as they are cooked. Place the cooked pieces on a sheet of heavy foil, off the grill. When all are done, close foil and return to grill for reheating.

3. To serve, pour sauce onto a warm platter. Arrange grilled vegetables on top in a pattern to suit your fancy.

# SHIITAKE MUSHROOMS
## *ALLA GRIGLIA*

Serves 4 to 6

Mushrooms are ideal for grilling. Use all kinds and decide which you like best.

### INGREDIENTS

1½ cups chicken stock
½ cup dry white wine
2 tablespoons butter
salt and freshly ground pepper
1 pound fresh shiitake mushrooms
¼ cup olive oil
2 garlic cloves, halved

1. Combine chicken stock and wine in a saucepan and boil over high heat until reduced by ⅔. Whisk in butter bit by bit and season to taste.

2. Trim mushrooms and cut stems so caps can lie flat on the grid. Place in one layer in a glass or ceramic container. Heat the oil in a small saucepan or skillet, add garlic and sauté until it begins to turn color. Discard garlic and pour oil over the mushrooms. When oil has cooled, rub it all over the mushrooms with your hands.

3. When the fire is ready, grill the mushrooms about 2 minutes per side. When ready to serve, spoon 2 tablespoons sauce onto each of 4 warmed plates and top with several grilled mushrooms. Salt and pepper to taste and serve immediately.

*Mushrooms*
*Mushrooms should be firm, clean and unblemished, without gray spots. Buy them loose, not prepackaged; as with strawberries, the top layer is often for show, with the lower ones of lesser quality. Besides, it's fun to reach into the bin and handpick each mushroom. It is not necessary to peel them; instead wipe or brush lightly. Trim the stems and use the trimmings in soups and stocks. There are wonderful varieties of mushrooms in the markets today, many of them imported and costly. Try shiitakes, porcinis and chanterelles — they all grill beautifully.*

## ONION PIECES
## IN PARCHMENT

Serves 4

Transferring grilled onions from grill to plate can be messy. This technique allows the onions to steam with butter, salt and pepper, and it makes a pleasant presentation.

### INGREDIENTS

4 medium onions, trimmed, peeled and each
　　cut into 8 wedges or slices
4 teaspoons butter
salt and freshly ground pepper

**1.** Arrange the onion pieces using the equivalent of 1 onion per serving on 4 sheets of parchment paper about 11 × 16 inches. Add a teaspoon of butter and salt and pepper to taste. Secure envelope-style (see page 18).

**2.** Make a charcoal fire but allow coals to burn down until heat is medium or less. Lay a double fold of foil on grid and place parchment packets on top. Close cover; thermometer should read around 400°F. Onions will be ready in about 20 minutes. (If temperature is lower, count on considerably more time before they cook.) Serve onions directly in packets.

## FRESH SHELLED PEAS
## WITH BUTTER AND MINT

Serves 6

This is a summertime dish but prepare it whenever fresh peas are available. It will also work with thawed frozen peas; use two 10-ounce packages. Vary the packet by adding 1 cup sliced water chestnuts or 1 tablespoon finely chopped candied ginger.

### INGREDIENTS

2 pounds fresh peas in the shell
2 small heads limestone lettuce, finely shredded
4 tablespoons unsalted butter, cut into ¼-inch
　　cubes
¼ cup finely chopped fresh mint
4 shallots or 6 green onions, thinly sliced
2 teaspoons sugar
salt and freshly ground pepper

**1.** Shell peas and place in a bowl. Add the shredded lettuce, butter, mint, shallots or green onions, sugar, salt and pepper. Mix well with splayed fingers.

**2.** Cut a sheet of heavy-duty foil about 18 inches square and pile pea mixture in center. Secure with a drugstore fold (see page 18). When fire is ready, place packet on grill 5 to 6 inches above heat source. Cook for about 20 minutes, turning once.

# ROASTED PEPPER AND EGGPLANT DIP

Serves 4 to 6 as dip, 1 to 2 as vegetable

Red or green peppers are grilled until their skins blacken; this brings out their flavor and makes them more digestible. Combined with baked eggplant, they make an unusual, rich-tasting puree that can be used as a dip, served with pita bread or as a side dish with grills, kebabs or cold meats. Nicola Cox has given us this recipe.

### INGREDIENTS

1 large eggplant
1 to 2 garlic cloves, halved lengthwise
2 red or green bell peppers
½ teaspoon coriander seeds
½ teaspoon salt
4 to 6 tablespoons olive oil
1 to 2 tablespoons fresh lemon juice

1. Preheat oven to 425°. Make knife slits in the eggplant and tuck in the garlic deeply. Grease a baking sheet and place the eggplant on it. Bake for 20 to 30 minutes until the eggplant is soft.

2. Place the peppers directly on the grill or over a gas flame and turn until skins are blackened all over and the peppers are soft and cooked. Wash the charred skins off under running water. Halve the peppers, removing the seeds and core. While the peppers are cooking, roast the coriander seeds in a heavy dry skillet over medium heat until fragrant, then grind them. Peel the baked eggplant, removing all the skin.

3. Place the prepared eggplant and peppers in a food processor and puree. Add the salt and coriander. With the machine running, trickle in the oil, which will be absorbed as in a mayonnaise. Adjust the seasoning, add lemon juice to taste and turn puree into a bowl. Serve warm or cold.

---

*Ways with Roasted Peppers*
1. *Dress ½-inch slices with oil and garlic and add to salads.*
2. *Add black pepper and herbs to thick slices and put on top of hamburgers.*
3. *Puree without eggplant and use as sauce with grilled pork, poultry or beef.*
4. *Add cubes of roasted peppers to vegetable recipes on pages 272, 279 and 281.*

---

Serves 4 to 6

The supermarkets are filled with varieties of pickled peppers. The cherry types are hot, but when grilled go well with grilled meats, especially pork. Sweet pickled peppers are also available.

### INGREDIENTS

8 to 12 pickled hot cherry peppers, green, red
  or both
2 to 3 slices of homemade, Italian or French
  bread, 1 inch thick
⅓ cup olive oil
salt and freshly ground pepper

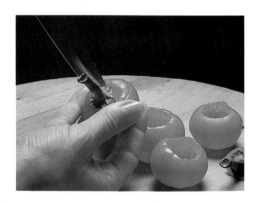

1. Cut out stems of peppers as if coring tomatoes for filling. Opening should be wide enough to receive a 1-inch bread cube. Discard stem and seeds.

2. Brush both sides of bread slices with some of the oil, then cut bread into 1-inch cubes. Toss peppers in remaining oil. Salt and pepper the bread cubes and place one into each pepper. Thread peppers on skewers from top to bottom.

3. When fire is ready, grill peppers for several minutes on each side, rotating until all sides show grill marks.

# GARLICKY POTATOES WITH CREAM AND CHEESE

Serves 6 to 8

Potatoes and garlic have an affinity for each other and go well with beef, chicken, pork, lamb — almost any dish. Try this with potato slices or with mashed potatoes (see variation); both versions are delicious.

### INGREDIENTS

2 pounds baking potatos (about 6 large)
1 cup heavy cream
4 garlic cloves, minced
6 tablespoons butter
¼ cup freshly grated Parmesan cheese
salt and freshly ground pepper
several fresh thyme sprigs

1. Boil potatoes until cooked, then peel and slice thickly. Transfer to foil pan.

2. In a saucepan, bring cream, garlic and 4 tablespoons butter just to boil. Remove from heat. Stir in cheese, salt and pepper. Pour over potatoes, tossing carefully to coat. Dot with remaining 2 tablespoons butter and cover with foil. Place on grill over indirect heat and cook for about 30 minutes. Garnish with thyme sprigs.

Variation: Mash the cooked, peeled potatoes and stir in the cream mixture. Reserve 2 tablespoons butter, as above, for dotting. Cover and place over indirect heat in covered grill for about 30 minutes.

# TZIMMES (SWEET POTATOES, CARROTS, PRUNES AND HONEY)

Serves 6

This is traditional for the Jewish Sabbath, at Rosh Hashana and on other Jewish holidays. The carrots, traditionally sliced straight across, represent the coins of prosperity. The honey, stands for the sweetness of life.

### INGREDIENTS

3 cups sliced cooked sweet potatoes
3 cups sliced cooked carrots
2 cups cooked prunes
1 tablespoon minced lemon zest
juice of 1 lemon
coarse salt
¼ cup honey
¼ cup vegetable oil

1. Make a double heavy-duty foil packet about $4 \times 8 \times 2$ inches or buy a foil pan about this size.

2. Layer the potatoes, carrots and prunes in the foil, dotting each layer with lemon zest, lemon juice and salt. Combine honey and oil and pour over all.

3. Close the packet or cover the pan with foil. Place on the grill about 6 inches over the heat source. Close the cover of the grill and cook tzimmes for about 20 minutes or until heated through.

## GRILLED POTATO AND GRILLED ONION SALAD

Serves 4 to 6

Potatoes and onions are certified companions; when grilled, they gain extra flavor. This dish is easy, may be made ahead and goes with almost any grilled food.

### INGREDIENTS

6 large boiling potatoes, cooked
vegetable oil
4 medium onions, peeled and cut into ½-
   inch-thick slices
½ cup olive oil
¼ cup white wine vinegar
2 tablespoons fresh lemon juice
1 tablespoon sugar
2 green onions, thinly sliced
1 tablespoon chopped fresh lemon
   thyme or 2 teaspoons dried
salt and freshly ground pepper

1. Peel the potatoes if you wish, although it is not necessary. Cut into slices about ½ inch thick, brush lightly with vegetable oil and grill on both sides until slices have grill marks. (This may be done when potatoes are either hot or cold.) Transfer to a large platter.

2. Brush onion slices with vegetable oil and grill until tender. Transfer to platter with potatoes.

3. In a small bowl, combine olive oil, vinegar, lemon juice, sugar, green onions, thyme, salt and pepper and mix well. Pour over the potatoes and onions and toss lightly to coat. Adjust seasonings if necessary. Refrigerate if salad is not to be served shortly, but for best flavor bring to room temperature before serving.

---

*Parmesan*
*Grana is the generic name of a group of Italian cheeses. The word grana means "grain"; it refers to the grainy texture of the cheeses when they are aged. There are two types of grana, Parmigiano-Reggiano and grana padano, both commonly called "Parmesan" outside of Italy. They come from Parma, Reggio-Emilia, Modena, and the region of Bologna.*

*In Italy, the cheese is made from mid-April to precisely November 11th. Domestic Paremesan, universally available in supermarkets, is made in the Midwest, and the cheese is also produced in Argentina.*

# WHOLE TOMATOES WITH PESTO

Serves 6

This dish is special when grilled but it is also delicious served cold as is. If served this way, core the tomatoes, plunge them into boiling water for a count of 10, then immerse in cold water and peel. Fill the tomatoes with pesto and place on a radicchio leaf.

### INGREDIENTS

6 medium-size tomatoes
salt
1 garlic clove, minced
1 cup fresh basil leaves
¼ cup pine nuts
¼ cup freshly grated Parmesan cheese
½ to ¾ cup olive oil
1 tablespoon softened butter
fresh basil sprigs, optional garnish

1. Wash tomatoes and core, making an opening large enough to receive 1 tablespoon filling. Cut a small slice off bottom of each tomato so they stand upright. Sprinkle salt inside core and invert tomatoes to drain while preparing pesto.

2. Combine garlic, basil, pine nuts, Parmesan, oil and salt to taste in food processor and blend until fairly smooth but still textured. Turn over tomatoes and fill each with 1 tablespoon pesto.

3. Cut a piece of heavy-duty foil, 18 inches square. Pour a little olive oil in the center and smear to cover center of sheet. Smear with butter also. Arrange tomatoes side by side on foil in 2 rows of 3 each. Secure with a bundle wrap (see page 18). Tomatoes may be prepared a day ahead to this point and refrigerated; bring to room temperature before grilling.

4. When fire is ready, put packet on grid, close cover and grill about 20 minutes. Garnish with additional fresh basil if desired.

---

*Tomatoes*
*Never ripen fresh tomatoes in direct sunlight; place them in a brown paper bag and leave the bag in normal indoor light. To remove tomato skins, drop the tomatoes (cored or uncored) in boiling water for 10 seconds, then dip them in cold water for 10 seconds. With the help of a paring knife, peel off the skin. When you need pureed tomatoes, run them through a food mill to separate the skin and seeds; do not use a food processor or blender because they pulverize the seeds with the pulp. In canned plum tomatoes, I prefer Progresso, Del Monte, Pope and Vitelli brands. Other good ones are Asti, Tana and Antonia Contorno.*

---

# GRILLED CROUTONS
# WITH TOMATOES
# AND BASIL

Serves 4

Alice Waters, a master chef of undeniable creativity, is often credited with the revival of grill cookery. The menus at her Berkeley restaurant, Chez Panisse, are fresh, bright and creative—the accent is on Italian and French but with a California touch. This summertime dish is a perfect example of Alice's cooking. If you wish, garnish with a confetti of edible flowers, such as rocket, borage or nasturtium. These croutons make a simple lunch, or a fragrant and fresh hors d'oeuvre.

### VINAIGRETTE

#### INGREDIENTS

2 small shallots or sweet red onions, finely
    diced
2 small garlic cloves, minced
salt and freshly ground pepper
2 tablespoons red wine vinegar
3 tablespoons extra virgin olive oil
16 opal or green basil leaves
8 medium-size ripe red and/or yellow tomatoes
4 large slices Italian-country style or
    sourdough bread
olive oil
1 garlic clove, halved

1. Combine the shallots, garlic, a large pinch of salt, a pinch of pepper and the vinegar and let stand for a few minutes. Stir in oil. Coarsely chop half the basil leaves and add to the vinaigrette; reserve the rest of the basil for garnish.

2. Prepare a small wood or charcoal fire. Thinly slice the tomatoes and season lightly with salt and pepper. Cut the bread into ½-inch-thick slices.

3. When the fire has burned down to medium heat, grill the bread for 2 to 3 minutes on each side until golden. Remove from grill and brush liberally with olive oil, then rub with cut side of the garlic.

4. While the croutons are still warm, arrange the tomato slices on top, overlapping slightly. Sprinkle with reserved basil leaves and spoon vinaigrette over.

# A VEGETABLE PACKET
# FROM THE FAR EAST

Serves 4 to 6

This goes well with the spit-roasted pork loin on page 226.

### INGREDIENTS

1 pound canned water chestnuts, drained
1 red bell pepper, stem, ribs and seeds removed, cut into ½-inch dice
⅓ cup slivered almonds
⅓ cup soy sauce
1 tablespoon sesame-chili oil (available at Oriental markets)
2 teaspoons sugar
4 green onions, thinly sliced
2 garlic cloves, minced

1. Pat the water chestnuts dry with paper towels. Combine with red pepper and almonds.

2. Combine remaining ingredients and mix with chestnuts, pepper and almonds.

3. Make a double foil package large enough to enclose the chestnut mixture. Secure with a bundle wrap (see page 18). Place on grill, cover and cook about 20 minutes.

**Nuts**

*This recipe calls for slivered almonds but other nuts can be used. I use enough nuts to buy them in bulk and freeze them. I even put frozen nuts straight into a food processor and have no trouble grinding or pulverizing them. Slivered almonds come pre-packed and may be frozen just that way. In this recipe whole almonds may be substituted, or other types of nuts. If you need to peel almonds, bring some water to a boil, add almonds and boil just for a count of 5. Drain and remove skins by pressing each almond between your thumb and index finger while still warm. The skin will slip off easily.*

*If you are unfamiliar with pine nuts, try them. These are the kernels of certain pine cones and are especially delicious and flavorful when lightly toasted. Pine cone nuts come cleaned and ready to use. They freeze well.*

*Walnuts and pecans are never blanched, but hazelnuts, as almonds, almost always are.*

# RUSSIAN RED BEANS WITH PLUM SAUCE

Serves 4

This uncooked vegetable dish is easy to make ahead of time as it may stay at room temperature for several hours. It's especially good with hamburgers, grilled chicken and steaks.

### INGREDIENTS

½ teaspoon red pepper flakes
2 teaspoons chopped fresh basil or ½ teaspoon dried
⅓ cup damson plum jelly
3 tablespoons red wine vinegar
2 garlic cloves, minced
salt and freshly ground pepper
1 can (20 ounces) red kidney beans, drained, rinsed and drained again

1. Combine all ingredients except beans in a food processor and pulse until garlic is pulverized and mixture is well combined.

2. Add to beans, stir well and allow flavors to develop for 2 to 3 hours at room temperature. Refrigerate if not using soon, but bring to room temperature before serving.

# UNCOOKED ONION AND DILL RELISH

Serves 4 to 6

A simple and invigorating relish that goes well with many grilled fish and meats. If you can, use sweet white Vidalia onions.

### INGREDIENTS

½ cup finely chopped fresh dill
1 teaspoon mustard seed
3 tablespoons powdered sugar
salt and freshly ground pepper
1 cup white wine vinegar
2 cups thinly sliced (in rings) white onions

1. Combine everything except the onions in a glass or ceramic bowl. Mix well and let stand for 30 minutes.

2. Add onions and stir well. Cover and marinate overnight in refrigerator.

# SPECIAL OCCASIONS

Americans love banquets and special dinners with a foreign accent. Here are seven such festive menus, for as few as four or six to as many as 100 people.

From the south of France, Richard Olney contributes an unusual, flavorful brochette of several meats, wrapped in caul and grilled to perfection over smoldering embers at the fireplace; a charcoal or gas grill can be used with equal success. A number of the steps can be done ahead, such as making the perillade and preparing the sweetbreads.

From Square One Restaurant in San Francisco, the inimitable Joyce Goldstein creates a magnificent Brazilian *churrasco*. Do a step at a time and the preparation is easier than it appears. Again, much of it can be made ahead.

The success of John Hettinger's paella, a wonderful thing to watch from start to finish, depends on building the fire(s) in the right location and preparing all ingredients individually. John Hettinger, Louise and John Imperiale, Linwood Boone and I once made eight paellas of this size; the only way we could do it was to have the ingredients in bowls, ready to throw into the paella pans at the right moment. Piles of wood were set next to the fires and added as needed.

Judith McMillen's roasts need large spits but they need not, of course, be reproductions of 18th-century pieces. Controlling the fire and balancing the beef are essential.

Lastly, a chicken dinner for up to 100 people is surely a possibility for anyone with a little experience at the grill. Again advance preparation is a must, but the main task is to figure out how to arrange for enough wire baskets and grill space. The grilled potato and grilled onion salad may be made ahead; so can the minted cucumbers.

Good luck and Happy Event.

# BROCHETTES FROM THE SOUTH OF FRANCE

Serves 6 to 8

Richard Olney, an American educated at the University of Iowa and the Brooklyn Museum Art School, has lived and worked in France for many years. Highly regarded in both countries as an authority on food and wine, he has written numerous books and articles, including the award-winning volume, *Simple French Food*. He was chief consultant for the Time-Life series, *The Good Cook*.

### INGREDIENTS

8 ounces veal sweetbreads, soaked for several hours or overnight in several changes of cold water

3 ounces lean unsmoked bacon or pancetta, cut into ⅓- to ½-inch squares

1 large garlic clove, peeled

large pinch of coarse salt

3 tablespoons chopped flat parsley leaves

2 lamb hearts, trimmed, split, rinsed and cut into 6 or 8 pieces each

1 short lamb loin and tenderloin, trimmed, the loin cut into 8 pieces, the tenderloin into 4

8 ounces lamb's or calves' liver, cut into 12 cubes

8 freshly plucked bay leaves (if available), halved crosswise

several green onions with tender green parts, very thinly sliced (or 1 small onion, finely chopped)

1 teaspoon mixed crushed dried herbs (thyme, oregano, savory, marjoram)

3 tablespoons (about) olive oil

salt and freshly ground pepper

8 ounces caul (if salted or frozen, soak in tepid water until supple)*

4 stiff 12-inch long rosemary branches, tufts of leaves left at one end, scraped smooth and sharpened to a point at the other end (if not available, substitute skewers)

a handful of fresh rosemary leaves or several additional rosemary branches

saffron pilaf (see below)

1. Place sweetbreads in a large pot of cold water. Bring to a bare simmer over low heat (water should be 180°F to 190°F) and cook for 20 minutes. Drain and rinse with cold water. Carefully remove fat, tubes and membranes, leaving lobe structure intact.

2. Place bacon in a saucepan of cold water and bring to boil. Drain, rinse and drain again.

3. For persillade, combine garlic and coarse salt in a mortar and pound to a paste. Add parsley and mix well.

4. Combine all ingredients except caul and rosemary branches in a large mixing bowl. Toss with splayed fingers until meat is evenly coated. Let marinate for at least 30 minutes.

5. Alternate the meats and bay leaf pieces on the rosemary branches or skewers so that they touch but are not packed; start and finish with a piece of heart, which is the firmest meat and will hold the others in place.

6. Spoon leftover marinade and chopped onions over skewers. Cut caul into 4 rectangles, each large enough to enclose a skewer. Cover each skewer with a piece of caul, twisting it at each end to seal completely. If brochettes are prepared more than an hour ahead of time refrigerate them, but return to room temperature before grilling.

7. Grill brochettes over hot coals for 12 to 15 minutes, turning every 3 to 4 minutes so that all sides are golden brown. The heart, loin and liver should remain pink inside. A minute or so before removing from the grill, throw rosemary leaves or branches onto the hot coals.

8. Accompany brochettes with saffron pilaf.

*Caul is a netlike membrane covering the lower intestine of a pig or sheep. Resembling a thick veil ribbed with white fat, it is used as a wrapper to keep ground meat (or pieces of meat) moist during grilling. It is available by the pound at specialty butchers, or by special order at regular butcher shops.

## SAFFRON PILAF

Serves 6 to 8

### INGREDIENTS

¼ cup olive oil
1 onion, chopped
2 cups long-grain rice
½ teaspoon salt
generous pinch of saffron
1¾ cups boiling water
4 tablespoons softened butter

1. In a large skillet, heat oil over medium heat. Add onion and sauté until soft, 4 to 5 minutes; do not let onion color.

2. Add rice, salt and saffron to skillet and stir until rice is coated with oil and appears opaque. Add boiling water and return to boil. Cover tightly and simmer for 18 minutes. Remove cover, add butter and toss lightly with two forks. Serve immediately.

---

*Bay Leaves*
*Originally from Asia Minor, the bay leaf became a Mediterranean staple in many ways at an early date. It was the symbol of wisdom and glory in ancient Rome and Greece, and emperors wore a crown of laurel leaves — i.e., bay leaves.*

*I've never seen a spice rack, in a supermarket or home, without bay leaves. This is one leaf that's better dried than fresh. Its most common use in grilling is on kebabs and as a flavoring agent in marinades and mops. Fresh leaves are too bitter to use as a culinary herb, so it's best to use the dried ones sold in jars. Very old dried leaves lose flavor — but some people keep them around because they are said to ward off lightning.*

# BRAZILIAN CHURRASCO: GRILLED MARINATED FLANK STEAK, PORK LOIN AND SAUSAGE WITH FRESH CORIANDER, GARLIC AND HOT PEPPER

Serves 6

The name "Square One" implies fresh beginnings every day. The restaurant serves seasonal foods and uses local produce whenever possible. The menu changes every day and features an international repertoire, with an emphasis on dishes of Mediterranean origin. Joyce Goldstein, the chef/owner, is a Smith College Phi Beta Kappa with a Master of Fine Arts from Yale.

### INGREDIENTS

1 pork loin (2 pounds)
¼ cup salt
½ cup sugar
3 bay leaves
1 teaspoon dried thyme
6 juniper berries, bruised
4 white peppercorns, bruised
4 black peppercorns, bruised
2 whole coriander seeds, bruised
2 whole cloves

Place the meat in a glass or ceramic dish. Combine about 1 cup water, salt and sugar in a small bowl and stir until salt and sugar are dissolved. Add the herbs and spices and pour over the pork. Add more cool water to cover the pork loin. Let marinate, refrigerated, for 1 to 2 days.

### BRAZILIAN PORK SAUSAGE
### INGREDIENTS

1½ pounds ground pork, about ⅓ fat
½ cup (about) chopped fresh coriander
2 tablespoons minced garlic
1 tablespoon hot pepper flakes
2 tablespoons water
½ teaspoon freshly ground pepper
1 teaspoon salt
a few feet of hog casing, if available

**1.** For sausage, combine all ingredients except the hog casing and fry a tiny sample, then adjust seasoning to taste.

**2.** Stuff the mixture into the casing and tie into 6 links. If you are unable to make cased sausages, form the meat into 6 long fingers and grill them as you would hamburgers.

### FLANK STEAK
### INGREDIENTS

1 large yellow onion, coarsely chopped
2 garlic cloves
½ cup fresh lemon juice
½ teaspoon salt
2 teaspoons ground pepper
2 flank steaks (about 1¼ pounds each)

Chop the onion and garlic in a food processor. Add the lemon juice, salt and pepper and pulse to blend. Pour this mixture over the flank steaks and marinate for 1 to 2 hours, turning the steaks once or twice.

### BLACK BEANS
### INGREDIENTS

2 cups black beans, soaked overnight (or covered with 6 cups water, brought to a boil for 1 minute, and allowed to soak for 1 hour)

2 onions, chopped
4 garlic cloves, minced
¼ small cinnamon stick
1 whole clove
1 ham bone or prosciutto bone
5 to 6 cups water
salt and freshly ground pepper

Combine all ingredients except salt and pepper in a large pot and bring to boil. Reduce heat and simmer until the beans are tender. Season with salt and pepper. Keep warm.

## RICE
### INGREDIENTS

14 cups salted water
3 cups basmati rice
8 tablespoons (1 stick) butter, melted
salt and freshly ground pepper

1. Bring the water to boil in a large pot. Add the rice all at once and cook over medium heat for 10 to 12 minutes, or until cooked all the way through but still firm. Drain the rice in a colander and rinse with warm water.

2. Preheat oven to 350°F. Place the rice in a 13 × 9-inch baking dish and drizzle with melted butter. Season with salt and pepper. Cover and bake for 25 minutes. Keep warm.

## GREENS
### INGREDIENTS

½ cup bacon fat
2 onions, finely chopped
4 garlic cloves, minced
6 bunches Swiss chard or kale, washed, drained and cut into fine julienne
salt and freshly ground pepper

Melt the fat in a large pan over medium-high heat. Add onions and cook until transparent. Stir in garlic. Add the greens gradually, stirring until they wilt. If they are dry, add just enough water to steam and wilt them. Season to taste with salt and pepper. Keep warm.

## SALSA
### INGREDIENTS

½ cup fresh lemon juice
4 garlic cloves, minced
4 jalapeño peppers, minced

Combine all ingredients and let stand at room temperature for 1 to 3 hours, or prepare ahead and refrigerate. Bring to room temperature before serving.

To assemble the Churrasco:

1. Prepare a mesquite fire; all the meats will be cooked over it.

2. Drain the pork loin. When the fire is ready, grill the pork loin for 8 to 10 minutes, turning every 3 minutes or so; the meat should be slightly pink inside when done. Keep warm after grilling.

3. Blanch the cased sausages in boiling water for 5 minutes. Drain and grill them until crisp on the outside and cooked through, about 8 minutes. Keep warm.

4. Drain the flank steak and grill it rare, about 2 minutes per side.

5. Slice the flank steak and the pork loin across the grain. Place a few slices of pork and beef on each plate with a sausage.

6. Add the beans, rice and greens and serve the salsa on the side.

# PAELLA FOR 25

This is a magnificent preparation of seafood, chicken and pork combined with tomatoes, rice, saffron and many other flavorful ingredients. It is cooked in a 2-inch-deep paella pan with top diameter of 28 inches and bottom diameter of 25 inches. These pans can be purchased at Casa Moneo Spanish Imports, 210 West 14th Street, New York, N.Y. 10011. They can also be ordered directly from Spain; write to Ramondo Ferdandez at El Corte Inglés (Paellera), Villa Verde 79, Madrid. It is possible to make the paella in two smaller pans, but in this case two fires will be required. Arrange three concrete blocks or bricks in the form of a tripod for the pan to rest on; the pan should sit 4 to 6 inches above the fire. John Hettinger, creator of this recipe, usually fuels the fire with small pieces of wood, no more than 2 inches in diameter, and feeds it as necessary. The *reposo* step of the procedure, during which kitchen towels are placed over the cooked paella, is important to the success of the dish and must not be overlooked.

### INGREDIENTS

2 cups olive oil
3½ pounds boned pork loin with some fat, cut into 1-inch cubes
15 chicken thighs
15 chicken drumsticks
6 medium tomatoes, cored, peeled and put through food mill
12 large garlic cloves, finely chopped
3 dozen fresh littleneck clams
3 dozen mussels
1 pound cleaned squid, cut into ¼-inch rings

6 quarts (24 cups) boiling water
6 tablespoons coarse salt
8 cups (3 pounds) long-grain rice
½ teaspoon Spanish saffron threads, crumbled into 1 cup warm water
3 dozen unshelled medium shrimp
1 package (10 ounces) frozen green peas, thawed
1 jar (4 ounces) pimentos, drained and cut into julienne strips
3 lemons, very thinly sliced

1. Place the paella pan over the fire; add and heat the olive oil. Add the pork cubes and brown lightly for about 5 minutes.

2. Add the chicken thighs and drumsticks and cook them with the pork for about 15 minutes, turning frequently until chicken is browned.

3. Add tomatoes and garlic and cook, stirring frequently, for 1 to 2 minutes; do not let garlic brown. Stir in the clams, mussels and squid.

4. Add the water and salt and bring the water to a rolling boil. This is the time to stoke the fire and add more wood.

5. Pour rice over ingredients in pan and cook for five minutes without stirring. Pour saffron mixture evenly over rice and cook for 10 minutes, again without stirring.

6. Add shrimp and peas. When the rice is cooked, about 10 minutes later, remove the pan from the heat, place it on the ground and cover it completely with 2 or 3 clean kitchen towels. Let stand for 5 minutes. This is known as the *reposo* (resting) period.

7. Remove the towels. Criss-cross pimento pieces every few inches apart over the surface of the paella. Arrange lemon slices around the outer edge. Transfer paella pan to a heatproof surface near the table and serve.

# RICHMONDTOWN SPIT-ROASTED TOP ROUND BEEF AND WHOLE TURKEYS FOR 75

You will need two spits, each 4 to 5 feet long. For the fire, use hardwood logs of your choice. To round out the meal, Judith cooks potatoes and seasonal vegetables, often green beans and corn, in large iron kettles on iron ring stands at the front edge of the fire. The kettles are about 15 inches deep and 24 inches wide. All meats and vegetables are cooked plain. They are served with salt and pepper and some freshly churned butter.

## INGREDIENTS

3 boneless whole beef top rounds (15 pounds each)
2 whole turkeys (22 pounds each)
salt and freshly ground pepper

1. Ask your butcher to bone the beef and trim off excess fat, and to dress the turkeys. Wipe off the beef; rinse and dry the turkeys.

2. Prepare a large firebed — about 4 feet in diameter — using kindling and hardwood logs. Erect two poles at the edge of the fire to support spits.

3. Arrange beef, pieces touching, on one spit by inserting it through center. Be sure meat is balanced on the spit. Do likewise with turkeys on the second spit.

4. When the fire is ready, put the spits in place and roast beef and turkeys for 2½ to 3 hours. First sear the beef all over to seal in the juices, pushing the logs closer to the meat with a metal peel or shovel. (Turkeys do not need to be seared, although they will take about the same amount of cooking time.) Move logs farther away from meat for remainder of cooking.

5. To test for doneness, insert a long, sharp knife into center of meat. If tip of knife against your cheek is cold, beef is still raw. If tip of knife is about body temperature, the meat is on its way to medium, yet still rare. If knife point is very hot, beef is probably overcooked. Seek a knifepoint between body temperature and hot for medium to rare beef. Turkey is done when legs move easily in the sockets and juices run clear at the point where the thigh joins the body.

*Judith McMillen*
*Six times each summer, Judith McMillen prepares an outdoor meal for 75 visitors to Richmondtown Restoration on Staten Island, New York. In full period dress (she is in charge of cooking and costumes), she roasts 50 pounds of top round and 45 pounds of turkey on a spit carefully reproduced by a local blacksmith from an early-19th-century design.*

*"We deal with historical accuracy here," she explains. "For example, we make rhubarb and cherry pies in July because the fruit was available at that time of year. We wouldn't make apple pie until late August." She adds, "We make one exception, and that is using vegetable oil on our salads. Vegetable oil as we know it today didn't exist 200 years ago. Did you know that Jefferson used sesame oil?" she asked. Judith's husband, William, has been Richmondtown's supervisor of restoration for 25 years. His father was one of its founders.*

# GRILLED BEEF TORTILLA

Serves 4

Some recipes are easier to extend than others. Here is a good one for just that. This is delicious, attractive and works well as a party dish. Use it on special occasions for four, as shown here; double it for eight; triple it for twelve and so on. This was created by Jimmy Schmidt, the innovative chef at The Rattle Snake Club in Denver, Colorado.

### INGREDIENTS

1 tablespoon chili powder
2 tablespoons olive oil
2 tablespoons ground cumin
1 pound sirloin or rib eye beef steak
8 blue corn tortillas
juice of 2 limes
½ teaspoon minced garlic
½ jalapeño pepper, roasted, peeled, seeded and minced
¼ cup olive oil
salt
2 cups romaine or red oak lettuce torn into small pieces
corn salsa (see below)
½ cup shredded queso fresco cheese
¼ cup pine nuts, toasted

1. In a small bowl combine chili powder, olive oil and cumin. Rub all over surface of steak. Allow to marinate at least 30 minutes. When fire is ready, grill or broil to desired doneness.

2. Meanwhile, reheat tortillas in a dry heavy skillet: put one tortilla in the skillet at a time. Heat one side, then the other. Transfer the tortillas to a towel, cover and keep warm.

3. In a medium blow, combine lime juice, garlic, jalapeño pepper and olive oil. Add salt to taste. Add lettuce and toss well. Cut steak into ½-inch cubes.

4. To assemble, lay one tortilla flat on each of 4 warm plates. Divide lettuce across them. Cover with steak pieces. Distribute corn salsa and cheese across. Top with remaining tortillas. Garnish with pine nuts.

### CORN SALSA

Makes about 1⅓ cups

½ cup fresh sweet corn kernels, cooked
¼ cup diced sun-dried tomatoes
¼ cup poblano peppers, roasted, peeled, seeded and diced
1 teaspoon chopped fresh coriander
½ teaspoon ground cumin
½ teaspoon freshly ground white pepper
3 tablespoons fresh lime juice
½ cup olive oil
salt

Mix all ingredients except olive oil and salt. Slowly add oil, mixing well. Season with salt to taste.

# GRILLED CHICKEN
# IN WHITE WINE MARINADE
# FOR 100

A food processor will expedite the chopping for the marinade. If you can gather enough hinged wire baskets to hold this much chicken, use chicken parts instead of quartered broiler-fryers; in this way you can grill thighs together, breasts together, and so on to achieve more even doneness. The fatty chicken skin will cause flareups on the grill, so it is best to remove some of the skin and to use covered grills (this will also help keep chicken moist). If using hinged wire baskets, check to see that they fit on the grill with the cover down.

### INGREDIENTS

4 large or 6 medium onions, finely chopped
¼ cup finely chopped garlic
½ to ¾ cup finely chopped fresh thyme or ¼
    cup dried
6 cups dry white wine
6 cups champagne vinegar
6 cups light olive oil
25 quartered broiler/fryer chickens or 125
    pounds chicken parts
salt and freshly ground pepper

1. In a 6-quart enamel, porcelain or glass container, or in two smaller containers, whisk together all ingredients except the chicken, salt and pepper.

2. Wash and dry the chicken pieces. Divide them among various nonaluminum containers (if you're using parts, keep like parts together) and cover with the marinade. Marinate at room temperature for about 3 hours, turning several times, or in refrigerator for 1 to 2 days. Bring chicken to room temperature before grilling.

3. When fires are ready, arrange chicken on grids skin side down, lower cover and grill for 15 minutes. Lift cover, turn chicken and brush with marinade. Lower cover and grill for about 20 minutes more, or until juices run clear. When they do, turn chicken, baste again and remove from heat. If you're using grills without covers, do not have the fire too hot or flareups may result. Baste chicken more frequently on an open grill.

4. Season with salt and pepper to taste after chicken is done.

---

*Grilled Chicken for 100*
*Chicken pieces are among the easiest things to handle for a large grill party. Most of the preparation is done a day or two ahead of time. Start the chicken on each grill some minutes apart, which allows time to go from one to the next (or recruit help from family or friends — I've found this easy to do.) Grilled potato and grilled onion salad (see page 279) is excellent with this, along with sliced red-ripe tomatoes and minted cucumber lengths. (Slice 25 peeled small cucumbers lengthwise and place in a large bowl. Cover with ice cubes and add about 2 cups fresh mint leaves. Add some fresh lemon juice and salt and toss with your hands. Let stand for 30 minutes to let cucumbers crisp and flavor.)*

# DRY-MOPPED BEEF BRISKET

Serves 12 to 20

The brisket should be seasoned with the dry mop at least an hour before cooking and left at room temperature. Do not overseason; too much mop can make the meat bitter. Sprinkle the dry mop over the meat and rub it in thoroughly, brushing off excess. Prepare the fire well ahead in order to reach a temperature of 200°F.

### INGREDIENTS

¼ cup sweet paprika
1 tablespoon freshly ground pepper
1 tablespoon salt
1 brisket of beef (12 to 15 pounds), trimmed

**1.** Combine the seasonings and rub evenly into the meat. Brush or shake off any excess.

**2.** Make a large enough fire in the smoker so fire will last a long time, although additional briquettes will be added during the cooking process to maintain a temperature of 200°F. Pour 2 cups water into the water pan and set in place under meat to catch drippings. Place the brisket on the rack in the smoker. Smoke at 200°F for 18 to 20 hours, basting every 30 minutes or so. Ten pounds of charcoal will maintain the temperature for about 10 hours, but check and add briquettes as needed.

**3.** Serve the cooked brisket in thin slices. If you wish, coat it with a favorite barbecue sauce and reheat before serving.

---

*Eileen Weinberg*

*Eileen Weinberg and Martin Yerdon own and operate Carolina, one of the best restaurants in New York for smoked and grilled foods. "We called it Carolina," says Eileen, "because we wanted something feminine, American and Southern."*

*Martin designed one of the most unusual smokers imaginable. About 6 feet high and 8 feet wide, it has four doors; each of the four sections contains five stacked trays to hold the food. Below these doors is the firebox, containing an inferno of smoldering lump charcoal, pecan, oak and apple.*

*Eileen says, "Just about everything is finished on the grill," which is near the smoker. It is about 3 × 6 feet and fired with the same fuel as the smoker. "There are three rules," she adds:*

*1. Immediately sear everything you put on a grill.*

*2. Keep the flames away from the meat; use a water sprayer if you have to, or close the cover.*

*3. For smoked food, it's better to use a mop than a marinade for flavor unless the marinade is an intense one.*

# MENUS

### NOTES FROM THE VINEYARD

*Store wine in a dark, cool place away from air conditioning vents, heating elements and drafts. Bottles should be on their sides to keep the corks moist. Dried corks are difficult to remove because they crumble—but more importantly, they shrink and let in air, which will spoil the wine.*

*White wines, champagnes and rosés should be served chilled. Put bottles in the refrigerator a couple of hours before opening time. Don't put them in the freezer. If you have an ice bucket for wine bottles, put in the bottle and ice about 30 minutes before serving.*

*Red wines should be served at room temperature. In my experience, very good wines do not need to be opened in advance, while wines of lesser quality benefit from being opened a half hour or so before serving. But there is no agreement on this in food and wine circles, so I suggest you experiment on your own. Most opened wine bottles do not fare well. They can be recorked and refrigerated but I find something is always missing. The best solution is to use leftover wine in cooking as quickly as you can. Opened bottles of fortified wines such as Madeira, Marsala, sherry, port and so on will keep a long time, but it is best to store them in a dark place and to be sure they are capped as tightly as possible.*

*Wine-based marinades are excellent for grilled foods. The wine tenderizes and flavors meats, and the alcohol burns off during cooking. (I never understand why anyone is hesitant to use wine in cooking; the goal is flavor, not alcohol.) Use good wines in the kitchen and at the grill—the kind you would be happy to drink.*

## MENU 1

Serves 4 to 6

Grilled Fennel Bulbs with Fresh Lemon Juice
Smoked Sea Scallops Marinara
Almond Meringues with Pine Nuts (recipe below)
Wine: Italian Pinot Grigio or California Pinot Gris

### MERINGUES

To make 2 dozen, toast 8 ounces slivered blanched almonds, cool and grind finely. Preheat oven to 350° F. Beat 2 egg whites and a pinch of salt to soft peaks. In another bowl, combine ¾ cup powdered sugar and ¼ cup granulated sugar and add by spoonfuls to the egg whites, beating until stiff. Add ¼ teaspoon almond extract. Gently fold in ground almonds. Drop by heaping teaspoons onto a buttered and floured baking sheet, 1 inch apart. Sprinkle tops with 1 cup pine nuts. Bake 15 minutes. Cool on racks. Store leftovers, if any, in an airtight container.

## MENU 2

Serves 4

Buttered fresh corn, if in season or Hot Corn
    Chowder with Water Chestnuts (recipe
    below)
Grilled Sea Bass in a Wire Basket
Fresh snow peas sautéed in butter
Fresh Pineapple Quarters on the Shell with
    Strawberries and optional white rum
Wine: Sauvignon Blanc

Make soup and prepare dessert before grilling fish. For chowder, sauté 2 finely chopped
bacon slices until golden. Add ½ chopped
onion, 2 cups peeled and cubed boiling potatoes and ½ cup water. Cover and bring to boil,
then simmer 10 minutes. Set aside. In another
saucepan, combine 2 cups corn kernels, ½
cup heavy cream, ½ teaspoon sugar and 4
tablespoons butter. Cover and cook slowly for
10 minutes. Combine ingredients in both
saucepans, adding 1 cup milk, salt and
white pepper. Add ½ cup water chestnuts cut
into ¼-inch dice. Heat through but do not
boil. Thin with more milk or chicken stock.

### DESSERT

Halve the pineapple lengthwise, slicing
through top leaves; cut each piece in half
again. Lay quarters skin side down and run a
knife between flesh and skin. Cut down into
flesh at ½-inch intervals, leaving the pieces
in place so pineapple appears uncut. Sprinkle
with light rum if you wish. Cover and refrigerate until serving time. Place each pineapple

quarter on a plate, being careful not to dis-
lodge the plume of leaves or the cut slices. Add
1 or 2 strawberries alongside pineapple.

## MENU 3

Serves 4

Pasta Salad (recipe below)
Grilled Prime Chuck Hamburgers with Bacon
    and Herbs
Fresh Fruit with Gorgonzola, Chèvre and
    Crackers
Wine: Red Rioja

Simple pasta dishes are good companions
for simple grilled meats. This pasta salad can
be made ahead and brought to room temperature by the time the burgers are put on the
grill. To serve 4, cook 8 ounces small pasta
(shells, butterflies, elbows, etc.), drain well
and add to a wooden bowl that has been
rubbed with a large garlic clove. Add 3 ripe
tomatoes, quartered, 12 shredded basil leaves,
1 small purple onion sliced in thin rings, ½
cup olive oil, and some fresh or dried oregano,
fresh lemon juice, salt and pepper to taste.

### DESSERT

Slice ripe honeydew or canteloupe; serve with
a lemon wedge, along with softened gorgonzola and Chèvre with crackers. See note on
crackers in Menu #23. Actually any other
fresh fruit (except citrus) will do, as long as
it is ripe and flavorful.

**MENU 4**

Serves 4

Spinach, Mushroom and Cream with Spaghetti
Grilled Lobster with Garlic, Ginger, Chili, and Butter Sauce
Raspberry Tart
Wine: Dry Chenin Blanc

Prepare the lobsters and sauce ahead; the grill time is not long. Serve the pasta first and let the guests wait for the lobster. It should go from grill to table.

**MENU 5**

Serves 2

Wine-soaked Sausage on Wine-soaked Bread
Grilled Marinated Filet Mignon of Tuna
Strawberry Sherbet and Ice Cream Parfait
Wine: Premier Cru Chablis or dry Chardonnay

DESSERT
In any kind of compote glass, alternate spoonfuls of sherbet and ice cream, adding sliced strawberries between layers. Serve slightly softened.

**MENU 6**

Serves 4

Shiitake Mushrooms *alla Griglia*
Grouper Grilled in Crushed Mustard Seeds and Peppercorns with Mussel-Saffron Sauce
Fresh Greens Vinaigrette
French Pastry or Melon
Wine: Riesling or Gewürztraminer

It is easier to make the mussel-saffron sauce ahead except for butter addition at end. In fact, may be made 1 day ahead if you need that lead time. Refrigerate before completing sauce. Also, the mustard seed preparation may be made ahead by as much as a day and refrigerated. Once these sauces are made, the rest is easy. Broil under a high flame.

Serve salad on a side plate so juices don't run into delicate, delicious sauces.

The fish sauces are rich so melon may be preferred. Yet the meal as a whole is reasonably light, so a Napoleon, or half of one, may be just right.

# MENU
# 7

Serves 4

Shrimp Remoulade
Grilled Sirloin Hamburgers with Soy, Sesame
   and Green Onions
Lemon sherbet with chocolate chip cookies
Wine: Red Côtes-du-Rhône or Chateauneuf-
   du-Pape

**O**ne cup of sauce is needed for 1 pound of shrimp, which will serve 4. Precook shrimp 1 or 2 days ahead, if you wish, or purchase cooked shrimp. Be sure they're not overcooked or they will be tough. Combine with the remoulade sauce, which also can be made several days ahead, and refrigerate until serving time.

---

*Options*

*For a heavier menu, add garlicky potatoes, page 278.*

*In place of lemon sherbet, serve sliced fresh oranges with almond cookies.*

---

# MENU
# 8

Serves 6

Tomato and Basil Soup (recipe below)
Marinated and Grilled Shell Steaks
Grilled corn
Strawberries with cream
Wine: Red Bordeaux or Cabernet Sauvignon

### SOUP
For 4, heat 1½ tablespoons each butter and olive oil. Sauté 1 garlic clove and discard when light brown. Add 1 small leek, 1 celery stalk and 1 onion, all chopped, and cook over medium heat for 10 minutes. Stir in 1 table-spoon sugar, 1½ pounds fresh tomatoes (cored, peeled, seeded and chopped) and 2 cups beef stock and simmer 30 minutes. Put through food mill and adjust seasonings. Add 3 tablespoons finely chopped fresh basil and the juice of ½ lemon. Garnish with fresh basil leaves. (Canned plum tomatoes may be substituted; use 3 cups, put through food mill to remove seeds.) Serve this soup hot or cold.

## MENU 9

Serves 6 to 8

Southern Barbecued Fillet of Beef
Baked potatoes
Sam's Cole Slaw
Blueberry tart
Wine: Red Côtes-du-Rhône

Make your own tart or find a good pastry shop. Add whipped cream if you wish. If serving company, be sure you know the quality of the bought tart. Don't ruin this otherwise delicious meal. If you use foil to bake potatoes, remember to remove foil before bringing to the table.

---

*Options*

*If a first course is desired, serve sliced ripe tomatoes with chopped basil and an oil and wine vinegar dressing.*

*If tomatoes are not ripe, use something else such as a small lettuce salad with a piece of goat cheese, Gorgonzola or Brie, room temperature.*

---

## MENU 10

Serves 4 to 6

Grilled Hot Cherry Peppers
Skewered Beef Tenderloin
Grilled Leeks
Salad of Arugula and Belgian Endive with
    Balsamic Dressing
Peach Sherbet with Zabaglione Sauce
Wine: Red Zinfandel

Select small leeks (2 per person) about ¾ inch thick. Coat lightly with vegetable or olive oil and grill whole. Salt and pepper after grilling, and add a little butter if you wish. If the grill is large enough, grill leeks along with the tenderloin.

To make a balsamic vinegar dressing, use a little less balsamic than you would red or white wine vinegar. Add oil, salt and pepper to taste. Do not add mustard; balsamic vinegar has a distinct, earthy taste and nothing should disguise it.

For zabaglione sauce, combine 4 egg yolks and ¼ cup sugar in the top of a double boiler. Over moderate heat, mix with an electric hand mixer until sugar dissolves. Heat ¾ cup dry white wine and add slowly, beating constantly, until sauce nearly triples in volume. Spoon around scoops of sherbet or ice cream. This makes enough for 4 to 6 servings.

## MENU
## 11

Serves 4

Grilled Belgian Endive, Italian Porcini Mush-
rooms and Japanese Eggplant with Ginger
Soy Sauce
Sirloin Strips, Grilled Korean Style
Onion Dill Relish
Sliced fresh Peaches in red wine
Wine: Red or White Côtes-du-Rhône

Make the Onion Dill Relish the day before.
It keeps well refrigerated.

Keep in mind that the sirloin strips grill
quickly, so don't put them over the heat source
until the first course is organized and grilled.

The peaches must be ripe. Let them marinate
in a hearty red wine for several hours at room
temperature. Serve a spoonful of the wine over
the peaches.

---

*Options*

*If a simpler appetizer or first course is desired, use
Shiitake Mushrooms, alla Griglia, page 272.*

*In place of peaches, use ripe pears in red or
white wine or sprinkle fresh, ripe apricot halves
with a few drops of apricot brandy.*

---

## MENU
## 12

Serves 4

Cold Cucumber Soup (recipe below)
Grilled Pork Satay
Grilled Buttered Turnips
Sliced Nectarines with Brown Sugar and Ber-
ries (recipe below)
Wine: Tavel Rosé or other dry Rosé

### SOUP

Peel, seed and chop 2 cucumbers. Puree in
processor with 1 garlic clove and 1 cup chicken
stock. Transfer to a large bowl. Mix in 2 more
cups chicken stock, 1 cup heavy cream, 3
tablespoons chopped fresh dill, ¾ cup sour
cream and salt and pepper. Before serving,
sprinkle 1 tablespoon chopped almonds, walnuts or hazelnuts over each bowl. Serve soup
hot or ice cold.

### DESSERT

Use 8 ripe nectarines; it isn't necessary to peel
them. Slice thinly, and place in a glass or
ceramic container. Sprinkle with 2 tablespoons
brown sugar and the juice of ½ lemon. Toss
well. Cover and refrigerate. When ready to
serve, add 3 or 4 strawberries or raspberries to
each serving.

### PORK

Reduce amount of pork to 1½ pounds. Marinade ingredients may remain the same.

# MENU
## 13

Serves 6

Orzo with Red Bell Peppers and Currants
Grilled Pork Tenderloin with Chili Red and
   Garlic Mustard Sauces
Fresh Shelled Peas with Butter and Mint
Lemon sherbet topped with crème de menthe
Wine: Dry Riesling or Merlot

Make sauces for pork ahead of time. Orzo may also be made ahead and kept warm with a little butter to keep from sticking to each other. To make enough orzo for 6, increase ingredients by one half – for example, use ¾ cup currant instead of ½ and so on.

The peas can be cooked along with the pork tenderloins. Make pea packages ahead, ready to place on the grill.

---

*Options*
*In place of orzo, use farfalle (pasta bows or butterflies). In place of chili red and garlic mustard sauces, slice grilled pork tenderloin and serve with Vegetable Packet from the Far East, page 282.*

---

# MENU
## 14

Serves 4 to 6

Various Fish en Brochette
Grilled Homemade Italian Sausauge
Grilled potato slices
Sliced Tomatoes with Mustard Vinaigrette
Raspberry sherbet with Oreos
Wine: Italian red, preferably Valpolicella

### SAUSAGE

This recipe makes 3 pounds of homemade sausage and will serve 8. To serve 4, grill only half the amount. The remaining sausage will keep in the refrigerator, uncovered, for 1 week or may be frozen for up to 2 months. Italian sausage may be bought in most butcher shops or supermarkets. Use 1½ pounds for 4, 2 pounds for 6.

The brochettes won't take long on the grill, so start the sausage first. Grill on low to medium heat. Tomatoes can be sliced and dressed an hour or two ahead of time. Leave at room temperature. The sausage is rich, so a sherbet is the perfect dessert.

## MENU
## 15

Serves 6

Grilled Eggplant with Capers and Anchovy
    Sauce
Grilled Spareribs with Birmingham Barbecue
    Sauce
Sweet and Sour Cole Slaw
Warm Deep-dish Apple Pie with Hard Sauce
    (recipe below)
Wine: Red or White Zinfandel

Prepare the first course ahead and refrigerate, but bring to room temperature before serving.

The recipe for cole slaw serves 8. To serve six, reduce cabbage to 1½ pounds, use small onion and bell pepper, ⅓ cup each of vinegar and oil, and scant teaspoons of salt, dry mustard and celery seed.

To make 2 cups hard sauce: Cream 1 cup softened unsalted butter with 1 cup powdered sugar. Beat in ¼ cup brandy a few drops at a time. When fluffy, add a sprinkle of nutmeg. Cool in refrigerator, but remove before the sauce becomes completely firm.

## MENU
## 16

Serves 4

Grilled Salmon Marinated in Juniper, Sugar,
    Salt and Orange
Grilled Thick Lamb Chops with Basil Butter
    Sauce
Grilled White Chicory with Olive Oil and
    Smoked Mozzarella
Brownies with a Triangle of Powdered Sugar
    (recipe below)
Wine: Red Graves or Pomerol

The salmon takes only a few minutes on the grill. To serve as a first course, omit the vegetables in the recipe. Add a spinach leaf as garnish.

To serve 4, reduce ingredients as follows: use 4 salmon fillets, 2 tablespoons salt, 4 tablespoons sugar, 2 tablespoons juniper berries, a scant teaspoon of pepper and a tablespoon of grated orange zest.

### DESSERT
Cover one diagonal half of each brownie with a piece of waxed paper. Sift powdered sugar over uncovered part. Remove paper. Serve with whipped cream or ice cream, if desired.

## MENU 17

Serves 4

Shrimp in Olive Oil and Lemon Juice (recipe below)
Grilled Lamb, Greek Style, with Vegetables
Baklava or Cherry Strudel (recipe below)
Wine: California Pinot Noir

### SHRIMP

For 4, use 1 pound shrimp (20 per pound). Throw into salted boiling water and cook until pink, about 2 to 3 minutes after water returns to boil. Rinse under cold water; shell and trim where necessary. Combine ½ cup olive oil and the juice of 1 lemon, adding more lemon to taste. Season with salt and pepper. Arrange 4 or 5 shrimp on a pretty lettuce leaf and spoon lemon dressing over them.

### DESSERT

Either pastry may be purchased, but here's an easy recipe for cherry strudel. Combine 1 cup pitted fresh or canned cherries (drained well) with 3 tablespoons melted butter, ½ cup sugar, 1 teaspoon grated lemon zest and ½ cup cake crumbs (or soft breadcrumbs sweetened with 2 tablespoons sugar). Lay 1 sheet phyllo dough on a sheet of waxed paper. Brush lightly with melted butter. Repeat with 2 more sheets. Spoon cherry mixture in a strip along short end. Lift waxed paper and use it to roll phyllo into a cylinder. Do not seal ends. Lay

strudel, seam side down, on a buttered rimmed baking sheet. Bake in a preheated 375° F oven for about 30 minutes or over indirect medium heat in a covered gas grill for about 40 minutes.

## MENU 18

Serves 4

Roasted Pepper and Eggplant Dip
Skewers of Lamb, Pineapple, Peppers, and Other Things
Fresh Green Salad (see below)
Strawberries with Sugar and Kirsch
Wine: Champagne or other sparkling wine

The pepper and eggplant is a flavorful dish that complements the lamb. Make it ahead.

### SALAD

Wash several varieties of greens; romaine, Bibb, arugula and watercress combine well. Place washed and drained leaves in a plastic bag and refrigerate. Prepare desired dressing and do not add to lettuce until the last minute. Trim berries early in the day and rinse quickly; never soak berries. Toss with sugar to taste; refrigerate. Add kirsch before serving.

**MENU
19**

Serves 6

Grilled Eggplant with Capers and Anchovy
   Sauce
Grilled Veal Chops with Balsamic Vinegar and
   Butter
Curly endive with lemon vinaigrette
Italian or French pastry
Wine: White Burgundy or California
   Chardonnay

Curly endive is one of the best greens for salad. Trim a head, separate leaves and put in iced water to crisp. Drain well and dress just before serving.

To use veal chop recipe on page 170 for 6, increase ingredients by approximately one half, as follows: 6 bulbs Belgian endive, 9 green onions, 6 veal chops, 6 tablespoons butter, ¾ cup balsamic vinegar, 1 cup white wine, 1 cup beef broth and 1½ tablespoons oil.

"We all prefer cooking from scratch" is a favorite saying of my friend Alice McAdams, and although there are many excellent pastries in the cooking literature, often there just isn't time to do everything. So visit one of your favorite bakeries and don't fret, for everything else on the menu is "made from scratch."

**MENU
20**

Serves 4

Three-Melon Soup (recipe below)
Grilled Calves' Liver
Onions in Parchment or Onion in Liver recipe
Orange Slices with a Sprinkle of Coconut (rec-
   ipe below)
Wine: California Merlot or Grand Cru
   Beaujolais

Make the refreshing soup 1 or 2 days ahead. To serve 4, combine 1½ cups fresh orange juice, 1 cup each chopped canteloupe and Cranshaw melons and ¼ cup fresh lime juice in a food processor or blender and puree (in batches if necessary). Blend in 3 tablespoons honey, 1½ tablespoons sugar and 1½ tablespoons chopped fresh mint. Transfer to a glass bowl and add 1½ cups sparkling wine and ¾ cup small watermelon cubes. Cover and refrigerate 3 hours or overnight. Garnish with mint sprigs.

The liver, with very little advance preparation, will be grilled in a few minutes, so concentrate on the onion side dish. Use parchment in foil to create a fine-tasting and elegant-looking dish.

DESSERT

Cut rind off oranges, removing all pith. Thinly slice oranges crosswise. Add a spoonful of Cointreau or other orange liqueur if you wish. Sprinkle a teaspoon of toasted coconut flakes over the slices. Moist, tender macaroons would make this a grand finale.

# MENU
# 21

Serves 6

Chili Red Pepper Soup (recipe below)
Buttery Barbecued Rock Cornish Game Hens
Smoked Fettuccine and Fontina
Assorted Fresh Fruit
Wine: Red Zinfandel or Côtes-du-Rhône

### SOUP
Grill or broil 6 red bell peppers until charred on all sides. Close them in a brown paper or plastic bag for 10 minutes. Peel and seed them, rinsing under cold water to remove charred skin. Puree 3 peppers and dice the other three. In a saucepan, melt 3 tablespoons butter and sauté 4 chopped green onions until tender. Put 1½ cans (28 ounces each) of plum tomatoes through a food mill and add to saucepan with 1½ cups dry red wine, 1½ cups tomato juice, 1½ teaspoons sugar, salt, pepper and pureed red peppers. Bring to boil, then simmer 20 minutes. Serve hot or ice cold, garnished with diced peppers.

### HENS
Double recipe on page 232 to serve 6 – this will provide ½ rock Cornish hen per person with 2 halves leftover for second helpings.

# MENU
# 22

Serves 4

Grilled Homemade Italian Sausage
Grilled Boned Chicken Breasts with Sweet Garlic on a bed of Curly Endive with Pine Nuts
Minted Fresh Cucumbers
Vanilla ice cream with chocolate chip cookies
Wine: Brunello di Montalcino

If you don't have time to make the sausage, find a good Italian meat market and buy *luganega* sausage, which is not tied in links. Ask the butcher to keep it in one piece so you can coil it into a spiral and grill it in a hinged wire basket. This is a first course here, so 1 pound should be enough for 4 or 6 people. Serve sliced, with 1 or 2 tomato wedges, or spear 1-inch pieces on wooden skewers after they're grilled.

## MENU
## 23

Serves 4

Sliced Fresh Tomatoes on a Bed of Tomato and
  Basil Coulis
Grilled Chicken Breast Pieces with Spicy Anise
  Sauce
Grilled Fennel Bulbs
Cheeses, crackers and grapes
Wine: Barolo

Use only red-ripe tomatoes. Avoid pink hothouse types, which are tasteless. Alternatively,
substitute grilled Belgian endive (see page 269)
and place 1 bulb per serving on the tomato/
basil coulis. Sprinkle freshly grated Parmesan
cheese over either vegetable.

Serve a ripe Brie, St.-André or Explorateur with
wholewheat crackers. (Carr's of Carlisle, made
in Great Britain and sold in a bright red package, are especially good.) Rinse bunches of
seedless grapes, or for a really special treat,
serve champagne grapes when in season.

## MENU
## 24

Serves 4

Cold Madrilène
Charcoal-grilled Quail with Warm Curly
  Endive Salad
Sliced Fresh Pears in Poire Williams
Wine: Red Burgundy

Good madrilène is available in cans.
Refrigerate the can(s) until ready to use; serve
with lemon wedges and a peppermill.

### DESSERT

Be sure pears are ripe. After peeling and slicing, coat them with fresh lemon juice to prevent discoloration. Poire Williams, an
imported pear brandy, is expensive but it goes
a long way as only a little at a time is used.
One tablespoon per pear is enough. If you
can't get ripe pears, substitute another ripe
fruit. Use kirsch (cherry brandy) with orange
or banana slices and framboise (raspberry
brandy) with strawberries or raspberries.

# SAUCES AND ACCOMPANIMENTS

## SAUCES

## AÏOLI

**Makes 1 cup**

Aïoli is a very thick sauce, almost a solid mass. It is heavier than mayonnaise, which it resembles. One could almost call this garlic and olive oil mixture "Friday sauce," because in the south of France it is made religiously every Friday and served with eggs, carrots, potatoes and many kinds of fish. In this country, we are learning that it makes an especially good sauce for grilled foods.

### INGREDIENTS

6 garlic cloves
2 small egg yolks
1 cup olive oil
1 teaspoon fresh lemon juice
salt and freshly ground pepper

1. Process the garlic almost to a paste in a food processor or with a mortar and pestle, or mince it as finely as you can.

2. Add the yolks and blend briefly in the processor. Add the olive oil a drop at a time, as in making mayonnaise, until all has been absorbed. Mix in the lemon juice, salt and pepper. (Mixing can also be done in a blender or by hand with a whisk.) Store aïoli in refrigerator up to 5 days.

## NO-COOK BARBECUE SAUCE EASTERN NORTH CAROLINA STYLE

**Makes 2 generous quarts**

This is served as a table sauce for barbecued meats.

### INGREDIENTS

2 quarts cider vinegar
6 tablespoons salt
1 tablespoon cayenne pepper
1½ tablespoons red pepper flakes
¼ cup molasses or ½ cup firmly packed
  brown sugar

Combine all ingredients in a nonreactive container. Allow to stand for at least 4 hours before using. Store in refrigerator.

# BRANDY and WINE SAUCE FOR HAMBURGERS AND STEAK

Makes 4 cups

INGREDIENTS

⅔ cup olive oil
8 anchovy fillets, washed and dried
⅔ cup finely chopped mushrooms
½ cup finely chopped onion
2 garlic cloves, finely chopped
⅓ cup brandy
2 cups dry red wine
½ cup tomato paste
1 tablespoon chopped parsley

**1.** Heat oil in a medium saucepan over medium heat. Add anchovies, mushrooms and onion and cook for 5 minutes. Add garlic and cook 1 minute more.

**2.** Add remaining ingredients and bring to boil. Simmer over medium-low heat, stirring frequently, for 15 minutes.

**3.** Strain sauce. Serve hot with grilled hamburgers and steaks.

# BUTTER AND CREAM SAUCE

Makes 2 cups

INGREDIENTS

1 cup dry white wine (or ¾ cup dry vermouth and ¼ cup water)
¼ cup white wine vinegar
½ cup finely chopped shallots
2 cups heavy cream
1 cup (2 sticks) softened unsalted butter
salt and freshly ground pepper
a few drops fresh lemon juice

**1.** In a nonaluminum medium saucepan, bring the wine, vinegar and shallots to a boil. Continue to boil over high heat until 1 teaspoon liquid is left, 5 to 10 minutes; be careful not to scorch the shallots. Add the heavy cream and boil vigorously until sauce is thick enough to coat a spoon.

**2.** Remove from heat and whisk in butter, about a tablespoon at a time, until completely absorbed. Season sauce with salt, pepper and lemon juice. Store in refrigerator up to 1 week.

# HORSERADISH CREAM SAUCE

Makes 1 cup

2 tablespoons grated fresh horseradish
2 tablespoons mayonnaise
1 teaspoon dry mustard
2 tablespoons fresh lemon juice
½ teaspoon chopped fresh mint or a generous
    pinch of dried
½ cup heavy cream, whipped

Fold all ingredients into the whipped cream one at a time. Continue to fold until the mixture is well blended. Store in refrigerator up to 1 week.

# MAYONNAISE WITH HERBS

Makes 1 generous cup

Delicious with many grilled fish and simple chicken dishes, this recipe incorporates dill but you can substitute almost any herb of your liking. Fresh basil, tarragon or thyme makes a flavorful mayonnaise. Add a little of the herb at a time until you reach the desired flavor.

INGREDIENTS

1 large egg
pinch of salt
1 teaspoon Dijon mustard
1 tablespoon (or more) fresh lemon juice
1 cup vegetable, peanut or corn oil or any
    combination
¼ cup finely chopped fresh dill

1. Combine egg, salt, mustard and 1 table-spoon lemon juice in food processor and pulse a few times until blended.

2. With machine running, add oil drop by drop until all is absorbed. Taste and add more lemon juice to taste. If a thinner sauce is desired, add 1 to 2 tablespoons warm water and pulse until well combined. Transfer mayonnaise to a small bowl.

3. Fold in dill or other herb with a rubber spatula. Serve immediately or refrigerate, covered, for later use. Mayonnaise is at its most flavorful when served at cool room temperature.

# VERMONT "B" MINT SAUCE FOR GRILLED LAMB

Makes about 1 cup

My friend, John Allen, the wizard of grilled lamb, suggests using Vermont grade "B" maple syrup—the "not-so-fancy" grade. He adds, "Keep the sauce in the refrigerator all summer, but triple and quadruple the recipe." Use this with grilled lamb and your family and guests will come back for third helpings.

### INGREDIENTS

⅓ cup white wine vinegar
⅓ cup maple syrup, preferably Vermont grade "B"
½ cup finely chopped fresh mint, tightly packed

Combine all ingredients, refrigerate and serve as needed.

# MUSTARD CREAM SAUCE

Makes 1 cup

This no-cook sauce suits almost all grilled meats.

### INGREDIENTS

⅓ cup water
3 tablespoons dry mustard
⅓ cup sour cream
⅓ cup heavy cream

1. Combine water and dry mustard and mix well.

2. Stir in remaining ingredients. If not using immediately, cover bowl and refrigerate. This sauce is most flavorful served at cool room temperature.

# REMOULADE SAUCE

Makes 1¾ cups

### INGREDIENTS

1½ cups mayonnaise (See page 309)
2 tablespoons (or more) heavy cream
4 shallots, finely chopped
1 tablespoon anchovy paste
3 tablespoons chopped pickled watermelon rind
  or sweet pickle
1 tablespoon chopped parsley
1 tablespoon chopped drained capers
1 tablespoon Dijon mustard
2 tablespoons catsup
2 tablespoons fresh lemon juice
1 teaspoon sugar

Combine all ingredients and refrigerate for several hours. Thin sauce as desired with more heavy cream. Mix well and refrigerate for up to 1 week.

# ROUILLE

Makes 1 cup

Crumbs of Italian or French bread have more body than American white breadcrumbs, and they make a better rouille.

### INGREDIENTS

8 garlic cloves, halved
2 teaspoons red pepper flakes or finely crushed
  dried chili peppers
1 teaspoon salt
1 cup breadcrumbs (made from fresh or day-
  old bread), soaked in water and squeezed
  dry
½ cup olive oil

In a food processor, blend garlic, red pepper and salt to a paste. Add the breadcrumbs and mix thoroughly. With machine running, add the olive oil a tablespoon at a time and process until smooth. (If using a blender, combine garlic, pepper, salt and breadcrumbs and blend for a few seconds; then add the oil a little at a time.) Store rouille in refrigerator up to 3 days. Variation: To 1 cup rouille, add 1 teaspoon finely crushed red pepper flakes (or dried chili peppers) and ¼ teaspoon saffron. Use less red pepper if you want a less fiery sauce.

# TOMATO AND BASIL COULIS

Serves 4

Several tablespoons of this sauce can be used as a base for grilled meat or poultry.

### INGREDIENTS

1½ pounds ripe tomatoes
3 tablespoons butter
½ small onion, finely chopped
8 fresh basil leaves, cut into ½-inch pieces
salt and freshly ground pepper

1. Bring a large saucepan of water to boil. Drop in tomatoes, count to 10, remove tomatoes and transfer to a bowl filled with cold water. Core and peel tomatoes. Halve them crosswise, squeeze out seeds and chop tomatoes into ½-inch pieces.

2. Melt butter in a skillet, add onion and sauté until limp. Add tomatoes, basil, salt and pepper and cook for 3 to 4 minutes, stirring frequently. Serve hot.

# GREEN TOMATO SALSA

Makes 6 cups

A wonderful Mexican touch with many grilled foods, especially beef, pork and chicken. Make it when your garden is filled with green tomatoes. The salsa can be served immediately, kept in the refrigerator for days or canned for longer storage. Be sure to give the jars a water bath for at least 15 minutes if canning.

### INGREDIENTS

8 cups coarsely chopped green tomatoes
1½ cups chopped yellow or white onions
1 cup cider vinegar
2 garlic cloves, finely chopped
2 teaspoons chopped fresh oregano or 1 teaspoon dried
2 teaspoons chopped fresh coriander
1 teaspoon celery seeds
2 tablespoons brown sugar
2 teaspoons coarse salt
¼ cup jalapenos or other hot chili peppers

Combine all ingredients and pulse in a food processor in batches until chopped; do not overprocess. Transfer to a large nonaluminum saucepan, bring to boil and cook 2 minutes. Serve warm or cool.

## SPICY CRANBERRY CHUTNEY

Makes 4 cups

I have not tasted a better cranberry preparation than this one prepared by my friend Joan Muessen.

### INGREDIENTS

4 cups (1 pound) cranberries
1 cup seedless raisins
1⅔ cups sugar
1 tablespoon ground cinnamon
1½ teaspoons ground ginger
¼ teaspoon ground cloves
1 cup water
1 medium onion, chopped (about ½ cup)
1 medium apple, peeled, quartered, cored and chopped
½ cup thinly sliced celery

1. Combine cranberries, raisins, sugar, spices and water in a large nonaluminum saucepan and cook for 15 minutes, or until berries pop and mixture thickens.

2. Stir in onion, apple and celery and simmer 15 minutes longer, or until mixture is thick. Cool. Store in refrigerator.

## TOMATO-MACADAMIA NUT CHUTNEY

Makes about 3 cups

### INGREDIENTS

3 cups chopped peeled plum tomatoes or one 35-ounce can, undrained
1½ cups sugar
1 cup red wine vinegar
¼ cup sherry vinegar
2 tablespoons minced fresh basil
6 garlic cloves, minced
2 teaspoons salt
pinch of red pepper flakes
1 cup whole macadamia nuts
½ cup currants

1. Bring first 8 ingredients to boil in heavy nonaluminum saucepan. Reduce heat and simmer, stirring occasionally, until thickened and reduced to 3 cups, about 2 hours.

2. Stir in macadamias and currants and cook 5 minutes more. Serve hot, warm, at room temperature or chilled.

# PLUM TOMATO CHUTNEY

Makes 3 cups

### INGREDIENTS

8 garlic cloves
½ cup finely chopped crystallized ginger
1½ cups red wine vinegar
1 can (35 ounces) plum tomatoes, undrained
1½ cups sugar
2 teaspoons salt
½ teaspoon red pepper flakes
1½ cups pine nuts
½ cup golden raisins

1. Combine garlic, ginger and ½ cup vinegar in food processor or blender and puree until smooth. Transfer to a large nonaluminum saucepan.

2. Add tomatoes with liquid, remaining 1 cup vinegar, sugar, salt and pepper flakes. Bring to boil over medium-high heat. Reduce heat and simmer until chutney coats a spoon, about 2 hours.

3. Stir in pine nuts and raisins and simmer 5 minutes more. Let cool, then store in refrigerator.

# PICKLED GINGER ROOT

Makes about ⅔ cup

Almost always served with sushi, this sweetened and pickled ginger root can be made at home. It is featured with one of the beef burgers on page 103, but it can be served with other meat and fish dishes if their marinades and sauces do not conflict.

### INGREDIENTS

1 large piece of ginger root (about 4 inches long)
1 tablespoon salt
⅔ cup rice vinegar
¼ cup water
1½ tablespoons sugar

1. Scrub the ginger root and pare away most of the skin. Place ginger in a flat glass or ceramic container, sprinkle with salt, cover with plastic wrap and let stand at room temperature for 1 to 2 days. Drain and transfer to a fresh container.

2. In a small nonaluminum saucepan, combine the vinegar, water and sugar and bring to boil. Immediately remove from heat and pour over the ginger. Cover tightly and let stand at room temperature for 1 week. Slice paper-thin to serve.

3. Tightly covered, pickled ginger will last for 3 to 4 months in the refrigerator.

## ONION RELISH

Serves 4

This relish prepared by Felipe Rojas-Lombardi, will keep in the refrigerator for up to a week. The recipe can be doubled or tripled easily to ensure having some on hand.

### INGREDIENTS

2 red onions, halved and thinly sliced
    lengthwise
1 hot pepper, seeded and finely julienned
3 tablespoons red wine vinegar
salt
⅛ teaspoon freshly ground white pepper
⅓ cup olive oil

1. Place onions and hot pepper in a bowl and set aside. In another small bowl, combine the vinegar, salt and white pepper and mix well. Add the oil and whisk thoroughly.

2. Add the dressing to the onions and peppers and toss. Let stand at room temperature for about 1 hour before serving.

## PASTA WITH BUTTER, CHEESE AND CREAM SAUCE

Serves 4 to 6

### INGREDIENTS

1 cup (2 sticks) butter
1 cup heavy cream
1 pound dried pasta
1 cup freshly grated Parmesan cheese
salt and freshly ground pepper
pinch of freshly grated nutmeg

1. In a large saucepan, combine butter and ½ cup cream. Place over low heat until butter has melted.

2. Cook pasta, drain well and add to butter mixture. Add remaining cream, Parmesan, salt, pepper and nutmeg and toss well. Taste and adjust seasoning and serve immediately.

# SPINACH, MUSHROOMS and CREAM with SPAGHETTI

Serves 4

### INGREDIENTS

4 cups shredded fresh spinach leaves
8 ounces fresh mushrooms
juice of 1 lemon
4 tablespoons butter
1 garlic clove, minced
2 tablespoons Marsala
1 cup heavy cream
salt and freshly ground pepper
8 ounces spaghetti, cooked
¼ cup freshly grated Parmesan cheese

**1.** Cook the spinach in boiling salted water just until tender, about a minute. Drain well and set aside.

**2.** Wipe mushrooms and trim stem ends. Slice thinly and toss with lemon juice.

**3.** Melt butter in a skillet, add garlic and Marsala and cook for 3 minutes over medium heat. Add mushrooms and cook 5 minutes more. Add cream and bring to boil. Season with salt and pepper. Combine spinach with cooked spaghetti, add cream mixture and toss well. Top with Parmesan and serve.

# TOMATO SAUCE WITH BUTTER FOR PASTA

For 8 ounces pasta, serves 4

### INGREDIENTS

2 pounds ripe plum tomatoes or 2 cups canned plum tomatoes
8 tablespoons (1 stick) butter, cut into 8 pieces
1 medium onion, quartered
1 medium carrot, peeled and quartered
¼ teaspoon sugar
1½ teaspoon salt

**1.** If using fresh tomatoes, wash well, halve and cook over low heat in a covered non-aluminum saucepan for 15 minutes. Put through food mill. If using canned tomatoes, put through food mill.

**2.** In a medium saucepan, combine butter, onion, carrot, sugar, salt and tomato puree and simmer over low heat for 40 minutes, uncovered. Stir frequently and be sure sauce does not boil.

**3.** Remove onion and carrot and serve sauce over freshly cooked pasta.

# PICKLED YELLOW, RED AND GREEN PEPPERS

Makes 2 quarts

"So simple and practical because it can be made ahead," says my good friend Joan Muessen, who makes this pickle often. "More importantly, the peppers are truly delicious with grilled meats and vegetables of all kinds."

### INGREDIENTS

6 yellow bell peppers
6 red bell peppers
6 green bell peppers
2 cups olive oil
⅔ cup red wine vinegar
1 tablespoon chopped fresh oregano or 1
    teaspoon dried
1 tablespoon chopped fresh rosemary or 1
    teaspoon dried
2 teaspoons coarse salt
1 teaspoon brown sugar
4 garlic cloves, halved
12 black peppercorns, cracked

1. Remove stems, ribs and seeds from peppers. Cut peppers into ½-inch-wide strips and place in a large saucepan.

2. In another saucepan, bring about 2 quarts water to boil. Pour over peppers just to cover. Return to a boil, uncovered, and cook peppers 5 minutes. Drain well.

3. Sterilize two 1-quart or four 1-pint jars and fill them with the cooked peppers.

4. Combine remaining ingredients except garlic and peppercorns and whisk until emulsified. Divide garlic and peppercorns into jars with peppers and pour oil and vinegar mixture into the jars. Close jars and let peppers marinate at least 1 day before serving. Serve at room temperature. Process jars in a hot water bath for at least 15 minutes if peppers are to be kept for longer than 1 week.

# RATATOUILE

Makes about 2 cups

This is the way Gerard Pangaud, chef at New York's Aurora, prepares it.

### INGREDIENTS

1 red bell pepper
1 green bell pepper
2 tomatoes
1 celery stalk
1 small bunch each of thyme, basil and sage
2 bay leaves
1½ cups olive oil
½ onion, finely chopped
1 small fennel bulb, trimmed and finely
    chopped
3 garlic cloves, crushed
salt and freshly ground pepper
1 eggplant, cut into 1¼ × ¼ inch sticks
1 zucchini, cut into 1¼ × ¼ inch sticks

1. Blanch the peppers in boiling water for 2 minutes. Refresh in cold water and peel. Cut into 1¼ × ¼ inch sticks.

2. Blanch the tomatoes in boiling water for 10 seconds. Refresh in cold water. Peel, seed and cut into sticks.

3. Make a bouquet garni of the celery and herbs; tie it tightly.

4. Heat oil in a large saucepan. Add onion, fennel and bouquet garni and cook for several minutes over moderate heat. Add

tomato, garlic, salt and pepper. Cover tightly with a foil seal under the pan's lid. Simmer until the tomatoes have disintegrated, about 10 minutes. Add the peppers, eggplant and zucchini, cover and simmer for 45 minutes.

# SOUR CREAM, GREEN ONIONS AND CUCUMBERS

Serves 4 to 6

Serve a bowl of this with grilled fish or, if preparing individual dishes, add a tablespoonful to each plate. It is also great as a condiment with potatoes, tomatoes or raw celery stalks, served as an appetizer.

### INGREDIENTS

1 cup sour cream
2 tablespoons cider vinegar or fresh lemon juice
1 small cucumber, peeled and cut into ¼-inch
    dice
2 green onions, including light green part,
    thinly sliced
salt and freshly ground pepper

Combine sour cream and vinegar or lemon juice and blend thoroughly. Mix in cucumber, green onions, salt and pepper. Serve slightly chilled.

# INFORMATION

## CONVERSION TABLES

T he following are conversion tables and other information applicable to those converting the recipes in this book for use in other English-speaking countries. The cup and spoon measures given in the book are U.S. Customary (1 cup = 236mL; 1 tablespoon = 15 mL). Use these tables when working with British Imperial or Metric kitchen utensils.

### LIQUID MEASURES

The Imperial pint is larger than the U.S. pint; therefore note the following when measuring liquid ingredients.

| U.S. | IMPERIAL |
|------|----------|
| 1 cup = 8 fluid ounces | 1 cup = 10 fluid ounces |
| ½ cup = 4 fluid ounces | ½ cup = 5 fluid ounces |
| 1 tablespoon = ¾ fluid ounce | 1 tablespoon = 1 fluid ounce |

| U.S. MEASURE | METRIC* | IMPERIAL* |
|--------------|---------|-----------|
| 1 quart (4 cups) | 950 mL | 1½ pints + 4 tablespoons |
| 1 pint (2 cups) | 450 mL | ¾ pint |
| 1 cup | 236 mL | ¼ pint + 6 tablespoons |
| 1 tablespoon | 15 mL | 1 + tablespoon |
| 1 teaspoon | 5 mL | 1 teaspoon |

* Note that exact quantities are not always given. Differences are more crucial when dealing with larger quantities. For teaspoon and tablespoon measures, simply use scant or generous quantities; of for more accurate conversions, rely upon metric.

### SOLID MEASURES

Outside the U.S., cooks measure more items by weight. Here are approximate equivalents for basic items in this book.*

| | U.S. CUSTOMARY | METRIC | IMPERIAL |
|---|----------------|--------|----------|
| Beans (dried, raw) | 1 cup | 225g | 8 ounces |
| Butter | 1 cup | 225g | 8 ounces |
| | ½ cup | 115g | 4 ounces |
| | ¼ cup | 60g | 2 ounces |
| | 1 tablespoon | 15g | ½ ounce |
| Cheese (grated) | 1 cup | 115g | 4 ounces |
| Coconut (shredded) | ½ cup | 60g | 2 ounces |
| Fruit (chopped) | 1 cup | 225g | 8 ounces |
| Herbs (chopped) | ¼ cup | 7g | ¼ ounce |
| Meats/Chicken (chopped, cooked) | 1 cup | 175g | 6 ounces |

*To avoid awkward measurements, some conversions are not exact.

| | U.S. CUSTOMARY | METRIC | IMPERIAL |
|---|---|---|---|
| Mushrooms (chopped) | 1 cup | 70g | 2½ ounces |
| Nut Meats (chopped) | 1 cup | 115g | 4 ounces |
| Pasta (dried, raw) | 1 cup | 225g | 8 ounces |
| Peas (shelled) | 1 cup | 225g | 8 ounces |
| Raisins (and other dried fruits) | 1 cup | 175g | 6 ounces |
| Rice (uncooked) | 1 cup | 225g | 8 ounces |
| (cooked) | 3 cups | 225g | 8 ounces |
| Spinach (cooked) | ½ cup | 285g | 10 ounces |
| Vegetables (chopped, raw: onions celery) | 1 cup | 115g | 4 ounces |

## DRY MEASURES

T he following items are measured by weight outside of the U.S. These items are variable, especially the flour, depending on individual variety of flour and moisture. American cup measurements on following items are loosely packed; flour is measured directly from package (presifted).

| | U.S. CUSTOMARY | METRIC | IMPERIAL |
|---|---|---|---|
| Flour (all-purpose) | 1 cup | 150g | 5 ounces |
| | ½ cup | 70g | 2½ ounces |
| Cornmeal | 1 cup | 175g | 6 ounces |
| Sugar (granulated) | 1 cup | 190g | 6½ ounces |
| | ½ cup | 85g | 3 ounces |
| | ¼ cup | 40g | 1¾ ounces |
| (powdered) | 1 cup | 80g | 2⅔ ounces |
| | ½ cup | 40g | 1⅓ ounces |
| | ¼ cup | 20g | ¾ ounce |
| (brown) | 1 cup | 160g | 5⅓ ounces |
| | ½ cup | 80g | 2⅔ ounces |
| | ¼ cup | 40g | 1⅓ ounces |

## OVEN TEMPERATURES

| Gas Mark | ¼ | 2 | 4 | 6 | 8 |
|---|---|---|---|---|---|
| Fahrenheit | 225° | 300° | 350° | 400° | 450° |
| Celsius | 110° | 150° | 180° | 200° | 230° |

# BRITISH EQUIVALENTS FOR AMERICAN TERMINOLOGY

Names and terms for ingredients vary from country to country. Here are some of the major American terms and their British equivalents.

## BAKING

all purpose flour is plain flour
baking soda is bicarbonate of soda
baking powder is bicarbonate of soda with a pinch of cream of tarter
cornstarch is cornflour
sugar is caster sugar, unless otherwise indicated
confectioners' or powdered sugar is icing sugar
dark brown sugar is soft brown sugar
light brown sugar is best substituted with demerara sugar
light corn syrup is best substituted with golden syrup
dark corn syrup is closest to light treacle

## DAIRY

cottage cheese is curd cheese
cream cheese is full-fat soft cheese
light cream is single cream
heavy cream is double cream
half and half is a 50/50 mixture of whole milk and double cream
sour cream is soured cream
plain yogurt is natural yogurt
butter may be either sweet or salted (most margarines are slightly salted)

## VEGETABLES

beets are beetroot
Belgian endive is chicory
chicory is curly endive
corn is sweetcorn
eggplant is aubergine
green onions are spring onions or scallions
snow peas are mangetout peas

## MEATS

meats are butchered differently in different countries; substitute the most appropriate cut depending on the preparation involved
ground beef and other meats are minced meats
beef flank steak is similar to topside; short ribs (cut from under the rib) are flat ribs; cube steaks are pounded slices from topside or silverside
lamb is all young spring lamb
lamb loin chops are cutlets from the saddle
lamb shoulder arm or blade chops are cutlets from the neck and shoulder
pork tenderloin is a long, narrow cut from the saddle; country-style spareribs are meaty, thick ribs cut from the best end of the saddle
smoked ham can be either brine- or dry-cured; most recipes for ham use a brine-cured, mild, moist ham with a faint smoky aroma, such as boiled ham
bacon strips or pieces are rashers, usually ½ to 1 ounce each. Canadian bacon is a long cylindrical cut from the loin that is sugar-cured and smoked
prosciutto is Parma ham; country ham is closest to York ham

## SAUCES/SEASONINGS

cilantro or Chinese parsley is fresh coriander, available in specialty markets
chili powder is a blend of spices, with red pepper (cayenne) as the base
chili sauce is bottled sauce with a tomato base and seasoned with a number of spices
garlic and onion powder are pulverized dehydrated garlic and onion, available with most other spices and seasonings
Liquid Smoke is a bottled commercial concentrate of smoke flavor, used to give a barbecued flavor to meats
Louisiana Hot Sauce is a bottled sauce similar to Tabasco onion salt and garlic salt are a blend of garlic or onion powder and salt
salsa is Mexican hot sauce, either green or red, usually sold in jars in shops carrying Mexican products taco sauce
and enchilada sauce are available in jars or cans (tins) in shops carrying Mexican products
tomato paste is tomato puree

## STARCHES/CEREALS/BREADS

wild rice is available in gourmet shops; long-grain and wild rice mix is a commercial blend with about a 2-to-1 ratio of white to wild rice
instant rice is quick-cooking rice such as Minute Rice
dry stuffing mix is a blend of bread cubes, dried herbs and seasonings. Italian flavor is strongly accented with oregano and basil; cornbread stuffing is made with cubes of baked cornbread instead of plain bread
flour and corn tortillas are unleavened Mexican breads, available in specialty shops with Mexican products. Corn tortillas are also sold in cans by El Paso products.

## DESSERTS

flaked coconut is desiccated or shredded coconut
sliced almonds are flaked almonds
pecans can be replaced by walnuts
vanilla or almond extract are the same as vanilla essence and almond flavoring

## UTENSILS/MATERIALS

paper towels are absorbent towels or kitchen paper
waxed paper is greaseproof paper
aluminum foil is kitchen foil
Cookware is measured in either volume or inches. For volume measures, see measurement tables on p. 319.

For inches, use the following:
⅛ inch = ½ cm
¼ inch = ¾ cm
½ inch = 1½ cm
1 inch = 2½ cm

6 inches = 15 cm
8 inches = 20 cm
10 inches = 25 cm
112 inches = 30 cm

# MEXICAN AND LATIN AMERICAN GLOSSARY OF COOKING

ACHIOTE: a seed used for seasoning and red coloring in Yucatan cooking, also called annatto. Antichuchos: Peruvian skewered barbecued beef hearts.

CHILES: a basic seasoning in Mexican and Latin American cuisine. Available fresh or dried, mild or hot.

ANCHOS: mild, deep red peppers that look like California chilies, but smaller. Often powdered and used like paprika. California chilies, also called *chile verde:* a fresh green chile, moderately hot. It is the green chile used in *chiles rellenos.* Chile tepín or pequín: very hot small chiles used to make red hot sauces.

COLORADO: sweet, mild, dried red chiles.

JALAPEÑO: small, green, usually very hot. Pickled jalapeño can be found in bottles or cans.

PASILLA: piquant dark brown chiles used in chile sauces.

POBLANO: large mild chiles like green peppers in size and use.

SERRANO: small and very hot; red when ripe, green unripe. Often pickled.

CHILI POWDER: a powder made from dried mild chilies including ancho and pasilla

CHIMICHURI: a spicy Argentinian vinaigrette sauce, served with barbecued meats

CHORIZO: A mexican cased sausage made of pork with lots of pepper.

CORIANDER: the parsley like leaves are used for flavoring and as a garnish; the fragrant seeds are used in savory dishes.

CUMIN: a popular flavor in Latin preparations. Of the parsley family and sold in seed and powder forms.

HOT PEPPER SAUCE: a very hot bottled condiment, derived from the pulp of hot red chilies.

MASA: also known as *masa harina,* and is sold in sacks like flour; used to make doughs for tortillas and tamales.

PEPITAS: pumpkin seeds, roasted to eat as snacks or ground to thicken sauces.

TACO: a meat or vegetable filling wrapped in a soft or fried corn tortilla.

TAMALES: eaten throughout Latin America, these popular cornhusk packages are filled with corn, cornmeal, vegetables and meat.

TAMARIND: a tart flavoring that comes from the curved flat dark pod of a leguminous tree.

TOMATILLOS: a tomatolike vegetable, small and green with a papery skin. May be bought fresh or canned. Used mostly in sauces.

TORTILLA: Mexican flat bread made of either corn or wheat flour.

# SOURCES FOR GRILLS, TOOLS, FUEL AND ACCESSORIES

The following manufacturers provide a wide line of grills and accessories. The first six companies were especially helpful; their products were used and tested by the author of this book.

HASTY-BAKE, Division of C. B. Simmons, Inc., P.O. Box 471285, Tulsa, OK 74147-1285: Maker of the Charcoal Oven, an attractive, efficient, solidly built charcoal grill.

MECO, P.O. Box 1000, 1500 Industrial Road, Greenville, TN 37744-1000: Charcoal grills: portable, standard and deluxe models, in attractive styles and various colors. Accommodate shelves, rotisserie, etc.

Water Smoker: single- and double-grid charcoal smokers, plus electric model in various colors.
Electric grills: tabletop and standard models in modern design and several colors. Accommodate rotisserie.

PREWAY INDUSTRIES, P.O. Box 534, Evansville, IN 47004-0534: Makers of the Falcon and Embermatic gas grills in a variety of outdoor models up to 44,000 BTU, including pedestal and cart types.

SUNBEAM, Howard Bush Drive, Neosho, MO 64850: Single- and dual-tank-capacity gas grills of various sizes, for both indoor and outdoor use, plus a single-burner tabletop model. Sold through Agway stores. Accessories available include rotisseries, gas grill covers, cooking grids, lava rock, etc.

THERMOS, Route 75, Freeport, IL 61032: Offers one of the best selections of simple to deluxe outdoor gas grills. Features include up to 42,000-BTU double burner, full-width window in cover, and heat temperature indicator. Among the most attractive grills available.

WEBER-STEPHEN PRODUCTS CO., 200 East Daniels Road, Palatine, IL 60067: Offers a wide variety of gas and charcoal grills in stylish designs, and many accessories including griddles, roast holders, drip pans, rib racks and so on. Features wagons, tabletop portables and cylindrical water smokers with two cooking grids.

## OTHER MANUFACTURERS

CHAR-GLO, % Thermador, 5119 S. District Boulevard, Los Angeles, CA 90040: For indoor use. Two models for use in wall, pass-through, peninsula, island and chimney installations. Special hood and ventilation required. Gas-fired grill unit, vented with an overhead hood and fan, has adjustable heat controls and comes in 19- and 29-inch widths.

CHARMGLOW, Turco, Inc., 501 S. Lime Street, Duquoin, IL 62831: Manufacturer of outdoor grills.

JENN-AIR, 3035 N. Shadeland, Indianapolis, IN 46226: Manufactures a variety of high-style indoor grilling equipment as well as other electric and gas appliances. They offer a 10-inch-wide grill cartridge that can be plugged into a down-vented convertible electric cooktop system; two units can be paired to make one large grill.

## ELECTRIC GRILLS

CONTEMPRA INDUSTRIES, 651 New Hampshire Avenue, Lakewood, NJ 08701: Indoor electric barbecue made of stoneware, with natural air convection. Goes from counter to table for serving. Quick heating element reflector system; unit is virtually smokeless and easy to clean.

GAGGENAU, 5 Commonwealth Avenue, Woburn, MA 01801: Offers an electric grill with 12 temperature settings as part of a modular cooktop arrangement.

JENN-AIR—SEE ABOVE

MAVERICK INDUSTRIES, INC., 5 Stahuber Avenue, Union, NJ 07083: Outdoor and indoor electric grills, basic to deluxe, including special Benihana model. Many accessories—lava stones, skewers, etc.

THE MAXIM COMPANY, 164 Delancy Street, Newark, NJ 07105: Portable indoor unit, 15½ × 10½ × 5 3/8 inches, with self-cleaning heating element and stainless steel body.

## ELECTRIC SMOKER

LUHR-JENSEN 7 SONS, INC., 400 Portway Avenue, P.O. Box 297, Hood River, OR 97031: Manufacturer of the "Little Chef" electric smoker (in several models) used by many home and professional cooks.

## PORTABLE CAMP GRILLS

L. L. BEAN, INC., Freeport, ME 04033: The unit works in the field or backyard with charcoal or wood, with or without a fire pan. Heavy-gauge aluminum, 9½ × 17½ inches.

## FUEL

LAZZARI FUEL CO., INC., P. O. Box 34051, San Francisco, CA 94134: Ten warehouses across the U.S. offer mesquite charcoal and wood as well as other woods including hickory, alder, apricot, etc.

HASTY-BAKE, Division of C. B. Simmons, Inc., P. O. Box 471285, Tulsa, OK 74147-1285: Makers of "Ozark Oak" brand hickory lump charcoal.

## BRUSHES

SPARTA BRUSH CO., P.O. Box 317, Sparta, WI 54656: Angled and straight brushes for barbecue and other kitchen uses.

## CHARCOAL STARTERS

EASY EMBERS, Alma Products, Inc., P.O. Box 2706, Evergreen, CO 80439: Chimney-type starter that lights charcoal without fluid. Indispensable.

Nu-Rod, Inc. Meteor Division , Monrovia, CA 91016

## CUTTING, CARVING and SERVING

J. K. ADAMS, Dorset, VT 05251: Maple barbecue stands, trays, cutting blocks, etc., in varying sizes.

## GASLIGHTER

STRUCTO/THERMOS, Route 75, Freeport, IL 61032: Offers reliable butane piezoelectric lighter with adjustable flame control. Indispensable.

## TOOLS

CHARCOAL COMPANION, 120 Linden, Oakland, CA 94607: Offers several unique products such as "tool and sauce holder" and a nontoxic grill cleaning solution. Also markets natural wood smoking chips.

KITCHEN BAZAAR, 4455 Connecticut Avenue, N.W., Washington, DC 20008: This large retailer and mail-

SASSAFRAS ENTERPRISES, INC., P.O. Box 1366, Evanston, IL 60204: Offers excellent and stylish barbecue tools as well as stones, peels and tiles for cooking pizza in covered grills.

TIN REFLECTING OVEN
WILLIAM McMILLEN, THE TINSHOP, Richmondtown,Staten Island, NY 10306: A roasting oven with spit that is brought right to the indoor hearth. Beautifully crafted and unbelievably efficient.

BLACKSMITH FOR CUSTOM-MADE SPITS
ALBERT ERIKSON, 417 Arthur Kill Road, Staten Island, NY 10306

# RECIPE INDEX

# INDEX OF CHEFS AND CONTRIBUTORS